For Pauline

Contents

Acknowledgements

Throughout this book I've given false names to people who might suffer if I used their real ones. Mostly they've had no say in this; last weekend at the May Day Celebration of Cannabis on Clapham Common I ran into 'David''s girlfriend, who said she didn't think of him as any kind of 'David'. Obviously there'll be more of this to come, so may I apologise in advance to those who hate their new names. I thought of using this page to thank them properly in person, but perhaps it's better not to.

Most of the people who've helped me feature in the text. In alphabetical order, I'd also like to thank Damien Abass, Matthew Atha, Jocasta Brownlee, Free Rob Cannabis, Chris Davies MP, Helen Dore, Helena Drakakis, Penny Edwards, Paul Flynn MP, Prof. Sabry Hafez, Dr David Harvey, Linda Hendry, Ian Hunter, Prof. Leslie Iversen, Stephen Jakobi, George Joffé, Danny Kushlik, Mario Lapp, Doug Lawrence, Sarah Leigh, Josie Lynwood, Monica Macdonald, Andrew Makower, Tim Malyon, Michka, Andy Miller, Nirvana Seeds of Amsterdam, David Reynolds, Matt Richell, Dominique Rogers, Allan St Pierre, Mark Saunders, Harry Shapiro and William Webb. Thanks, too, to my mother and my sister for their support. I have a nagging feeling that this list isn't comprehensive, but given the subject matter I'm sure that anyone left out will understand about short-term memory lapses.

Finally, I'd like to mention the exceptional amount of input that's come from Tim Barklem and his partner, my (ex) sister-in-law Lulie Biggs.

1

Wine of Haydar

Any sensible person would envy this project: weed enthusiasts who see someone being paid for work they'd gladly do for love, other writers wondering why they didn't grab the idea first. Almost without exception people tell me I must have enjoyed the research and give me a look that suggests I'm a bit of a black sheep. It's a lot to live up to and, rather than risk a later collapse of my reputation, I'd better start by gently deflating it.

I haven't been stoned all the time. Although I used to smoke quite a lot in my twenties, I pretty much gave up after my children were born. And even after I'd begun working on the book I was worried, as I'd been as a final-year student, that it would make me lazy. (This is the same anxiety that politicians feel when they think about the effect on society of legalization.)

But were my fears well founded? In fact, my notebooks for the last ten months are dotted with bursts of productivity which coincide with encounters with weed. Perhaps if I'd smoked every day I'd have found it harder to get up in the morning and write. But since I had young children it's alcohol I've found to be the real enemy of work, a couple of beers plus stress and tiredness making for a rapid exit from consciousness.

Next, the question of what I mean by 'cannabis culture'. I could glibly say that the West has a cannabis culture because we consume such a lot of it. Here in Britain 40 per cent of young people have tried pot; it's a huge business which is worth, on different estimates, $1–3 billion a year in this country and is the fourth cash crop by value in the United States ($15.1 billion in wholesale value, and the largest crop in California, Kentucky and Virginia). The spur for the book was finding that so many of my north London neighbours smoked, whether black or white, and whatever their social class. I admire the Marxist idea that the key to understanding a society is studying its habits of consumption, production, distribution and exchange. And if it's revealing to examine the social role of cod and tulips, how much more so in the case of a commodity whose purpose is to change consciousness?

But it's not as easy as in the late 1960s when there was a well-defined 'underground' culture with dope as a badge of identity. With groups like hippies or Rastas it's tempting to believe that a drug is making them the way they are – especially when this is what they tell you. But there's so much of it about these days that it's hard to describe what contemporary cannabis users are like, any more than we can talk about a wine-drinking class or generalize about people with mobile phones.

Does cannabis even *have* a culture? If nothing else it has connoisseurship, a set of expectations, a way of talking about the experience, the rituals of sharing joints and an idea of how stoned to get and how to behave when stoned, all of which matter. Without this social dimension, drugs are just a check-list of physical changes, and without it they seem to be especially dangerous, whether as prescription anti-depressants or wine ordered by the case for solitary consumption. People who take illegal drugs usually try to compensate for the lack of labelling, quality control, or legal comeback on dodgy suppliers by becoming as well informed as possible; this active consumer culture may be one reason why even the more dangerous illegal drugs kill only a small fraction of the number who die through using prescription drugs and alcohol and tobacco.[1]

Alcohol and tobacco always feature in the argument: how can

governments send people to prison for using pot while raking in funds from two drugs that are proven killers? Rather than staking out my own position I'd have preferred to lie low, at least till the end of the book, so as not to get bogged down in a stale debate. But in passing let me share the answer to the old alcohol-and-tobacco poser that was given to me at Scotland Yard in February 1999 by a superintendent in their Drugs Directorate. He told me that if these substances appeared tomorrow they would certainly be banned: a discouraging prospect to put before me as a paid-up member of the Circle of Wine Writers. In a more perfect world, in other words, my wine-making heroes in Alsace, Burgundy or Tuscany would be behind prison bars – or at least be undergoing counselling, as prescribed for arrested pot smokers under current Government plans.

Meanwhile the drinks firms are aggressively keen to 'demystify' what they sell – stripping it in effect of the ritual which helps limit its potential for harm. Wine has had a makeover to turn it into something for drinking without food. New products like alcopops and ready-mixed cocktails are targeted at club-goers and designed to wean them off drugs and back to booze: something that's been done quite successfully. Demystification has a long history; Europe did it successfully with tobacco, which in America before Columbus was a sacred herb which helped transport shamans into altered states of consciousness[2].

Of course cannabis is dangerous. It can cause acute anxiety, especially with inexperienced users; the risk for experienced users is that people who get stoned all the time can tend to let things slide. But cars and bicycles are dangerous, many sports are dangerous, family life is dangerous – and alcoholic drinks certainly are. Traditionally the media have dealt with cannabis as a social, health or criminological issue while considering wine and other alcoholic drinks as aspirational lifestyle subjects. Yet both cannabis and alcohol have health benefits as well as risks. The most significant difference is that alcohol, unlike cannabis, has historically been part of the culture which now dominates the world. And while cannabis and alcohol have very different kinds of effects, culturally they're second cousins.

As a wine writer, I'd expected my colleagues and contacts to be embarrassed when I told them about my new project. Instead I found that the people I most respected in the business formed a closetful of pot-heads. 'Please don't get anyone going on the subject of what I'm like when I'm stoned,' one particularly live-wire importer asked me. One of her older colleagues said he thought pot was 'a very good thing', and asked my opinion on whether a twenty-year-old lump of hashish in his kitchen dresser might still be worth smoking. Another guru of the wine trade told me: 'I'm one of the few people I know who still smokes it. I get it from one of my customers. One of the best growers is a Chianti producer in Tuscany, though his stuff is so strong I can barely smoke it – it sends me to sleep.'

The medieval Arabs used to argue about the respective merits of wine and hashish, whose discovery they attributed to a Sufi mystic called Haydar. One well-known ode goes:

> Give up wine and drink from the wine of Haydar
> Amber-scented, green the colour of emerald . . .'[3]

The American orientalist Franz Rosenthal uncovered a huge body of writing when he started investigating hashish in the medieval Arab world in the late 1960s. In his classic study, *The Herb*, he says he suspects 'that nearly every poet and productive amateur writer of verse, from the thirteenth to the sixteenth centuries, wrote at least some playful poems on hashish'. Today the rivalry between wine and weed that was such a marked theme of medieval Arab poetry has often been replaced by mutual tolerance. For years Serge Hochar, Lebanon's great wine maker, shared the Bekaa Valley with the most famous hashish plantations of the Middle East, which the Syrian authorities have now suppressed in response to American pressure. 'At least it wasn't heroin,' he said, and told me of a bas-relief on one of the vast ruined Roman temples at Baalbek showing a vine and a cannabis plant side by side.

Vines are long-lived woody climbers whereas cannabis is an annual, growing quickly to maturity and going to seed in a single season. Even so, the two plants have a surprising amount in common. They grow most strongly on flat ground, but for top quality rather than high yields are often best planted on hill slopes; they both deteriorate if they're over-fertilized and they're equally vulnerable to waterlogging. In each case the weather will determine whether it's a good or a bad vintage year. The best wine and the best pot come from dedicated growers working on a manageably small scale. Both have to be processed before they can be sold to the consumer, but success or failure is guaranteed by the grower; you can't make great hashish from poor plants or outstanding wine from mediocre grapes.

Writers on wine are inspired by its potential for diversity; but cannabis, like any natural product, can also take any number of forms. The different names are poetic: Thai sticks; Nepalese temple balls; Acapulco gold; Durban poison; Ketama Double Zero – or the modern American strains commercialized in Holland: Haze Skunk, Northern Lights. And you could no more mistake hand-rubbed charas – black, gummy and pungently aromatic – for Red Leb than you could confuse Mosel and Tokay.

You don't even have to consume wine and cannabis separately. It was Randall Grahm, the proprietor of Bonny Doon vineyards in Santa Cruz, California – top marijuana breeding country in the 1970s – who first told me about marijuana-

infused wine, made, apparently, at some of the top estates not by
the wine maker, but by cellar hands who grew the weed
between the rows of vines. The plants were then steeped in
the wine: ideally a chunky tannic red which could stand up to
the taste of the gummy marijuana buds.

It's traditional in Jamaica to make ganga tea, which is taken as
a medicine even by respectable people who wouldn't dream of
smoking it. But as cannabis doesn't dissolve in water tea isn't
ideal (probably in Jamaica the condensed milk dissolves the
cannabinoids, the active ingredients such as THC (tetrahydrocannabinol) which are fat-but not water-soluble). The cannabinoids dissolve readily in alcohol, however.

(The editor of a supposedly 'youth-oriented' Californian wine
magazine rubbished the idea that these marijuana cuvées existed
and told me off for harming the image of wine by associating it
with an illegal drug. This is a typically panicky American
reaction. Soon afterwards I met an Englishman who had personally drunk dope-infused wine in New York.)

It isn't only wine culture that hybridizes with cannabis. The
then head of one of the London auction houses' wine depart-
ments told me that the same thing goes on among cigar makers.
After being given a stogie with a marijuana core, he had once
gone on to conduct a tutored wine tasting, and found himself
gripped by lust. The lady he made a pass at was not at all
offended: 'She wouldn't leave me alone for the next three days;
it was a bit difficult to explain the situation to her.'

Hashish experts repay the compliment, though these days the
highest tribute they can pay to the grape is *not* to put any hemp
products in it. Just after the 1998 Cannabis Cup, the competition
organized annually in Amsterdam by the American magazine
High Times, I went to the city's Hemp Hotel to meet the
American author and botanist Rob Clarke at a signing of his
long-awaited magnum opus *Hashish!* He was late, so I'd gone to

the bar; everyone was drinking hemp beer, which contains extracts of THC-free hemp for flavouring. The idea is that as hops, which are related to cannabis, are used for flavouring, cannabis itself could also make a great additive. But, as Rob points out, hops have been selectively bred for this purpose for more than 1,000 years; hemp adds an oily, vegetal character. I asked if there was any ordinary beer, and encountered a questioning gaze from the grizzled Americans sitting along the bar. 'Do you have a problem with hemp, buddy?' one asked. Fortunately Rob saved my face; when he arrived he was holding a bottle of southern French red and boasting, 'It's hemp-free!'

It wasn't long into my research for this book that I started experiencing *déjà vu*. The way that experts talk about cannabis can be not just similar but actually identical to wine-speak. I first discovered this on a warm summer night in Brixton outside a pub that's steeped in history – Brady's, also known as The Railway, where Jimi Hendrix had a residency in the mid-sixties and where The Clash filmed *Rude Boy*. I was waiting for David, a friend of a friend of a friend who had been arrested a year earlier on a substantial pot-related offence and who I wanted to talk to about his experiences with the law.

As David was delayed I got chatting with his older brother Jim, who turned out to have spent many years in India – including eight months in a regional prison – and in consequence spoke fluent Hindi. His passion was the Kulu district in the Himalayan foothills, 3,500 metres above sea level, which is to pot connoisseurs what the Côte d'Or is to wine lovers. One of the valleys is named after Shiva's wife Parvatti: a legend says that the couple took up residence there and planted it with cannabis seeds. Jim and David had rented a field many years running, grown the local speciality, a wild plant called jangli that seeds itself from year to year, and made small quantities of top-quality charas, or hashish, by hand-rubbing the living marijuana plants.

Wine growers are interested in genetic diversity. In Burgundy especially traditionalists reject the clones introduced over the last quarter of a century and argue instead that you get more interesting wine from vines which naturally vary, giving different flavours, different quantities of grapes and fruit of slightly different degrees of ripeness. For vines read cannabis plants: Jim is equally convinced that jangli, the traditional wild cannabis, is better than the cultivated strains called bagicha that have now largely taken over. 'When we used to run through the fields you'd find that literally every plant smells different. *Sativa* plants are more mango, strawberry, very fruity smells. *Indica* – it's something like roast beef.'

David turned up a bit later, with a ponytail and an understandable trace of a careworn look. I had to leave and we agreed to meet another day at his flat. It was there, a couple of weeks later, that I learned that, as well as insisting on genetically diverse plants, Jim and David made hashish by the method that most of the world has abandoned. The standard modern technique is the one I saw on a visit to Morocco in the 1970s: the female plants are cut when ripe, after the males have been discarded, and they're then dried indoors for months. Hashish is not made from pollen, which is produced by the males in their small green flowers, but from resin glands on the female flowers. When the plants are dry these microscopic glands are loosened by shaking or beating the plant over a sieve, through which they fall as powder. The powder becomes hashish when the resin is freed from the cell walls of the glands – either by simple pressing, or by heating or wetting.

But the brothers have stayed with the Himalayan tradition of hand-rubbing. This has points of resemblance with hand-harvesting grapes, especially in regions like Sauternes where the pickers return repeatedly to remove individual grapes as they develop the prized 'noble rot' which concentrates sugars. To make charas like this requires practice and a sensitive touch; a harvester must stroke the flowering tops with enough pressure to get the palms of the hands covered with resin, but not so much as to bruise the plants and make them sappy. Only relatively tiny quantities can be made at a time and the process of getting the goo off the hands is tiresome. Another disadvantage is that bad weather can mean the complete loss of the harvest; plants for sieving can be cut down and brought in to dry under shelter before the weather breaks, but living plants risk rotting in the field before the resin glands have matured. 'It's really all about the taste,' explains David. 'There's just nothing in the world as sweet as hand-rubbed charas. Almost all hashish tastes rough by comparison – it catches in your throat.' Another of their obsessions is with what the French would call the *terroir* of these valleys: the importance of the extreme altitude, tempered by a perfect exposure to the sun on the south-facing slopes of a valley running from east to west.

Soon after this book was commissioned I went to the world's most famous hashish-producing village, Ketama in the Moroccan Rif (a visit during which, as I'll describe later, events overtook my indecision on whether to smoke pot or just write about it). There's a saying that 'Ketama loves only *kif*,'[4] this means that no other commercial crops will grow in this mountain valley with its long cold winters – one reason for the licence granted the area around 1890 by Sultan Hassan I. On the slopes of Mount Tidiguine, terraced with stone walls, everything happens late. Sowing can't be carried out until well into May, six weeks later than at lower altitudes, and the harvest which elsewhere will be under way in July can be as late as September.

Five years before I went there, a team working for the European Union had visited this region. The researchers, from the Paris-based Observatoire Géopolitique des Drogues, describe in a restricted-circulation report[5] how they had used personal contacts to get an invitation to the guarded residence of an important trafficker. He had shown them a hashish-processing workshop and garages that adapt vehicles to carry the standard trading unit of 250 kilos. The report describes a strict hierarchy in the Moroccan hashish business, of growers, middlemen who purchase the harvest, processors, wholesalers, carriers, Moroccan retailers, drug barons who control the whole process and official protectors at all levels of the Moroccan state, from local customs officers right up to individuals close to the palace.

I spent most of my time in Ketama with different members of a family based in the village of al Azila which, they told me, has grown 'al Qinnab al Hindi' ever since it first came to Morocco (at least 600 years ago). Aziz had a processing facility and also a small plot of land near the village on the ancient terraces. Like his neighbours, he claimed that because of the unique growing cycle Ketama and the other local hamlets are the ideal *terroir* for cannabis, and he was outraged by the new lowland plantations near Tetouan on the Mediterranean coast.[6] His view that high altitudes bring quality would be endorsed by any wine grower: the longer plants take to reach maturity, the longer they can work as chemical factories, adding flavour compounds in grapes, THC and other cannabinoids in cannabis.

When I was in Ketama I increasingly felt that the *kif* farmers lived in a kind of parallel universe to wine growers. One similarity was the insecurity felt by the farmers who made the best hashish and *kif*. 'Ketama' has been a brand-name for top Moroccan hashish since the 1970s, like 'Burgundy' or 'Nuits St-Georges' for red wine, but, as with wine before the advent of legal protection in the 1930s, the farmers of Ketama have no way of stopping others from cashing in on their reputation. The EU report's authors estimated the total area growing cannabis in Morocco as at least 64,000 hectares – more than a ten-fold increase of the traditional zone of cultivation.

The approach to new technology was also familiar. Just like a young *vigneron*, Aziz contrasted his generation with 'the old guys who didn't really known what they were doing. It's the attention to hygiene plus new technology that's brought about the big improvements in quality,' he said. This technology is imported: high-quality sieves from Japan; high-temperature plastic to seal the blocks of hashish from Holland, plus some selected high-yielding seed strains. And, again like French wine growers, the farmers in Ketama are worried about the help that technology will give their rivals in compensating for their lack of an ideal *terroir*. After dark I mooched around the dusty fringes of the village with Tammam and a second grower also called Tammam, while they fretted about a visit to Holland. What upset them was that the Dutch growers were diversifying from sinsemilla buds into hashish: 'Have you seen it? They dry the plants just like we do. Soon there's going to be nothing left for us.'

In hashish as in wine, the nicest people to spend time with are the producers who are small enough both to grow and process the crop. They speak scornfully about the makers of bulk hashish or 'resina'. This is made with the coarse, greenish powder that can be beaten from the dried plants after the best stuff, the 'double-zero' powder that's almost pure resin glands, has been gently tapped through a fine sieve;[7] because of its low resin content cheap hashish is often stuck together with adulterants. Salesmen like to impress clients by showing that like the top-quality product, it holds a flame when lit – but this isn't surprising considering that wax is commonly used to stretch it. This stuff, dark and oily-looking when compared to tradi-tional average-quality Moroccan hashish, is called 'soap bar' because it's usually shaped like Cussons Imperial Leather (the other 250-gram shape is known as a 'passport').

Britain is a major market for low-grade soap bar, and it can undergo further stretching after importation. I met a former prisoner whose cellmate had worked with a gang who mixed it with bitumen as used in surfacing roads (perhaps hashish, like cigarettes, should have a warning about tar levels). '100 kilos would go in; 115 would go out,' he told me. Dutch coffee shops won't touch soap bar, though some go in for a milder deception: I heard of coffee-shop workers being asked to cut Moroccan hashish into different shapes in order to sell it under a variety of brand-names.

Tammam took me to meet a quality-oriented producer called Abdul Hayy on his smallholding beside the road to the outlying village of Talata Ketama. The sun had set when we got there, but as well as the vivid stars there was a full moon revealing the jaggedness of the mountain landscape, with pines, cistus and a forest of countless pointy-headed cannabis plants scrambling up peaks in every direction. The drive had been dusty; the tap-rooted cannabis is worsening the soil erosion that began when the occupying Spaniards brought in chain-saws to fell the forests during their protectorate of Eastern Morocco.[8]

Abdul Hayy was a small, oldish man with a twinkly smile. He offered a hashish joint, made with the local black tobacco, but wasn't offended when I also didn't want to sample his *kif*, saying, 'It's not good to get too stoned.' He told me he'd cut down the forest to create his farm; I tut-tutted on ecological grounds and unsettled him further by asking the questions you ask wine growers: how many hectares did he have and how long had he been there? He shot a questioning glance at Tammam and said apologetically, 'I'm sorry; I have a little paranoia.' ('Paranoia' and 'hassle' are two words that have passed straight from English into modern Moroccan Arabic.)

The harvest had started, and Abdul Hayy took me up onto the flat roof of his house to show me the bundled stooks of plants that had been put to dry before being taken downstairs for further drying. One worker was chopping some flowering tops with a knife to make proper old-fashioned *kif*. This is the way Moroccans traditionally smoke cannabis, in a pipe: the long pencil-like sabsi topped with a small disposable clay end called, tongue-twistingly, a shkef. The effect is more like having a small glass of beer than blowing your head off with a joint of double-zero; groups of Moroccan men can usually be seen with a sabsi at dusk in parks and other public open spaces. People like Abdul Hayy have made a living selling top-grade hashish to discerning Westerners who would come to buy the odd kilo. Again, there is an analogy with wine growers who do most of their business selling a case or two at a time to loyal customers from the nearest big city.

But since the early 1990s the region has experienced a 'War on Drugs'-type crackdown partly directed, in the view of the researchers who wrote the 1994 report for the European Union, at eliminating competition with the big-scale producers and smuggling rings which enjoy official protection. The middle-sized growers are suffering from this and from the 'paranoia' of potential customers. Almost all the best-selling guides to Morocco say that it's standard practice for dealers to tip off the police, earning them both a reward and the return of the confiscated stash. I mentioned this to Aziz. He replied with an expression of pain that I think was genuine, 'I would never do that; no one would ever sell a customer. He is putting himself into the fire. I would do anything to help him.' I believed him – although I wouldn't want to try the experiment.

As Muslims, the Moroccans have always regarded cannabis as having greater legitimacy than alcohol. In 1959 their Government threatened to implement a complete ban on *kif* throughout the traditional growing region. The Rifi farmers rose in revolt, saying they would accept a ban on *kif* only if the Government brought in a corresponding crackdown on alcohol. Aziz told me: 'If you drink alcohol you can fight and you can steal. You can't go and steal if you're stoned. *Kif* makes people calm and it makes them honest. We know it very well. A drug is something strange, something new, like heroin or cocaine. This is not a drug.'

Any number of people have told me that cannabis isn't a drug: one of those 'Yeah, right' statements that don't seem worth the bother of arguing over. But you can see what they're saying: that pot belongs in a category of everyday mind-altering substances like tea, coffee and alcohol. I certainly don't think that within this category alcohol deserves any greater legitimacy: both come from cultural traditions that deserve equal respect. Just as European food and wine lured my parents' generation out of a sense of insular superiority, hashish and grass have been the bait to bring Europeans and North Americans into contact with Mexicans, North and West Africans, Afghans, Thais and Indians, with a sense of exploration and equality. Today cannabis activists from both sides of the Atlantic often like to dress and talk like Rastas and listen endlessly to tunes that were hits in Jamaican dance-halls in the mid-1970s. This can create a feeling of a time warp, but so what: there's something civilized in seeing Europeans and white Americans and Australasians acknowledging a cultural debt.

David went to Morocco with his girlfriend soon after I met him, on a short holiday intended to make the most of his last weeks of freedom. He admitted that he'd 'become a bit Indocentric' but he was impressed by the best Moroccan hashish. He went to Chefchaoen, a town in the western Rif largely built by Muslim refugees from the Christian reconquest of Andalucia and strongly reminiscent of southern Spain. Unlike Ketama it is not regarded as beyond the pale, and it's as clean and picturesque as Ketama is shabby and garbage-strewn. David was offered double-zero-grade hashish; the proposed deal would have involved placing an order on the spot, but taking delivery and making the actual payment in Malaga, at a price that reflected the expense of smuggling it to the coast and into Spain. The main difference he found was the greater commercialism of the Rif. Himalchal Pradesh is now famous or notorious for charas, but the northern Indian farmers have not yet turned cannabis into a huge cash crop on the scale of Morocco.

What they and their counterparts in the Rif have in common, however, is a pride in what they produce and a refusal to be browbeaten into according alcohol any greater legitimacy. The cannabis culture originates in India, where Shiva, in legend the divine planter of the cannabis fields of the Kulu district, is described as 'The Lord of Bhang', the drink made of cannabis leaves, milk, sugar and spices. The phrase comes from the *Athar Veda*, one of the Sanskrit hymns written down in the twelfth century but forming part of an oral tradition going back around two millennia. Bhang is part of India's living culture. One historian of cannabis[9] writes how 'without bhang on special festivals like a wedding, evil spirits were believed to hover over the bride and groom, waiting for an opportune moment to wreak havoc on the newlyweds'. In the late 1970s the social anthropologist David Jones became familiar with modern Hindu villagers' use of bhang. He spent time both in Nepal, carrying out fieldwork for his M. Phil degree in religious change in that country, and across the border in Himalchal Pradesh. From observing the ritual of preparing bhang, pounding cannabis in a pestle and steeping it with milk, he is strongly inclined to believe that bhang is the same thing as the plant beverage called soma, whose ritual preparation is the subject of the 200 or so hymns that make up the ninth and probably oldest section of the *Rig Veda*.[10] *Soma* is both the offering to the god and the god itself; historians and scholars of Sanskrit have endlessly debated which plant the hymns refer to.

Clifford Wright, Professor of Sanskrit at the London School of Oriental and African Studies, sounded depressed at the suggestion that soma was cannabis. A previous candidate has been some kind of fermented alcoholic drink, and researchers are still recovering from a thirty-year-battle to refute an identification with the red and white-spotted Fly Agaric mushroom. Many scholars now think soma was made from *Ephedra*, a plant species with an amphetamine-like effect, but admit that there's no evidence.

But why, asks David Jones, now keeper of Human Resources at Ipswich Museum, should a ritual drink used in medieval and modern times by Himalayan peoples not be the same as the one celebrated by their remote ancestors? He thinks there are two reasons why people won't make what he regards as an obvious connection, having discovered that the preparations described in the *Rig Veda* correspond to what he saw in Himalayan villages. One is that Sanskrit scholars try on principle to ignore current Hindu practices and concentrate on the study of ancient texts. The result, he believes, is that they probably don't know how bhang is made, and so are unable to see an obvious parallel. Another is that modernizing and reform movements in Hinduism feel obliged to explain away such awkward parts of their heritage as animal sacrifice and the use of cannabis, even when these have scriptural authority. 'Why look for something else? There are people who say that when the Bible mentions wine it means unfermented grape juice, but if you look at the people who say that, they usually turn out to be teetotallers. If you have modern Christians and Jews using wine liturgically, why strain the evidence and say "It wasn't wine, it was lemonade"?'

To many Hindus cannabis still has the religious importance that wine has to Christians celebrating the Eucharist. David described to me how his friend Donald had smoked chillums, or stemless pipes, of charas with the crowds at the festivals called Kumbh Mela that circulate between eight of the great historic cities of North India. He had also given away charas to Saddhus, or Hindu mystics, to smoke in the prayer ceremony called Puja. 'It's one thing the Saddhus like about Westerners,' said David. 'We're apparently well known for having better-quality charas.'

It's a pity there weren't more visitors like Donald at the greatest Kumbh Mela, at the holy city of Benares, or Varanasi, on the Ganges when this was held for the first time after cannabis was made illegal throughout India. Dominique Rogers, a Frenchwoman who lived for some time in Goa, told me how some fifteen years ago, the worshippers were joined by a tall, red-haired English friend of hers called Robin Brown. Brown, who writes on India, received a coveted invitation to serve as a tea boy to the chief Saddhus in the large marquee where they traditionally offer Puja. The trouble was that the recent prohibition meant there was no hashish available for the holy men. The Saddhus refused to invent a hashish-free version. The Benares police soon learned of the problem and were aghast at the prospect of riot and mayhem should 15 million pilgrims learn that the Saddhus were unable to perform Puja.

As there was no chance of finding enough hashish in Benares, the city's police chief sent a buying team in a truck to Delhi, 450 miles away. There, to their relief, they found that expatriate Afghans had what they were looking for. They loaded a ton and a half of black hashish into the truck and returned in triumph to the Saddhus' marquee. But when they unwrapped the haul the Saddhus were outraged rather than grateful. The pieces of hashish were individually stamped with markings showing that they came from an Islamic state – and it was only when the police agreed to sit down to scrape the stamps off every single 250-gram slab that they were finally mollified.

It's appropriate that India has become the place of secular pilgrimage for Western cannabis lovers since the 1960s. Despite what many people believe, the plant is not native to Africa or the Americas; researchers suggested that it first grew wild in Central Asia, from where the nomadic Scythians of around 1500 BC spread its use as a drug into the mountains to the south in modern Iran, Afghanistan, Pakistan and India. When you visit India you realize how much late-sixties hippie style was taken straight from the subcontinent: not just beads, henna and joss-sticks, but the long dishevelled hair and beards that made kids from American and European suburbs into a fair approximation of Hindu holy men. But that was a fad: one direction that fashion briefly took. Today, after innumerable swings of the pendulum, weed has settled down in Britain, as familiar as Vindaloo, barely more foreign than coffee or gin (in their day thought of respectively as Turkish and Dutch). This process has gone on throughout my life – and I've seen some of it at first hand.

2

Mugglesborough

Things I remember about my first joint: the hot smoke produced by loosely re-rolled cigarette tobacco smoked in and around a phone box at the South Kensington end of the Fulham Road; a rasping taste; the erratic way it burned. It was a weak grass joint and I can't remember any effects. Afterwards, the friend I shared it with probably went to a party and I would have gone home to my mother and sister.

My motive was the same as any English public schoolboy's before or since: the quest for cool. At least it seemed a better bet than my earlier interests (London Underground rolling stock followed by dogmatic Trotskyism). Dope has stayed in favour in the 'better' English fee-paying schools because it shows that you're not trying too hard, as required by their gentlemanly code. One high point of those years was when an acquaintance returned, not from university or a crammer's, but from prison, and hung out in the school yard showing off a packet of cigarette papers marked, I think, 'HM Government Property'.

'Cool' may not have been that different from the 'good form' required of the English officer class at the time of Waterloo, but of course the language was different. 'Man', 'bread', 'hassle', even the stuff about 'keeping on trucking', all came from black American street-talk of about a decade or two earlier, just as 'underground' music did with 'British Blues' and its note-for-note copies of Elmore James. Compared to modern Britain (which is a kind of melting-pot, however uneven), and unlike the working-class mods and skinheads, the first flowing of hippiedom was a consumer phenomenon, rather disappointed when it came face to face with itself at pop festivals.[1] The clothes, the language, the politics came from far away, via records, *Easy Rider*, John Peel's *Perfumed Garden* radio show, the underground press. Did it lack 'authenticity', whatever that means? Well, I did.

Still, it was better than the alternative of fogeyism. This was a period of noble aspirations, clumsily or crassly expressed: school-boys playing Roy Harper's 'I Hate the White Man' as an act of subversion at morning prayer assemblies, or Richard Neville, the *Oz* editor, telling readers of his book *Playpower* that 'dope blackens the white man'. It's true, of course, that the modern use of cannabis does come from among the subject peoples of Britain and America rather than their imperial masters – hence this stereotype.

Even these days this kind of lazy thinking persists, as shown in the case of a forty-something lecturer on my girlfriend's university course. He joked that a dreadlocked black student, who'd had to go out for a moment, was 'going to phone his dealer'. The class told the student, who doesn't take drugs, and he then demanded a public apology. The lecturer's blunder came about through trying too hard – through wanting to seem at home in a culture he saw as symbolized by cannabis, but missing the one important thing about it: the ability to ditch preconceptions and treat people as individuals.

In fact almost any generalization about cannabis and race turns out to be oversimplified. Over the last half-century cannabis has moved into the British mainstream, from two originally separate groups of user: college students and the West Indian immigrants who the yellow press of the 1950s saw as threatening to engulf Britain with reefer. In fact, up until the present day there's been a separate market for black people; one of the people who supply it, a motherly ex-restaurant owner, has been known to generations of African students. But British weed smokers at any rate now talk like Jamaicans: spliff and ganga have entered the language.

The word ganga is itself a reminder that no one people has a monopoly on the weed. For Rastafarians, 'herb' and the rituals of smoking come from Africa and form part of a heritage they find celebrated in numerous passages of the Bible. The Rasta version of the past is an explanatory narrative, describing the kind of people they are, and comparable with the work of the Roman state poet Virgil or Old Testament stories about the origins of Israel.

But like them it isn't a historical record. In fact, cannabis smoking seems to have come to Jamaica with the Indian indentured labourers brought over by the British in the mid-nineteenth century – even though modern Indian communities in the West Indies no longer smoke it. Ganga is the word for weed in both India and Jamaica, and the Jamaicans, like Indians, smoke ganga in chillums, the stemless pipes, which they call kutchies, as well as in water-pipes. Top weed is called cally, which sounds like a piece of forgotten homage to Kali, the Indian goddess of destruction.[2]

These connections are pointed out by Lambros Couiras and Vera Rubin, an American social anthropologist who in the 1960s carried out a definitive study of the role of ganga in Jamaican life. Their work is a great antidote to clichéd thinking. For example, they found that farm workers did not work less hard if they were heavy smokers. But ganga was far from being accepted universally – the middle and upper-middle classes disapproved, and because it was illegal, it was as much an adolescent rite of passage for young male Jamaicans as it is in English public schools.

In the United States too, the marijuana habit took some unpredictable detours as it spread between the Mexican and black communities and white hipsters. One of the key links was Milton 'Mezz' Mezzrow, a white jazz saxophonist in the 1930s who claims in his autobiography[3] to have turned black Harlem on to the habit, bulk-buying 'muggles', as they called it then, from a Mexican importer in the South. He wrote:

> Overnight I was the most popular man in Harlem. On the Corner I was to become known as the Reefer King, the Link between the Races, the Philosopher, the Mezz, Poppa Mezz, Momma Mezz, Pop's boy, the White Mayor of Harlem, the Man about Town, the Man that Hipped the World, the Man that Made History, the Man with the Righteous Bush, He who Diggeth the Digger, Father Neptune.

It's because cannabis has been spread through personal contacts that it comes with such rich associations. Thirty years ago, when the process had barely begun, the hippie media drooled over non-European cultures with roughly the same level of insight and discrimination that Peter Mayle brought to his year in Provence. Anything that didn't conform to a cliché was invisible. One of the biggest changes since then has been the fashion for contemporary black music (rather than for the extinct masterpieces of Blues and R'n'B). Since reggae first crossed over in the 1970s, and again with rap in the 1980s, followed by jungle in the 1990s, mass audiences have experienced black cultural movements more or less as they happen, instead of with a time delay.

One effect is that everyone knows that cannabis can be a symbol of protest instead of escapism. For Bob Marley in Jamaica, as for Fela Kuti, the dissident star of Nigerian music,

weed represented the culture of the poor majority against the
élite put in place by the departing colonialists. Nigeria's rulers
sentenced Fela Kuti to eleven years in jail ostensibly for cannabis
offences – really, in most Nigerians' eyes, to silence a political
dissident. As we get Third World societies in focus, we see ways
of using cannabis that turn out to be startlingly different from the
passivity of the Fabulous Furry Freak Brothers.

Take Egypt. The criminologist Ahmad M. Khalifa[4] describes
small circles of friends who gather round a water-pipe, with one
of them acting as the 'sultan' who takes care that the pipe is
loaded up, that the water is clean and that the charcoal is
replenished. The participants, says Khalifa, are 'amused by the
slightest matters and exchange jokes and words of endearment'.
From studying Arabic at university I remembered Naguib
Mahfouz, the Nobel Laureate novelist, writing quite affectio-
nately about the 'gruff laughter' of hashish smokers in his 1940s'
novel *Midaq Alley*. And just before I visited Egypt in 1982 a
movie comedy called *al Bātiniyya*, about life in the hash dealing
quarter near the al Azhar mosque, had been a huge popular hit.

In 1989 I'd gone to Cairo to interview Mahfouz, filming him
at one of his weekly meetings with the group of now elderly
friends who called themselves '*al Harafish*', 'the street people'.
But I had never got round to asking him what he thought about
pot. To make good the omission, I got in touch with a friend of
his to ask at second hand for the views of the Arab world's
greatest novelist. I was pointed to his 1960s' novel, *Tharthara
fawqa al Nil*, translated as *Drifters on the Nile*; this is about a civil
servant who meets with a circle of friends for regular sessions
round a water-pipe on a moored house-boat. After flicking
through the book I asked what attitude Mahfouz would take to
his characters' hashish-smoking. 'Don't you see?' his friend told
me. 'This book is a description of al Harafish and the main
character is Mahfouz.'

I was given a crash course on hashish in modern Egypt. 'You know the political jokes that go around? They all come out of these sessions where once you get high, the collective mind takes over from the individual mind and people have this quick repartee and become empathetic. Hashish is also an excuse to protect them; people can say, "They're not in their right minds – they're not conscious of what they're saying." They can say things for which if they were sober they'd go to prison.'

Mahfouz's friend, who is a professor of Arabic literature, and who does not himself smoke hashish believes that it's this political aspect of cannabis which has always made it unpopular with Egypt's rulers. It was in Egypt during Napoleon's occupation that a European power first enacted prohibitionist laws, and at the international Opium Conference of 1925 it was the Egyptian delegation that insisted on extending the ban to cannabis. But the religious scholars, the *ulema*, don't share this prejudice, and have always ruled it more acceptable to Islam than alcohol, which is explicitly banned in the *Qur'ān*. And he said there was no popular feeling against hashish smokers, whilst it was disgraceful to be *bitaa kubeyah* – someone who uses a wine-glass.

Of course creativity and wit weren't exclusively confined to Harlem in the 1930s or the DJ artists of 1970s' Kingston; as well as pomp rock and lots of versions of Neil from The Young Ones the psychedelic era did have some high points. And you don't have to be white and middle-class to go catatonic when stoned. In the 1970s the children of the first generation of West Indian immigrants took up ganga, generally to their parents' disapproval, and began spending their evenings barely swaying in front of sound systems (in the disco era this was great for diffident white dub fans, who didn't have to risk trying to dance). Reggae artists tended to be militant about their enthusiasm for ganga (Peter Tosh's 'Legalize it', etc.).

By a quirk of history all this coincided with punk and the new consensus – uniting The Clash, the Socialist Workers Party and Julie Burchill – that joint-smoking hippies were passive, pathetic and boring. Mick Farren and Charles Shaar Murray, who had been the reigning gods of *New Musical Express* in the early 1970s, get a working-over in Julie Burchill's 1998 autobiography, *I Knew I Was Right*, for their hair-cuts (the frizzy style she christened the 'Izro' (i.e. a Jewish Afro) and for filling the adjoining cubicle in the *NME* offices with clouds of dope. (She and Tony Parsons, the other 'hip young gunslinger' hired in 1976, felt this justified a rain of lighted matches thrown over the partition to try to set light to their colleagues' Izros.) I don't know what Murray and Farren were like to work with, but I can identify irritating bits of an early seventies' cannabis world view still lodged in my own personality. There's the lazy blankness, the self-absorbed manner, recalling the effects of too much therapy and the belief that one's own thoughts and insights are uniquely profound.

Dope stopped being a mark of fashion but it didn't go away. The Legalize Cannabis Campaign got going in 1978. Unlike in America, consumption continued to increase,[5] until today more than 40 per cent of people under twenty-five have at some time had a puff on a joint. I discovered that 'straight' people were starting to take it up during the late 1970s when I was a trainee reporter on a weekly local newspaper in north-west London, and had just been for Christmas lunch with my colleagues at the local Esso Motor Hotel. The only other young male reporter had short hair and wore a Crombie-type overcoat and a neatly tucked-in scarf, and was the last person I'd have expected to suggest, as he did, that we share a festive spliff on the fire escape outside the office, above the Gas Showroom.

John Peel once got some notoriety for saying it was the English folk music clubs rather than the hip labels sprouted by the record majors that represented a genuine underground culture. Cannabis went underground in this unglamorous sense, eclipsed by amphetamine sulphate in the late 1970s, by cocaine in the 1980s and by Ecstasy in the 1990s, but growing steadily. The heartland was no longer confined to Kensington, Notting Hill, Brixton and the university towns, but was spreading to what George Orwell, writing in 1941,[6] called 'the place to look for the terms of the future England . . . the new townships that have developed as a result of cheap motor cars and the southward shift of industry . . . Slough, Dagenham, Barnet, Letchworth, Hayes . . .'

Gangsters helped meet the demand when they began organizing imports by the containerload. In the 1960s, according to the Government inquiry chaired by Baronness Wootton which reported in 1967, importation was piecemeal, largely by individual travellers returning from producing countries. As late as 1979, Don Aitken, then of Release, could characterize smugglers as 'the man who goes to Morocco or Afghanistan with £2,000 in his pocket' and talk about the widely felt distrust of drug-dealing's money-making potential – 'most proponents of alternative culture still have uneasy feelings about this type of activity' – which he contrasted with the more relaxed West Indian attitude to financial success.[7]

But by this time weed was becoming part of the way of life of the established criminal class. As early as the 1960s the Krays had discovered the stuff, and taken to it with enthusiasm. The son of one of the bouncers at their clubs told me that they'd diversified from amphetamines into cannabis importing, and that without it Ronnie 'would have been even nuttier than he was'. (I asked him for more details and he conferred with his dad, who advised me to leave the subject well alone: 'No one writes about the Krays without their permission.') In the 1970s the profits that could be made from cannabis were starting to attract gangs who were interested in avoiding the long jail sentences handed down for armed robbery.[8] The murder of the black teenager Stephen Lawrence in south-east London in 1993 put the spotlight on this new kind of dope dealer. Clifford Norris, the father of one of the racist suspects, was a major smuggler, who, according to the Lawrence family's legal team, managed to induce corrupt police to bungle the investigation deliberately. The five suspects belong to a social category undreamt of in the 1960s' Summer of Love: violent pot-smoking racists.

When my children were very young, in the mid- and late 1980s, I hardly ever came across dope – though cannabis helped fuel the romance that brought them into existence. (When I came home on my first date with their mother, I woke up another member of my shared household who I knew had a stash.) But in 1995 I inherited money and we moved into a big house in a smarter street; we could afford to pay not just builders to do structural work, but a decorator. One day my wife had a surprise: quite a big piece of black hashish that she'd found in the toilet where Andy, the painter, had been working. We asked Andy if he'd lost anything and he accepted the lump back (now nibbled away a bit) on behalf of 'one of the other blokes who might have dropped it' – but later he owned up.

   Andy turned out to be famous for his love of spliff; when the other builders couldn't find, say, some rawlplugs, they'd guess that 'Andy's smoked them'. He'd work conscientiously, the room filling with smoke, refusing to apply any paint without days of 'prepping'. This was the way he'd been taught to work by his father, but it brought him into endless conflict with his scrimping employers whose incompetent plumbing drenched our house and rotted the plaster. Despite his late-sixties look (centre-parted hair and John Lennon glasses), he is a dealer who buys from old-established criminal families. All his suppliers are in 'firms', as in 'Jonesie's firm' or 'the Reynolds' firm'.

These guys have nothing in common with the alternative culture of the 1970s. As Andy described them, they're most likely to be found on a golf-course, mobile phone in hand, and the drugs they'd be most likely to take would normally be body-building steroids. 'The higher up they are, the less drugs they do themselves personally, but then they'll do big weekends, special occasions, and they'll go absolutely bonkers. They'll never do none during the week but then they'll be like doing a bender, doing lines and drinking.' His main current contacts were 'a Paddy firm: these geezers who was night-club bouncers in Bedford. You remember them four geezers that was shot; you must remember – it was in a Transit van. Oh no, it wasn't – it was in a Landrover.'[9]

In larger-scale dealing there isn't the socializing that goes with buying a quarter of an ounce. 'You'd be meeting in the streets and in pub car parks. You'd go round to the other boot, get the bag out and fucking get in your car.' But his experience has been that even small-scale dealing isn't always particularly friendly, especially in the depressed provinces. 'It's where you get people selling the ounces, ticking out an eighth to dole people. They'd get their puff on tick till they got their dole money, then they spent their dole money. Their mates would fucking beat them up and turn them upside down to get their money out of them.'

Though he's a nice person, Andy is a liability in terms of the public image of cannabis. 'I think you should try everything,' he told me. 'Have you tried smack? I have, three times. The first two times I was shitting myself that I was going to be addicted, but the third time I'd got a bit used to the type of thing that was going to happen.' In his experience drug users who smoke and nothing else are 'a minority – about 10 per cent, and there's a minority who do one particular thing, like coke or speed or Es, and another 10 per cent just do Es and the rest do everything.'

I mentioned to Andy that David's friend Donald had a few

ounces of what he was claiming as the best hashish in the world: 'cream' – top-grade hand-rubbed charas from the Parvatti Valley. He leapt at the opportunity to go round and sample it, and I was intrigued to see two drug cultures meet head-on. Andy wasn't disappointed with the charas: 'Fucking wicked gear,' was his verdict afterwards. I'd been as tense as anyone who introduces people who may or may not get on. There was a bit of bonding; David was there and able to compare notes on police raids. Andy told David that a friend of his had just been arrested by police in flak jackets who'd kicked the door down – 'Loudest sound they'd ever heard in their life,' said Andy. 'BANG!' Unlike David, who'd been woken at dawn, this had happened at 6.30 on a Friday evening. 'They were probably hoping to find some action going on,' David guessed. He and Donald went on to reassure Andy about his mate, taking the moral high ground about pot. 'When you want to stop it, you just stop like that. Not like fucking chemicals, man.' I prayed that Andy wouldn't mention the Es also stashed in his friend's house.

In fact he only reacted to the purist atmosphere when we were out in the street: 'They were real puff smokers weren't they, like you was saying.' Then back in his car we started debating dealers' codes of practice. The charas was selling for £10 a gram, which would work out at £350 an ounce – very steep, even for 'the world's best'. Andy had been refused a discount he wanted for an eighth of an ounce (dealers have to be a lot better than me at metric-avoirdupois conversion), and suspected that the penny used on the scales had been weighted. I thought this was no more likely than that a wine importer would water down *grand cru* Burgundy. You leave it to the mystique to inflate the prices. Andy just said 'He's a dealer' and wouldn't accept there was more than one way of doing things: 'otherwise you're a mug'.

★   ★   ★

Jail helped create the new cannabis culture. Peter Timms, governor of Maidstone Prison from 1975 to 1981, remembers the change. 'I suspect that if you looked at disciplinary reports in the late seventies and early eighties you'd start to find less reports about alcohol and more about cannabis than five or ten years earlier. It's a bit of an institutional game to beat the authorities making hooch, and the game changed in a way.' Making illegal alcohol involved bulky equipment, and the stuff smelt. So of course do burning joints, but the smell could be camouflaged behind the pungency of prison tobacco. Cannabis was routinely smuggled in – 'On open visits it was relatively easy for men to secrete in a variety of orifices.' Timms denies turning a blind eye to cannabis, but says that it was something dealt with as and when it arose rather than actively sought out. 'If you started going on purges on anything that was the road to disaster. You give it an attraction it doesn't deserve whatever it happens to be.'

In those other closed communities, fee-paying schools, cannabis stayed popular – not just among the pupils but sometimes among their parents as well. In 1998 Caroline Noortman, a former BBC radio journalist who is the mother of two public school boys, set up an organization called the London Lecture Group to lay on conferences on the issue of drugs in school. She says that there are pot smokers among the parents concerned enough to book places: 'You can get even quite nerdy-looking, quite anoraky parents who see giving a joint to their kid as a sort of rite-of-passage thing.'

It's the well-off who are the biggest drug users. The Institute for the Study of Drug Dependence[10] pulled together statistics on drugs in Britain for *Social Trends*, the Government's annual guide to the way the country is changing. It found that the richest group in society, who in today's jargon are called the 'thriving', are the second most likely group to use drugs between the ages of sixteen and twenty-nine, though their level of use falls to the lowest in the thirty to fifty-nine age group. The poorest class, the 'striving', show a less marked decline as they get older, from 24 per cent having used drugs in the last year, falling to 7 per cent in the group aged thirty and over. But the astonishing figure is the one related to the 'rising' class, defined as 'prosperous professionals in inner-city areas and better-off executives in metropolitan areas'. This class is most likely to use drugs when young – meaning predominantly cannabis – and more than six times as likely as the seriously rich to continue using when over thirty.

It's not often that you get all the different cannabis tribes under a single roof. But that was what was achieved by Britain's biggest retail cannabis operation of recent times. Most people only heard of the Back Beat Club on 2 December 1998, the day after 500 police armed with stun grenades and sub-machine-guns stormed the three-storey building in Denmark Place, a cul-de-sac leading off the Charing Cross Road in London's West End. But during the course of the year its reputation had grown steadily. For Zelda and Daniel, who were colleagues in a local office, it was like going to the pub after work on Friday, except that both liked to stay till 6 a.m.

Daniel: 'I think for me it was the convenience. After a hard day's work you could leave Tottenham Court Road, the traffic, and go somewhere and totally forget about it all. Basically we'd go to a wine bar, get totally hammered on alcohol, and then sit and buy a draw. You could get all the supplies you need: buy your weed, buy your Rizla behind the bar, sit down at a table and roll your spliff.'

Zelda: 'You had this room where you could chill out and play your own music and just sit there for hours stoned off your trolley. On the dance floor there was a lot of really young people off their faces on Ecstasy and cocaine. One of the guys did sell Ecstasy but the main thing was weed.'

Daniel: 'We used to call it the United Nations. There were more foreigners there sometimes than English people.'

Zelda: 'It was just like a local shebeen, but you don't see white people in those apart from white prostitutes with Yardie pimps . . . This was men, women, black, white, Indian, Chinese. It was totally multicultural. You can't believe that a place like that would be in the West End.'

Daniel: 'It's a high-profile place for tourists, but you've got this operation which is 100 per cent illegal. But they got away with it and more and more people actually get away with it.'

In fact the Back Beat mixed not only races and nationalities but classes and age groups. There were City workers in suits, middle-aged train-spotter types, with anoraks and unfashionable glasses. In the late autumn, when it was obvious that a raid must be imminent, the regulars eyed each other nervously wondering if the respectable-looking ones were Drug Squad officers playing a game of double bluff. The operation was protected with CCTV cameras with a view not just outside the door but up the Charing Cross Road.

But the club itself was being watched. For six months, according to the *Evening Standard*, there had been surveillance teams in the EMI publishing offices opposite. For the final assault, timing was crucial to catch the dealers with the drugs. One team threw stun grenades after abseiling from the roof; another burst from an apparently broken-down lorry and swept in from the street, armed with sub-machine-guns and wearing flak jackets. Scotland Yard's press briefings led journalists to believe they'd find guns and hard drugs. But later in the week the story had scaled down; they'd only found cannabis. An *Evening Standard* team described how this was dealt out through a hatch, in £10 deals at a time of 'black' or weed: none of the punters were allowed inside to see the scale of the operation.

★   ★   ★

Except for my interviewee Zelda. She's a small, mischievous, mixed-race woman of thirty, who moved to an outer suburb to be able to bring up her two children away from guns, Yardies and drugs. 'Their father moved too – to prison.' Her passions are weed and excitement, which she sometimes finds in spur-of-the-moment sex with acquaintances of either gender. She rapidly bonded with the doormen at the Back Beat, first by discovering that they'd been at school together, and a little later with successive encounters in the locked stock-room at the top of the stairs. 'I didn't want to take them home: I just wanted to have sex with them.' She doesn't accept my description of her as 'queen of the Back Beat', but she did enjoy certain prerogatives, like walking to the front of queues, knowing from experience that the doormen would throw out anyone who objected.

But Zelda's writ only ran on the bottom floors of the club, with the doormen and the barmen, who were black English. Outside the drugs room was a man who wore a glove even during the hottest weather to protect himself from 'residue' – powder traces from firing a hand-gun. Inside the room, as she found out, the drugs were guarded by recently arrived Jamaican gangsters. She didn't enjoy her experience there.

'Jesus, that was just mad. I'd been downstairs with my friends and we were completely pissed. We'd taken a bottle of Jack Daniels in with us and we were drinking Jack Daniels all night. I said, "I'm going upstairs and buy a draw." I went upstairs and knocked. There was this guy sitting outside the hatch, and I put my money through, and all of a sudden the door swung open. There was three Yardies in there. The guy just sitting in front of the hatch helped me into this room. There was mountains, piles of weed like I'd never seen before, coke like I'd never seen before, and security TV screens.

'This guy said, "What do you want?" I said, "I just want to buy a draw." He said, "Have it." I said, "I'll pay for what I

want." You don't get nothing for nothing. I knew they were
Yardies because of the way they spoke: they were definitely just
off the boat. I know what Yardies are like and I know what
they're like with English women, whether they're black or
white. They expect a certain thing from you. I want to fuck
someone because I want pleasure, but the Yardies are into their
little gang-bangs and shoving fucking bottles up women. They
like to see violence and all sorts of shit.

'He said, "What do you suggest we all do?" They kept talking
in that fucking Yardie slang they thought I couldn't understand.
I thought I'd play stupid. They said, "Do you want a drink? A
double whisky?" I was going: "Fuck this shit. I don't need this.
I'm the nearest to the door. Is the door open or locked?" I
walked out of the room when the guy came in to give me the
whisky. He stopped me going down the stairs and sat me down
on the stairs and was kissing my neck – he was so ugly as well.
He's like saying, "I want to fuck you. I know you want to fuck
me. You can have as much weed as you like." He's got his image
of this stupid little girl that I'd made myself out to be. He had me
in this grip, but I just managed to break out of it and I just ran
downstairs and came back to my friend Daniel.'

This story would have been a gift to the scriptwriters on *Reefer
Madness*, but it's more about prohibition and its consequences
than cannabis itself: I can't imagine Al Capone's men being any
more chivalrous in the same situation. The Yardies were among
the people arrested on 1 December, but were given bail –
inexplicably – and are unlikely to be seen again. The black
English doormen mingled with the crowd during the raid and
escaped. The very day after the raid, Zelda claims, they were
offered their old jobs back on double pay. For a while they held
out, then capitulated. She has heard that at the time of writing –
seven weeks after the raid – the Back Beat is back in business,
though in new premises and only as a cash-and-carry operation.

A cry that's often heard is 'Take it out of the hands of the gangsters'. At a conference I heard someone call for licensed shops where pot would be sold together with non-alcoholic refreshments (and, if the speaker had his way, organic whole-foods and Third World handicrafts). But Zelda doesn't want to stop buying from her dealer: 'I want to support him and I want the best in quality; I don't want to pay taxes on it.' Apart from anything else, she's a bad girl and wants to stay that way.

I know it's wrong, but I do find criminals glamorous – from a comfortable distance. It's an attitude that pisses off people campaigning for a change in the law, like the Exodus Collective. Zelda used to go to this group's free raves when she lived in Bedford in the early 1990s. Like the police who briefly closed down the Back Beat, Exodus specialized in timing: at breaking into a warehouse and rigging it for power, lights and sound in under an hour. She remembers good DJs and a tactical sense that left the police outnumbered and powerless and made Exodus a local legend in the 'new townships' described by George Orwell, cut off from London by the Green Belt but linked by the M25. 'They're not just ravers,' said Zelda. 'They're like a little community by themselves. They weren't just total wasters and off their faces all the time – they wanted to do something.'

Exodus came out of the council estates of South Luton – the least glamorous end of a prosperous but charmless light industrial town, and the part where the West Indian community was concentrated. There was a local dub sound system called Ge-mini, with two celebrated MCs: Federal Billy (now Prince Malachi) and General DC. Among 200 black reggae fans would be a handful of white guys, including Glenn Jenkins, now the best-known member of Exodus, getting off on the ganga, the late hour and the music. Prince Malachi told a Radio I doc-umentary in 1998:[11] 'He is white and I am black and we are from different cultures, and he is coming into my culture to seek, and respect to him for it.'

There were eight people behind the first party put on in June 1992 by the group which soon after would call itself Exodus. Some of them had been drug dealers, but soon moved from selling drugs to a form of drugs activism. Specifically, they became militantly hostile to hard drugs and evangelistic about cannabis. 'Our whole culture is spliff,' one of them told me. This doesn't isolate them from the wider drugs culture; they say a shared interest in spliff makes it easy for them to convey their message when they meet hard drug dealers. (They're relaxed about a middle category, including Es and speed, whose negative effects, if any, affect the individuals who take them rather than by whole communities.)

When I went to visit Exodus it was because they were planning to turn their particular skills to the cause of cannabis legalization. Michael Anthony was one of those working on a plan to squat a large number of empty shops simultaneously in order to sell cost-price weed openly. 'We had this idea of twenty different coffee shops all opening at ten o'clock. We'd all be masked up, wearing Clinton and Jack Straw masks. It would be £6 an eighth, totally non-profit-making. When the police turn up, whoever's serving up would jump over and everyone would make their stand. That's how it happened in Holland: there was 149 coffee shops. That's how they legalized it, or decriminalized it. So the police turn up – twenty different Drug Squads – and you say that next week there's another twenty opening up. We ran it by Release's solicitors. They say the maximum would be eighteen months for intention to supply. That sounds to me like a holiday. I'd get myself a little garden job, and there are some really good books I'd like to read.'

A non-profit operation and the risk of jail sounds pretty far removed from a weekly turnover of £300,000 defended by armed gangsters. As a former weed dealer, Glenn Jenkins has had to work hard to shake off the hostile perception that Exodus had been funded by dealing. 'Fuck the dealers,' he told me. 'We're not doing it for the dealers. We're doing it for the smokers.' But though against 'gangsterism and corporatism', Glenn instinctively lined up with the Back Beat against the armed crackdown. 'I say respect to them, even if they were taking a profit. They showed up the police with that hysterical response of theirs.'

Not taking a profit is a central principle. Exodus have the expertise to grow and sell large amounts of highly potent weed (the Brotherhood of Eternal Love in California in the 1960s offer a precedent for idealistically motivated drug dealing). Instead they offer seeds to encourage people outside Exodus to grow their own. The principle of selling at cost means that as a visitor you feel that you've defrauded them when you pay ridiculously little for a huge fried breakfast or a goat curry (made with the meat on the bone and marinated for several hours). This is served in the canteen of a former old people's home to the north of Luton which the Exodus members first squatted, then bought with a bank loan. The sprawling single-storey complex of buildings is now called Haz Manor (HAZ = Housing Action Zone) and houses fifty families. The whole collective helped convert the individual homes, which their owners have decorated and personalized. At first glance it looks familiar – chickens, kids, long hair – but suburban Luton isn't the deep rural version of hippiedom that my middle-class university contemporaries went in for. As Glenn says, 'We're not tuning in, turning on and dropping out. We're the bods. We're from right bang smack in the centre of the community.'

Many Exodus people live off Haz Manor in estates defended by the council's security cameras. They speak like Londoners – although Luton is an old town,[12] most of the population are fairly recent emigrants from the capital – and dress in trainers, combat trousers and hooded sports tops. Their vocation is 'to link the culture to the mainstream – not to stay out on the fringe'. Steve Jacobs: 'Most middle-aged men between forty and fifty, working-class people, have accepted it.' Glenn Jenkins: 'I know people are up for this message on cannabis. I like it when it's Mr and Mrs might have some of that – not an Eco warrior.'

Glenn Jenkins worked for ten years as a train driver. He was an ASLEF shop steward, and his heroes include Tony Benn as well as Bob Marley, though he doesn't suppose Benn would give Exodus a whole-hearted endorsement. 'He was anti-cannabis-smoking because he thinks it makes you drop out of work activity – which is generally true – and therefore you're dropping out of the struggle, because the struggle for rights is in the workplace.'

Exodus is dedicated to a different sort of struggle outside the workplace, but Glenn keeps an interest in the low-wage, electronically monitored work on offer to school-leavers through New Labour's 'New Deal'. One of his favourite books is Robert Tressell's *The Ragged Trousered Philanthropists*, the classic text of pre-World War I socialism. The book is set in 'Mugsborough', a thinly disguised version of Hastings, where its author worked for a firm of slapdash and money-grabbing builders, looking with longing desperation towards a socialist dawn while excoriating the corrupt local establishment. Glenn feels similarly about Luton, a town dominated by Vauxhall Motors and by Whitbread, the brewers. He once worked at the former Bedford Commercial Vehicles, rechristened IBC, which has operated Japanese work disciplines since Isusu 'bought' it in 1983 from General Motors – although, it transpires, Isusu was at the time 40 per cent and is now 90 per cent owned by General Motors. 'Our local MP assisted General Motors in creating a climate of fear that Bedford Commercial Vehicles was about to close. That's a cost to Luton of 6,000 jobs and this massive fear went through the town. Then this Japanese company Isusu say, 'We can save this place' and everyone says, 'Thank fuck for that.'

The local bourgeoisie are the enemy, whether imposing 'Roman working conditions', through blackmail and coercion, or in the form of 'Sam Whitbread, knocking out drugs': more precisely ethanol in the form of beers, wines and spirits, as sold in Luton's pubs. Back in 1992 Glenn claimed there had been a 40 per cent drop in pub takings when Exodus were playing, not to mention a 6 per cent drop in crime. 'The pub landlords were going to Sam Whitbread and Sam Whitbread went to the police. We were forced to look at the background.'

Exodus have made enemies, but also allies. The police have been round Haz Manor, seen the outdoor cannabis plants and been told about the ten-per-person rule. They have clearly decided not to descend in force to uphold the law. And for what it's worth, the Church of England diocese of St Albans thinks they're a good thing. It's difficult not to like them. When I was with them I found myself almost as a reflex taking up their funny handshake, which then ends up as a hand-clasp with the fingers threaded together. I also felt I should manage at least a token puff when a spliff was going round – and as a spliff always was going round, and I hadn't built up much tolerance, conversations seemed to happen in a dream. (Mick Anthony claims I hit a particularly taxing day, as a new crop was being assessed, and the conversation about cannabis put them in the mood.) I have notes, but I can't put faces to them, or I can remember faces but couldn't tell you what they said.

Perhaps because I kept doggedly writing, Steve, Mick and Glenn's conversation mostly took the form of a tour of Exodus's philosophy. All three, and others who joined in, agreed on every point, so I won't worry too much about my uncertainty about exactly who said what. There's a precise question I'd like to have asked, but didn't. This was whether they thought their anti-capitalist, 'spiritual' outlook came from 'chuffing' ganga[13] – reflecting the state of mind you get into when you're stoned – or whether it was the other way round. Equally it could be that the collective's socialist principles had steered them towards a drug that lends itself to being produced on a non-profit basis and doesn't cause addiction or crime. They themselves are very willing to give credit to ganga, seen as expressing the will of a quasi-conscious planet. 'Weed-smoking is a natural response to the dangers posed by the attitude of humanity. We're saying it's a drug that makes you think naturally, slows you down from Babylon speed. If the earth's got a self-defence policy, it's the weed. The way it's so easy to grow – it's a God-given plant for sure.' They talk about how weed is helpful in giving up addictive drugs, something that has been asserted in the medical literature. But I suspect they're underplaying the importance of their ideology. Cannabis isn't enough in itself to guarantee social harmony; after all, the 1960s' psychedelic revolution went in exactly the opposite direction to Exodus, starting with weed and then being engulfed in a blizzard of chemicals.

With all the ganga in the air, everyday chores become pregnant with significance. One strand of the conversation comes from Glenn's absence for a few hours to get a dog to scare away burglars; he's chosen a sweet-natured but fierce-looking English bull terrier from a local dog's home: 'While it's violent out there we're going to need our dogs.' It's the art of non-violent defence against burglars, gangsters and the police. 'I'd rather accept their violence than give it back to them any time the police come and weigh in, with sirens, uniforms, all these things that are military images designed to make it look as though there's more troops than there really are. Uniforms do that. When they bang their sticks on the floor . . . You can go up to a line with them nose to nose with you. If you're not prepared to fight violently there's a warrior sense that that's cowardly. That's a Roman attitude that they've bred into you. To take but not to give it back, that's a lot harder. If you're a Roman you just go with the flow.'

They sum up Exodus as: ganga + rave + Bob Marley, now a kind of Christ figure in much of the Third World.[14] 'Reggae music is spiritually aware because of black slavery. Because black slavery was the worst atrocity. So for someone to come out amongst the murder and the blood and not be hateful and vengeful but saying One Love and Stand Up For Your Rights, that's the sign of a spiritual movement . . . 'Rasta is the only spiritual warrior. Every one else is a spiritual but not a warrior. A Buddhist will take himself into the quiet of a contemplation. What about the screaming? What about the warring?' Exodus is multi-racial, but its white members don't try to talk like Jamaicans. 'We aren't sitting with dreadlocks saying Rastafari. What's happened is that the religion is alive and well in Jamaica, but I see us as a mutation of that; we're a spiritual movement but we are not Rastafarians. Spirituality is about, to do good for others. It's that moral life – like you're part of a whole rather than an individual, whereas Babylon is about doing well against each other.'

All the talk of Rome and Babylon sounds Rastafarian, but Exodus also gave me a sense of English traditions. Sometimes I was reminded of Robert Tressell's socialists, but at other times there were much more distant echoes – almost of the soldiers of Cromwell's New Model Army who sang as they marched:

> For God begins to honour us
> The saints are marching on
> The sword is sharp, the arrows swift
> To destroy Babylon.[15]'

The English Civil War spawned scores of groups of working men who like Rastas derived their world view from the Bible: the Quakers, Shakers, Fifth Monarchists, Levellers and Diggers. The Behmenists, followers of Jakob Boehme (1576–1624), popularized the idea of the coming of the New Age, of spiritual liberty for the children of God. The Quakers are still around; the Muggletonians survived until the 1970s and the death of the last follower of a seventeenth-century tailor named Ludowick Muggleton. In *Witness against the Beast*, the historian E. P. Thompson describes how this last member of the sect allowed him to examine the Muggletonians' archive, and how this enabled him to understand the ideas underlying William Blake's prophetic writings.

Though Exodus live on the edge of the law, they appear more respectable these days than the precursors of the Muggletonians, the Ranters, who flourished briefly in the 1650s, and were noted for blasphemy, free love and smoking tobacco, then still novel and controversial.[16] Or after a long enough ganga session could we even see Exodus as reincarnated monks (communitarianism and voluntary poverty)? Not that there's any claim to hair shirts. Glenn admits that they are 'British; English; comfortabilist. In the world that we live in poverty is relative. If you lived in Somalia and had to adapt in solidarity with the poorest people you wouldn't be able to struggle.'

Exodus's current campaign is to create what they call their 'Ark': in planning application terms, a community centre in a disused warehouse in the middle of a housing estate, creating workshops and entertainment areas. Their members, many of whom originally used drug-dealing as a way out of alienated employment, have developed a multi-racial cannabis culture that feels home-grown and here to stay, with the same powerful, imprecise appeal of Blake's 'Jerusalem'. Glenn says: 'I think now is the time for the victory of hearts and minds over misery – and

England is the prime place. It's class-ridden, but in England we don't hurt each other that much.'

This discourse, high-minded in every sense, isn't the way Exodus people talk all the time. They're also as addicted as Egyptians round a water-pipe to what they call 'ramping', or piss-taking. I find them convincing and impressive; not so Zelda, who preferred their earlier guise. In fact, the more I tell the little cynic about their idealistic views, the more irritated she becomes, finally snarling, 'That's all bollocks, that is. You'd better not get me in a room with them guys.' But plenty of other people, including their local police commander, are ready to applaud Exodus for going from small-time hustling to alternative politics and for their campaign against Class A drugs. Their achievement is to create a fully fleshed-out, home-grown version of ganga culture, which now co-exists with that other new phenomenon: the movement for medical cannabis.

3

'Medi-Pot'

In an Amsterdam hotel it isn't odd to overhear someone asking where to find a coffee shop. When you check in at the Hotel Ostade you in any case get given a map and advice on where to find the drugs area and the red light district. The young woman who'd made the request had a sensible English voice and smart clothes, but then pot-smoking couples often consist of a dishevelled male and a well-turned-out girlfriend. It just seemed rather early to want to get stoned – 9.30 in the morning, when she'd just arrived on an all-night coach trip from London.

This was the last day of the Cannabis Cup and hundreds of Americans were in town. A Frenchwoman who'd spent all week on the French stand at the Cannabis Cup's Hemp Expo helped out with a couple of names but warned 'neither of them are open till 11'. The Englishwoman and her boyfriend found another one in their guidebook – the Green House, in Tolstraat, not too distant and opening at 10 a.m. Off the couple went; the girl, I noticed, was on crutches. Cicely turned out to have MS and to be a medical cannabis user – the first I'd met.

Next day at breakfast I sat at her table. We were both drinking too much tea and coffee to pretend that either of us felt quite OK. She was no longer on crutches and we took turns in making fresh cups on a scarily hissing piece of equipment. She said, 'I feel as bad as I did yesterday. My head feels this big' (indicating an imaginary goldfish bowl). But she was up for a conversation.

What intrigued me was that such a straight-looking girl should be smoking weed, even for medical reasons.

'When I was at university I was a real "drugs are for mugs" nerd – in fact I moved three times because my housemates smoked dope. It's really sad, isn't it? I look back and think – what a precious little girl. It was the way I was brought up, I suppose: drugs of any kind were no good. Plus I was asthmatic and I didn't like people smoking in the house – and I don't like people behaving like morons. I thought it was the effect; I'd rather missed the point that they were morons before they smoked.'

It was her family doctor who'd suggested she try cannabis, and other doctors had since agreed that it was a good idea. 'The one who suggested it was female; she'd just had a baby. Of course she said, if you get caught don't mention my name. Then there's the one I've got at the moment – he's a Pakistani male – and an orthopaedic surgeon who's English through and through, and they're all up for it. It was quite convenient as my fiancé Liam had smoked for three years. I now roll four joints a day.' Cicely demonstrated how she makes them; very long, it seemed to me. 'Well, they're very thin and elegant. We buy a couple of ounces every two months, which should come to £30 a week, but we pay less because we buy in bulk. But in England you get really ripped off and the hash at the moment is so bad that it makes me retch. "Soap bar" – yerchh.' The words 'soap bar' still sound strange coming from Cicely (who asked me not to use her real name so as not to upset her mother).

'With dope I get my medication down to about a tenth of my usual levels. I'm prescribed around twenty drugs. One of the main ones is dihydrocodeine, which is an opiate one step below morphine. I've found that having dihydrocodeine and dope isn't a good thing – that it has negative effects.

'Dope is an anti-spasmodic: the effect is to make everything work correctly. It's also excellent for when you're bored: there was a period of time when I couldn't get out of bed or function in any way. I'd actually prefer to have the pain-killing without the mental effect, though it's still nice sometimes to have the freedom to just go with it. What it does do to people is to make them slightly more remote, and I don't think that's a bad thing. If I moaned to Liam as much as I feel I want to I'd drive him round the bend. And I can actually work on it. I'm doing a degree in biochemical sciences – laboratory medicine – and this last year I actually allowed myself to smoke while writing my assessment exams and report, and my marks have gone rocketing through the roof.'

Cicely turns out to be quite representative of many cannabis users who, in Europe at least, only began smoking after the onset of an illness. In Holland, where it could hardly be easier to buy cannabis in one of the specially licensed coffee shops, there is a large operation supplying marijuana through pharmacists; 400 of the country's 1,500 chemists' shops sell 25-gram tubs of high–THC weed for the equivalent of £100, restricted to patients with a doctor's prescription. Marcel de Wit, the chairman of Maripharm, which grows and packages cannabis, told me he started the company in 1994 in response to a demand from patients who wouldn't go near a coffee shop.

'Most of the time the patients are very old people and people who have money. It's like the time that alcohol was forbidden but only the rich got it on doctor's prescription. So our group of patients don't want to have anything to do with coffee shops and recreational use and they're very angry if they see a young kid smoking a joint and laughing. So they're very serious; they want to cure their symptoms and they don't want to get high.'

Marcel de Wit runs a curious business; two of his colleagues outlined their work in a presentation to the International Cannabinoid Research Society in July 1998. They described how they'd succeeded in growing plants with high levels of the psychoactive THC (delta-9 tetrahydrocannabinol), and with less than 0.1 per cent variation between batches, and how after harvesting the female flowering heads they sealed them in plastic tubs and gamma-irradiated them to kill any fungal spores. Such spores can be a danger for patients with weakened immune systems, but Maripharm's product beats coffee-shop weed in that it can be guaranteed free of contamination. They grow a strain of cannabis called 'Plant 1001' under grow-lights and use no chemical sprays. For quality control the company sends regular samples to a Dutch Government lab which carries out tests and analyses which guarantee that the weed is free of pesticide residues. Medical cannabis is available under the Dutch equivalent of the National Health Service, in which insurance companies refund the cost of patients' supplies. And the whole operation is in breach of Dutch law and operates without any official Government tolerance.

At the time I spoke to Marcel de Wit early in 1999 there were rumours that even the tolerant Dutch might be on the point of ending these legal anomalies and closing down the Maripharm operation until it has created the licensing framework required by international treaties. The Dutch Government has only issued one such licence, to an Amsterdam company called HortaPharm for its own project to develop a medical marijuana strain, which has now come to the end of its term. A toughening line on medical cannabis has aborted the clinical trials on cannabis for MS patients that Maripharm were running with a leading Dutch teaching hospital.

Now it's in the United Kingdom rather than in liberal Holland that medical researchers are soon going to evaluate cannabis. There is a long list of conditions in which it is thought to help, including migraine, glaucoma, nausea induced by chemotherapy, depression, anorexia, AIDS wasting syndrome and even, surprisingly, some lung disorders including asthma and emphysema. However, the first clinical trials will concentrate on two of the best-attested applications, in relieving chronic pain and the symptoms of MS.

Until I met Cicely, cannabis as a treatment for MS had been an abstraction; part of a bundle of scientific and political arguments I could find my way around while staying neutral on the central proposition. Few anti-cannabis campaigners are even troubled by doubt: medical use is, in the words of Professor Gabriel Nahas, 'a fraud', a 'scandal' and a 'hoax'. Peter Stoker of the National Drugs Prevention Alliance talks about a 'Medi-Pot scam' perpetrated in order to give credibility to the legalization lobby.

Seen in this light, the pot-using patients must either be committed members of the lobby or have been duped by it. A parallel conspiracy has to be assumed among doctors, since respectable people would hardly start taking an illegal drug simply on the say-so of some hippy. The reputation of cannabis partly rests on word-of-mouth among patients, backed up by self-help groups like the Alliance for Cannabis Therapeutics and, as in Cicely's case, supported by a developing consensus among doctors. One reason for their interest is the discovery of how cannabis works (described in the next chapter); among other things, this discovery has helped to explain the drug's extremely low toxicity. It's virtually impossible to die of an overdose, and unwanted effects such as possible anxiety and short-term memory loss go away when the dose wears off.[1] Cannabis doesn't kill off brain cells, as some people think, though you may give that impression if you're stoned all the time.

I've been advised to smoke pot by a doctor. It was in my personal crisis of the summer of 1997 when my wife had left to move in with her boyfriend. An ex-girlfriend of mine, now a professor of Community Medicine, suggested I smoke a joint or two, but avoid prescription tranquillizers or anti-depressants. In the event, I thought that any drugs, or too much drink, would stop me holding things together. Now we've reversed roles; I've just visited her two days after she underwent surgery to remove a small breast cancer, and seen her battling to get enough pain relief, after only a single day on morphine. The doctors in the specialist pain team are held back by the toxicity of most pharmaceutical anaelgesics. Although I'm completely unqualified, I find myself burning to tell the staff everything I now know about the effectiveness of cannabis, its low toxicity and its apparent synergy with opiates given in tiny quantities.[2]

This is a message that doctors were increasingly prepared to listen to during the 1990s. In 1997 there were separate reports published by the British Medical Association, the US National Institutes of Health, and the British Medical Association. In 1998 a committee of the House of Lords made up of distinguished retired scientists took written and spoken evidence over a period of months and in November produced a report. Professor Leslie Iverson, the scientific advisor to the committee and Visiting Professor of Pharmacology at Oxford University, told me that the biggest impression had been made by the personal testimony of MS patients. This of course was anecdotal evidence rather than hard science; however, it was given weight by a scientific paper documenting the claims made by 112 cannabis-smoking MS patients, which concluded in favour of taking these claims seriously and investigating them further.

Several of the stories forwarded to the Lords' committee carried an extra emotional charge because they took the form of handwritten letters. One described growing three cannabis plants in the greenhouse among the tomatoes and making the dried leaves into shortbread. Eaten before bedtime, this green-coloured biscuit guaranteed a peaceful night for both the writer and her husband. Otherwise, she wrote, 'Violent muscle spasms in my left leg would make me cry out in pain, and my leg would jerk and bounce in the bed.' Another was from a seventy-five-year-old patient who had had MS since the age of thirty; she wrote: 'I am in a wheelchair, which means it has to be brought to me, which means my supplier is running a risk. I have dreadful spasms in my legs and can take pills like diazepam without any effect. Half a cigarette a day doctored with cannabis stops the spasms within ten minutes. I have to pay £30 for a piece as long (mainly) as my little finger and half the thickness. I find it very difficult because I only have my pension and mobility allowance.' The conclusion: 'When, oh when, is it going to be legalized and put on prescription?'

The committee recommended that until more conventional cannabis-based medicines could be developed, patients should be allowed to possess herbal cannabis, provided they had a doctor's prescription. The Blair Government immediately ruled this out, but the very fact of the recommendation will have had an impact. My solicitor told me that his parents-in-law are constantly at odds over the issue. His mother-in-law would like to smoke pot to relieve the symptoms of her MS, but her conservatively-minded husband objects. 'Now at least she can quote the House of Lords as being on her side,' said my solicitor, who is professionally inclined to be impressed by House of Lords rulings. Similarly, Cicely now has a defence if her mother discovers her puffing on a joint.

In Britain, however, the medical cannabis issue dovetails with people's disinclination to get very worked up about this particular drug of abuse. Among the two-fifths of people under thirty who have smoked a joint at some time[3] are a large number of future doctors: a study at Newcastle University Medical School published in 1998 found that more than twenty-five per cent of medical students were pot smokers. Although I believe that the medical and recreational arguments about pot are different, there is an overlap. Six of the nine medical marijuana witnesses to the House of Lords had not smoked before they became ill, but three had (which looks like a fair reflection of the national statistical picture). For a novel treatment, cannabis has a flying start; people are receptive in a way that they surely wouldn't be if, say, crack cocaine started being touted as a cure-all.

There is a lobbying group on each side of the Atlantic; both organizations are called the Alliance for Cannabis Therapeutics (ACT). The British version was founded by an MS patient living in Leeds, who took the pseudonym Clare Hodges to protect her two young children. She describes the ACT as 'a loose affiliation of patients, doctors and politicians', inspired and helped by the longer-established organization based in Washington, DC. Clare Hodges told the House of Lords that when she first discussed cannabis with her doctors they had been sympathetic but not well informed: 'They all said it couldn't do me much harm in moderate doses and was probably safer than many of the medicines they could prescribe.' The House of Lords backed the ACT's objective of making cannabis available immediately on a doctor's prescription. It probably helped that Clare Hodges spelt out that she was not campaigning for general legalization: 'Even if cannabis were legalized we would still be campaigning, as we think seriously ill people should get their medicine from their doctor and not have to provide it for themselves.'

As well as a British ACT there's a struggling and persecuted counterpart of the buyers' clubs that supply around 100,000 patients in the United States. The man behind it is Colin Davies, a young-looking forty-year-old joiner from Stockport, Manchester. Before the bizarre events of the night of 26 December 1995 he was a successful contracts manager for a firm of shopfitters which worked, among other clients, for British Home Stores and MotherCare. On that Boxing Night he had gone out for a drink with his parents at a scenically situated pub, whose garden looked out over a steep valley.

'I'd gone outside with my father to get a bit of fresh air, because everybody was packed inside, and to get a cigarette. We was both talking – there was a mill opposite that we were reminiscing about – then my father said, "I'll go and get the drinks." It's very dark, this place, and I was just stood there. I could hear footsteps on the gravel. I didn't turn round because I was deep in thought, and the next thing somebody grasped the back of my waistband and said, "See how you like this, you fucking bastard." '

That was the last thing Colin remembers before coming round in hospital. He had been rushed there after being found unconscious in the valley below the pub the following morning by someone out walking his dog. (His parents had left assuming he had gone on somewhere else on the spur of the moment.) He was paralysed, his spine was fractured in three places and his shoulder was shattered. Since then he hasn't worked, though he can walk again. There is more he could say about the assailants who left him for dead, but legal proceedings are under way. He has been left in constant pain. 'I've had bolts put in and taken out. My shoulder's in bits; I've got pieces of bone fragments around my spinal cord and now and then they interfere with my spinal cord and then I'm in extreme pain. If you can imagine having a huge splinter between the bones of your spine . . . even breathing you feel a pain and movement is even worse.'

Although his appearance doesn't suggest any stereotyped idea of a pot smoker, Colin had before his injuries smoked a modest eighth of an ounce or less a week. While still in hospital he met people in wheelchairs as the result of road injuries who told him that cannabis relieved chronic pain. He found that it worked. Without cannabis he takes the maximum recommended dose of eight tablets of Tylex, a codeine and paracetemol mixture which leaves him nauseous. But he can halve his intake of pills if he smokes four joints a day, and he says they make him relaxed rather than outright stoned. But getting hold of those joints hasn't been easy. Perhaps he attracted attention by going to well-known dealers: one morning at 10 a.m. the Stockport police broke down his door and searched the flat hoping, he thinks, to find cannabis by the kilo. Instead they uncovered just one plant, for which Colin was arrested and cautioned. This haul was modest enough; a second police raid caught up in its nets Colin's unassuming companion, his grey African parrot Mary.

'When I came out of hospital I was on Disability Living Allowance but that was stopped two years ago, and I couldn't afford to buy any because I was on £64 a week, so I decided to grow my own, and this was where the second bust came. I had eighteen plants and when I was taken to the Magistrates Court I was pleading Not Guilty. I'd got the seed from the parrot food and I didn't know if it was actually cannabis.' No one ever found out; the police had allowed the seized material to decompose, and the magistrates threw the case out.

Then there was a third prosecution, which took place in June 1998 and involved another batch of eighteen plants. Now the saga moved to a higher plane. The facts weren't in dispute, and the prosecution told the Manchester Crown Court jury that having taken an oath to give a true verdict according to the law, they had a duty to return a Guilty verdict. But they didn't. After the judge had explained that a defendant might be justified in breaking a law to avoid death or some other extreme threat, the jury deliberated for forty minutes and then declared Colin Not Guilty. Afterwards an expert witness at the trial, Matthew Atha of the Independent Drugs Monitoring Unit, declared that the verdict would bring closer the day when cannabis for medical purposes would be legalized.

After the resulting publicity, Colin was contacted by two

activists with MS from Edinburgh and Huddersfield, West Yorkshire respectively. Soon afterwards the three of them publicly launched the Medical Marijuana Co-operative, run from Colin's flat. The inspiration was the American buyers' clubs that have flourished, especially in Californa, since state voters passed Proposition 215[4] on 5 November 1996 declaring medical marijuana lawful. The system in California works rather like the Dutch pharmacies supplied by MariPharm (who offered Colin moral support, though not supplies). Patients bring personal identification and a doctor's letter to the club. This is then verified and a check is made that the doctor is a *bona fide* practitioner before issuing the marijuana. As the three got the co-operative under way, planting a crop of plants and designing ID cards for members, Colin phoned for advice from Scott Imler of Los Angeles' Cannabis Research Center. 'I think what I told him was *not* to do it until there's some type of law there,' is Scott's memory of their three conversations.

The LA buyers' club, which serves 580 patients, has stuck meticulously to rules designed to restrict supplies to genuine medical cases and has prospered – unlike six clubs in Northern California which were raided by the Drug Enforcement Administration (DEA). The state referendums have created an interesting conflict between state and national law, which continues to ban all use of marijuana (except for a federal programme supplying a handful of experimental patients, which dates from the 1970s and has been deliberately run down). Washington counterattacked on two fronts: by threatening to withdraw the right to prescribe from doctors who recommended marijuana to their patients, and by sending (DEA) agents as *agents provocateurs* to try to buy marijuana with insufficient or bogus documentation.

Perhaps the Northern Californian clubs had become complacent. Terence Hallinan, the San Francisco District Attorney in the years before Proposition 215 was passed, was an ally, a believer in decriminalization on the Dutch coffee-shop model and a friend of Dennis Peron, the gay activist who wrote the text of 215. (Hallinan had been famous for his policy that if Assistant DAs wanted to prosecute for marijuana, 'The cases had better be big and the defendants had better be bad.') After the Oakland Cannabis Buyers' Co-operative was raided, the city authorities attempted to keep it going by giving its staff the same status as city police, who are legally protected from prosecution under a statute intended to give immunity to undercover officers.

In Los Angeles, where they lacked the support of the local administration, Scott Imler and his colleagues were alert enough to spot the fake papers carried by the DEA investigators and refuse to serve them. Scott, a former special needs teacher who uses marijuana to relieve his epilepsy, is troubled by Dennis Peron's much-reported claim that 'All marijuana use is medical.' 'That's not what the voters voted for. I understand that marijuana legalization is his agenda, and I think it's incredibly disingenuous. There are many people from the drug legalization movement who got on the medical issue bandwaggon and supported it; they don't have the right to change the meaning of the law after it's passed.'

The LA Cannabis Research Center grows 146 pounds in weight of marijuana a year, which accounts for 60 per cent of its turnover. The pot is grown under lights and Scott says it's so fresh that the problem of fungal contamination does not arise: 'Fungus is a product of the black market.' Three-quarters of the members are AIDS patients and virtually all are people who Scott says would have used marijuana before falling ill. In America the views of older people were formed in the 1940s and 1950s, and they're still too influenced by the press and movie campaigns of that era to risk a bout of reefer madness.

*　　*　　*

Colin Davies obviously wasn't persuaded by Scott Imler's advice to hold fire with his medical marijuana co-op and wait for a change in the law. In November 1998 the police raided him for a fourth time after waiting, Colin suspects, till the Government had decided to reject the House of Lords' recommendation that medical cannabis should be legalized or tolerated. But while one lot of medical cannabis plants was being seized from Colin Davies's flat, a much larger number were thriving, with Government approval, in a glasshouse complex in the South of England. Their owner was a forty-four-year-old Englishman called Dr Geoffrey Guy.

I first saw Geoffrey Guy in the ornate but dignified setting of the House of Lords' Committee Room No 3. He was sitting facing the semi-circle of peers and offering an impromptu seminar on the science of cannabis smoked in joints. Although smoking obviously wasn't medically acceptable, a joint actually worked very well as a delivery system. Inhalation bypassed the liver, meaning that the THC was not broken down as it was when you eat it, producing the even more hallucinatory by-product 11-hydroxy-THC. Also, as the effect was immediate, patients could adjust or 'titrate' their dose, so that they'd get enough of the drug into their bloodstream to relieve their symptoms without, he said, actually getting stoned. Next, he argued in favour of giving patients cannabis rather than cannabis-derived medicines; experience showed that they preferred the whole plant to pure THC (which is prescribed quite widely in the United States under the brand-name of Marinol), and it was likely, as with other whole-plant medicines, that the sixty different cannabinoids found in the plant interacted and modified each other's action.

The lords on the committee clearly took a shine to the young medical entrepreneur and in their published report they 'warmly welcomed' his initiative. Afterwards, in the high-ceilinged, wood-panelled corridor that runs down the upper floor of the Houses of Parliament, I competed for his attention with other members of the world of cannabis lobbyists and pressure groups.

'You're writing a book about cannabis – another one?' he asked. I batted the question back: 'Are there lots?' In reply he tugged at his briefcase to suggest the physical weight of the rival tomes. 'So what line are you taking? Is the main angle about Britain or America – I mean, are you calling it "cannabis" or "marijuana"?' Why did I have to tell him that my current working title was 'dope' (which sounds old-fashioned anyway)? Perhaps in response to the Victorian surroundings I'd unconsciously structured this encounter along the lines of one of those nineteenth-century *Punch* cartoons which end with the phrase, 'collapse of stout party'. In fact a cloud did briefly pass across his good-natured features, and later his PR people wrote expressing concern that there should be any blurring of the issues of legalizing 'medical' and 'recreational' cannabis. But actually the non-smoking, non-drinking Dr Guy was developing a certain relish for the subject. I told him that I had recently been in the hashish-producing Rif region of Northern Morocco. 'Ah,' he said, suspecting not just research but indulgence. 'Soap bar, eh?' Geoffrey Guy was interested in soap bar, not because of its naff reputation, but because of the high ratio of the less well understood CBD (cannabidiol) to THC in Moroccan hashish.

Quite soon afterwards he gave me an interview at the offices of his PR company over sandwiches and Chilean Sauvignon Blanc (he drank water). He'd set aside an hour, but didn't then tell me my time was up, so I stayed and stayed, filling a whole notebook with a kind of outsider's guide to cannabis. Many cannabis experts spend years or decades talking to the converted, with little expectation that they'll make a difference. Geoffrey Guy, after only a year, has been faced with the task of persuading the Home Office and the Medicines Control Agency to accept him, in effect, to run Britain's medical cannabis programme. The result was that he was firing on all cylinders. We talked about hashish in Indian and Arab culture; the work of Dr William O'Shaughnessy, the Indian army surgeon who in 1842 introduced cannabis into the mainstream of British medicine; the sociology of the legalization and anti-legalization lobbies; the progress of Proposition 215 and other state initiatives in America; the intrinsic difficulties of getting whole-plant medicines accepted by the regulatory bodies; the new systems of cannabis receptors recently discovered in the brain, and lots more.

Geoffrey Guy has a good CV for the job he's invented. As a multi-millionaire he could contemplate spending £10 million of his own money on the project should other investors fail to bite. The main outlay has gone on leasing the glasshouse complex with its capacity to grow 20,000 plants, and high-security defences against all kinds of criminal predations including ram-raiding. 'It doesn't look like a World War II concentration camp,' he explained. 'More like something between Greenham Common and Porton Down.' You can imagine that a pharmaceutical company would blush at having to explain such an investment to its shareholders and the press – though Geoffrey Guy envisages that he may sell his products to the major names in the business if it all works out. The other necessary qualifications have been belief in the project, and experience of running clinical trials in getting medicines licensed.

It was also important that Guy spent a formative period in France, a country whose policy-makers have a phobic dislike of cannabis, as it happens. In 1981, at the age of twenty-seven, he threw in a career in obstetrics and instead went to work for an old family-run company called Pierre Fabre, based at Castre, near Toulouse in southern France. This firm's core business was in plant-based medicines, but Guy's job as Clinical Trials Co-ordinator was to launch the company's new range of synthesized drugs in Britain, and in particular to prepare the dossiers on them required by the Medicines Control Agency. The experience showed him that modern synthesized single molecule medicines were being promoted for reasons that did not necessarily relate to their effectiveness.

Medicines are evaluated according to the criteria of quality, safety and efficacy. 'And it's important to understand that it's in that order of importance,' said Geoffrey Guy. 'If you're unable to make your product consistently, even if it's safe and effective it won't be approved. After all, not all drugs are safe: take steroids or cytotoxic drugs, for example. And that's why synthetic chemicals are deemed to be good starting points, not only because you can get patents, but because you can test your quality. Plant extracts were frowned on quite heavily in the late seventies and eighties. Most Anglo-Saxons were saying "typical French" – but things are changing now.'

The new climate of the 1990s allowed Geoffrey Guy to develop a plant medicine for eczema. Increasing numbers of children suffer from it in a severe form, and find steroids, the only existing treatment, either to be ineffective or to cause bad side-effects. He had heard stories of children being cured by Chinese herbal medicine. But although a particular herbal mixture seemed to work it could never become a licensed prescription medicine, because it varied from batch to batch and from practitioner to practitioner, and because of fears that some of the rather obscure ingredients such as 'Yellow Emperor's Extract' might be con-taminated or even toxic. His former company Phytopharm has created a standardized form, which has been put into clinical trials at the Children's Hospital, Great Ormond Street. One measure of the new attitude is commercial; Phytopharm has sold the licence for a plant-based anti-obesity medicine to Pfizer, the makers of Viagra, for no less than £32 million.

It was a conference at the Royal Pharmaceutical Society in

1997 that parachuted Guy into the new area of medical cannabis
– which, he comments, is hardly unexplored territory. 'What's
extraordinary is to have so many reputed applications for something that doesn't even legally exist as a medicine.' It was
following this conference that he made the vital connection
with HortaPharm, a friendly rival of Maripharm run by expatriate Americans. HortaPharm had for a period been licensed
by the Dutch Government to breed cannabis, but as outsiders
felt they were unlikely to get an illegal supply network unoffi-
cially condoned. The British Government, meanwhile, continues to smile on Geoffrey Guy. His programme means that
officials can go on opposing legalization without appearing
heartless in the face of the demands of MS patients and other
campaigners for medical cannabis. On the other hand, although
he's never going to be a hero of the legalization, his project is
helpful to medical marijuana around the world. Until now,
especially in America, campaigners have been called irrespon-
sible in asking for a treatment that hasn't been clinically proven;
yet governments have placed severe restrictions on anyone
wishing to make an illegal drug the subject of clinical trials.
Guy's work promises to break the log-jam.

I came to see him as a kind of representative figure: John Bull
introduced to Señor Marijuana, in a turn-of-the-century *Punch*
cartoon. Though the epitome of 'straightness', he feels comfortable with the legalization lobby. 'I'd thought it was quite clear
that there would be a medical scientific group and the illicit
group, but it's actually very difficult to make this distinction.' He
told me about a major forthcoming event – a conference on
'Regulating Cannabis' ('regulating' in this context means 'legalizing') organized by both Release and the American Lindesmith
Center, which is funded and supported by the billionaire
financier George Soros.[5] This was subsequently held at Regent's
College on the Inner Circle in Regent's Park, formerly part of

the University of London (see Chapter 11). As an ex-medical student he chiefly remembered that it had 'a terrific bar', though I'm not clear that he ever drank alcohol. He sat next to me while awaiting his turn on the platform, offering a stream of bluff asides, such as 'The French would string the lot of them up', referring to the session with Dutch coffee-shop owners, growers and campaigners. His own speech offered little to the assembled lobbyists and drug workers; in fact, with its emphasis on novel delivery systems like inhalers, patches or suppositories, and a generous tribute to the Home Office, it was rather coolly received, I thought.

But there's no mistaking the relish for his new work. 'I've got beyond the point of being surprised by anything that this amazing plant can do,' he told the Lords, on being asked about some medical application or other. He's also a kind of bridge-builder between cannabis users and the world of science: and among pharmacologists, biochemists and neurologists, cannabis is currently a hot subject.

4

The Hard Science

Whatever the fluctuations in public opinion, I'd guess that there is a bedrock of support for pot for MS patients, and equally solid opposition to pot for schoolchildren. But a lot of sixteen-to-nineteen-year-olds have already smoked cannabis – a third of them, according to the figure for 1996 collected for *Social Trends*. Fee-paying schools aren't immune: a report for their Head-masters' Conference in 1998 found that 43 per cent of sixth formers had tried drugs at some time, one in eight in the last week. Parents paying between £8,000 and £15,000 a year find that their kids are as likely to be taking illegal drugs as they would be at the local comprehensive, or more so. Caroline Noortman, who took matters into her own hands in 1998 and organized a self-help group for independent school parents, told me that fee-paying schools were often less clued up than state schools; too often they were anxious not to scare away business, and they weren't obliged to include drugs education in the curriculum. Her first meeting, held at the House of Commons and addressed by the junior Home Office minister George Howarth, among others, was packed and over-subscribed. The second, in the spring of 1999, was held at Westminster, my old school, and the speakers included my ex-headmaster, Dr John Rae.

John Rae is a bruised veteran of this arena. As he remembers in his autobiography *Letters from School*,[1] he arrived at Westminster from a country public school without ever being told that cannabis was endemic. He moved to an automatic expulsion policy, but still frets at using bluff and plea-bargaining to secure confessions and denunciations. It worked, though: after a time no one would dream of taking a joint within a square mile of the school. Ben Golomstok, who was there in the 1980s, was sitting in a day room with a group who decided, as one does, to incinerate a tea bag in a toaster, creating an ambiguous smell. This was what the authorities had been training for and masters and prefects came running in seconds, not minutes.

But when public school headmasters try to persuade pupils to Just Say No, they must expect to be asked – Why? Over a pot of Earl Grey in the Warldorf Hotel, Dr Rae told me that he wished that scientists could produce a simple summary of the relative riskiness of cannabis. 'If they could just show that it's harmless, then fine.' He had tried bringing in various speakers, but none were satisfactory. 'The trouble with the policemen was that some of the pupils knew much more about the subject than they did.' On the other hand a psychologist had given the impression that it was all a fuss about nothing, which hadn't helped either.

Many British public schools these days turn to the services of a grizzled New Zealander called Trevor Grice, who's the co-author of a book called *The Great Brain Robbery*. He is also working on a drugs information CD-ROM in which more than large sums have been invested, but which, given the size of the potential market, is expected to show a handsome return. One of his chief claims is to have succeeded in getting the relevant scientists to express their findings in language that's accessible to the young.

I sat in with fifth formers at The Leys School, Cambridge, a Methodist foundation where he had been invited by the head, the Revd Dr J. C. A. Barratt. (The reverend doctor, a somewhat tough egg on first acquaintance, had according to the *The Good Schools Guide* 'been brought in to put the school straight after a shaky period.') Trevor Grice was older and shorter than I'd expected, but racily dressed in a dark blue shirt and magenta tie. The tone had been set from our first encounter in the chilling setting of the waiting room outside Dr Barratt's study. He said: 'With adolescents there's absolutely reliable evidence of their faster absorption rates and less efficient metabolic systems. But with adults, as for interfering with free will, I'm totally opposed to that. I'd rather see everybody smoking a joint.'

And in this spirit, his opening gambit to the assembled pupils was to assure them that he wasn't there to tell them not to take drugs. 'All I want to do is to share some things with you that I've been privileged to learn.' This included masses of stuff on the easily documented hazards of alcohol, some very detailed information about the structure of nerve cells and their branching structure of axons and dendrons, some thoughts on the intimacies of adolescence, and a 'desiderata'-type poem carved in an eighteenth-century Baltimore church, concluding with thanks 'for being a wonderful audience'. ('When they just sit in silence like that it's a sign that they're taking it in,' he confided afterwards.)

But what was missing was the 'hard science', to use his phrase, about the health risks of pot. His book doesn't fight shy. He quotes a now-deceased professor of pharmacology at Oxford, citing a study 'that found brain atrophy in youthful marijuana users equivalent to people aged seventy to ninety' and continues: 'To date clear-cut, quantitative, neuro-anatomical evidence of brain ageing in the hippocampus has been found in connection with chronic exposure to only one drug of abuse – and that is THC (the main psychotropic drug in cannabis).' I rang Leslie Iverson, currently the Visiting Professor of Pharmacology at Oxford, for an opinion. 'Unscientific rubbish,' he snorted.

Trevor Grice had been one of Caroline Noortman's speakers at the House of Commons. 'In fairness to him,' she said, 'I think he is genuinely concerned to protect young people.' There's nothing wrong with this aim, but I do feel that it would be more honest of Mr Grice to illustrate *The Great Brain Robbery* with pictures of Sir Harry Secombe and Sir Cliff Richard rather than, for example, a moody shot of Bob Dylan circa 1965 with the line 'He not busy being born is busy dying' (written, as it happens, at the height of Bob's amphetamine period.)

Especially since the rows surrounding attempts to introduce genetically modified foods in Britain, people have become aware of the limits of scientific neutrality. Those who pay for research tend to seek a return for their investment. An environmental chemist I know was once employed by a toxic waste facility to provide data for the regulatory authorities, which was also published in scientific journals. One of his jobs was to measure levels of poisons around the perimeter. Sure enough, these showed raised levels, indicating that unpleasant things were leaking out. The solution was to scour the countryside for other polluted sites; the high levels found there were then presented as 'UK background levels', beside which the soil contaminated by his employers looked comparatively healthy.

Until very recently, most research into cannabis has been funded, as Geoffrey Guy told the House of Lords inquiry, 'primarily to get evidence against the use, medical or otherwise, of cannabis'. The funding comes from the US National Institute on Drug Abuse and the effect of its 'politically motivated research' has, he said, been to 'seed misinformation into the medical and lay literature'.

This trend can be traced back a quarter of a century to a meeting in Washington, DC of a group called the Crusade Against Moral Pollution. (Fundamentalist Christians have been very active in the War on Drugs; at the level of individual treatment, they are often successful with the most stubborn cases of self-destructive multi-drug abuse.) After this meeting in 1974 three of the men who'd been present had an informal chat: the pastor of Washington's French Protestant Church in Washington, Dr Gabriel Nahas, an anaesthesiologist and anti-marijuana campaigner, and David Martin, the official investigator for the Senate Sub-Committee for Internal Security. All three were concerned at a tendency towards social tolerance of pot which they felt had been confirmed by the findings of the Shafer Commission, set up in 1971 by the new Nixon administration. They succeeded in getting a new set of Senate hearings, chaired by Senator James Eastland. Selected witnesses raised questions they felt had not been answered by the earlier report, whose findings, Nahas felt, 'would only compound the prevailing general confusion about marijuana'. His 'response to its bland conclusions was a determination to study the immune system'.[2]

Gabriel Nahas is an extraordinary person. He was born in Alexandria to a Lebanese father and French mother. He holds decorations from both the French and British Governments for helping Allied airmen to escape from occupied France. He has had a real influence on the course of history, providing a rationale for Reagan and Bush's war on marijuana, and stiffening France's resolve to fight *la toximanie* as President Chirac's special adviser on drug policy. Peter Stoker of Britain's National Drug Prevention Alliance runs into him at international anti-drug gatherings, and refers to him fondly as 'Gabby'. Trevor Grice quoted him to me as an authority on cannabis. Nahas clearly inspires affection: two eminent scientists joined Jacques Cousteau in writing introductory notes to the 1983 edition of his book *Keep Off the Grass* – although they express caution about his anti-pot conclusions and recommend reading more widely. This book is actually a good introduction to the subject, which is prevented from being effective propaganda by its candour, as above, when Nahas reveals his political agenda in studying THC's effects on the immune system.

Nahas has been demonised by legalization activists. Dana Beal, an AIDS activist and contributor to the pro-cannabis handbook *The Emperor Wears No Clothes*, describes him as a member of a clique of ex-members of the OSS (the wartime predecessor of the CIA) including Kurt Waldheim and the right-wing maverick Lyndon Larouche. Perhaps because the purpose of this cabal is bit unclear, no writ has been issued. In 1996, though, Nahas did sue Michka, a French writer and cannabis activist, over a piece she wrote describing him as a discredited figure (winning only token damages of a single franc). The most damaging criticism, for which he has not successfully sued, was published in a learned journal in 1994[3]. Two members of the University of Sydney's Department of Pharmacology checked the citations made by Nahas and his co-author C. Latour in a paper entitled 'The human toxicity of marijuana' which they had published two years earlier in the *Medical Journal of Australia*. They reported that at least twenty-eight of the thirty-five citations from other research were inaccurate, and that all the inaccuracies tended to find an adverse effect.

Geoffrey Guy cryptically calls Nahas 'a very special type of person'. From her courtroom encounters Michka remembers an elderly, short and irascible figure, with staring brown eyes. He frequently wears a bow-tie and favours a white coat for media appearances. I've spoken to him on three occasions on the phone in the course of which our relations steadily deteriorated and I lost my chance of a face-to-face. I regret this. His intense, embattled quality is somehow endearing (I've also spoken to a pro-marijuana documentary maker who has filmed him and feels the same way).

Nahas studied the effects of high doses of THC on animal cells, such as white blood cells, or on live laboratory animals. After scores of experiments by various researchers a disturbing pattern emerged: cell function was disrupted; animals, especially those directly injected with THC, developed a range of symptoms from brain damage to infertility and physical addiction. These findings were reviewed in 1982 by the US Institute of Medicine and the World Health Organization, and after this date the US Government built up its support for marijuana research; the National Institute on Drug Abuse spent about $3 million in this area in 1982 but $26 million in 1990. In the year ending September 1998, the last for which figures are available, the NIDA marijuana budget was still running at $21.4 million.

But cell damage is no longer the prime issue that secures funding for cannabis research. (After all many, if not most, drugs, including valium, caffeine, aspirin and alcohol, produce similar changes in the laboratory.) The House of Lords committee, drawing on the previous year's World Health Organization report 'Cannabis: a health perspective and research agenda', simply stated that 'there is no evidence that cannabis adversely affects human fertility, or that it causes chromasomal or genetic damage'. 'Our side is losing,' Dr Nahas told me. The focus has moved from toxicology to the medical applications that he discounts – or, as Geoffrey Guy put it, 'This subject will now move independently of the pro and anti lobbies, and out of the hands of what the Americans call the "piss testers" who controlled the ground a few years ago.'

The turn-round has caused ripples that can be felt in secondary school drugs education – Trevor Grice's opening remark on cannabis was a prediction that one day it would be the source of wonderful medicines – and among pro-pot activists: Free-Rob Cannabis told me that it was a substance naturally found in the body, so how could it be bad for you? This isn't quite right; researchers are starting to appreciate how different the cannabinoids in the cannabis plant are from the substances in the brain that switch on the same brain receptors.[4] Put more accurately in the words of Professor Trevor Robbins, giving evidence to the

Lords on behalf of the Medical Research Council: 'Cannabinoid pharmacology has exploded in the past decade . . . opening up all sorts of exciting possibilities.'

Put simply, the old theory was that THC had its effect by dissolving in the membranes which surround body cells and 'perturbing' them: disrupting the flow of signals between cells. This is the way that both alcohol and general anaesthetics work. But the theory didn't explain why if THC could be effective at such extraordinarily low doses – one-thousandth of that needed for alcohol – its action on cells was essentially the same.

The anomaly was explained in 1990 when Tom Bonner and Liza Matsuda of the US National Institute of Health in Bethesda, Maryland proved the existence in certain cells of a 'receptor' activated by THC. A receptor is a single protein, made up of about 500 molecules, which sits on the cell wall and can create alterations in the cell's activity – but only if it is triggered by certain chemical substances which 'bind' to it. An analogy often used is with a lock that can only be opened by certain chemical keys.

It had been a chance discovery for Bonner and Matsuda, molecular biologists with no special interest in cannabis – unlike the man who now, at the age of sixty, picked up the baton. For a drug to act on a receptor it has to have certain structural similarities to a chemical used in the transmission of the body's own nerve impulses. Heroin and morphine act by mimicking the action of the 'neurotransmitter' named endorphin, which produces its pleasurable effects when, for example, we take exercise or go to sleep. Professor Raphael Mechoulam of the Hebrew University of Jerusalem renewed his quest for what he calls 'the chemistry of emotion', and began to hunt for a neurotransmitter chemically similar to THC.

The professor, whose family escaped to Palestine from Nazi-occupied Bulgaria, had still been in his early thirties when he transformed our understanding of cannabis by discovering THC. This substance wasn't the first of the cannabinoids (the chemicals found only in cannabis) to be isolated; this had been cannabinol, which was found in 1895 by a team at the Cambridge University Medical School. The end of the previous century had seen a burst of work led by Walters Ernest Dixon, the Salters Research Fellow, who took a benign view of smoking cannabis, which he said could be placed 'in the same category as coffee, tea and cola. It is not dangerous and its effects are never alarming, and I have come to regard it in this form as a useful and refreshing stimulant and food accessory.'[5] In fact cannabinol is a degradation product – none is found in fresh cannabis – and it's only a tenth as psychoactive as the new substance Raphael Mechoulam isolated in 1964.

'We were the first to oftain THC in a pure form and to demonstrate its structure. I thought cannabis was a good topic to work on because it was the most prevalent drug in the world, even then in the 1960s, but the active compound had never been isolated. People had worked on opium and discovered morphine about 200 years ago, and cocaine was discovered in the mid-nineteenth century. They are both easy to obtain using nine-teenth-century techniques. But the cannabinoids form a horrible complex mixture. There are about eighty, and we've identified about twelve major compounds. They have to be separated by techniques that weren't available many years ago.'[6]

Mechoulam's skills of analysis were called on ten years ago by archaeologists excavating a Roman site twenty kilometres south of Jerusalem. They had found the remains of a fourteen-year old girl who had died in childbirth, together with something that had been burnt on a brazier beside her bed. 'When we analysed the ashes we found traces, not of Delta 9 THC, which you find in cannabis, but of Delta 8 THC. When you burn cannabis part of it is converted to Delta 8, which is extremely stable. In fact it had been there for 1,600 years. They had burnt cannabis next to the bed: at that time people had used cannabis to reduce pain or help in childbirth.' The discovery strengthened Mechoulam's belief in the medical potential of cannabis – a belief that would create some coolness with his old friend Gabriel Nahas.

Then came the discovery of the receptors that were 'switched on' by THC, found largely in cells in the brain and the spinal cord. Mechoulam's team began looking for a substance in the brain that would bind to them. The original experimental material was cows' brains, but it wasn't until the team moved over to the un-kosher alternative of pigs' brains that they were able to collect measurable amounts of a promising-looking candidate.

This substance bound to the receptors, but this was not proof that it switched them on. ('Ligands' – chemicals that bind to receptors – can be 'agonists' which create changes in the cell, or 'antagonists' which have no action but stop the receptor being triggered by an agonist.) Mechoulam turned to a British colleague, Dr Roger Pertwee of Aberdeen University Medical School, for help.

Aberdeen has seen a surprising amount of research and innovation in the last quarter of a century. There is the offshore industry with its novel technologies for extracting oil from the sea bed at great depths; more recently the biologists at the Rowett Institute were in the news after the saga of Dr Arpad Pusztai, the rats and the genetically modified potatoes. And this northern city has also been home to fundamental work in brain chemistry. Roger Pertwee arrived in 1974 after working on cannabis at Oxford since 1968. He had been appointed as a lecturer to replace John Hughes, who was leaving to pursue his search for the natural substances that activate the body's morphine receptors – the endorphins.

In 1992 Pertwee was based in Marischal College in one of the

main streets of Aberdeen; this monumental granite building –
supposedly the largest such structure in the world – also housed
his colleagues researching the endorphins and other substances
that work on the so-called 'opioid' receptors. This research
group had developed a test for opioids, using a mouse's vas
deferens (the tiny length of tube through which it ejaculates its
seminal fluid).

   Like Raphael Mechoulam, Roger Pertwee was galvanized by
the news from America. He soon found that the minute piece of
dead mouse so prized by his colleagues was full of receptors for
THC as well as for opioids. To measure the effect of THC on
living tissue, the technique involved putting the vas deferens of a
newly killed mouse in a 'physiological solution': a sort of
chemical soup kept at a body temperature with life-giving
oxygen bubbling through it. The piece of tissue, resembling
an undersized elastic band, was wired up and given a small
electrical jolt every ten seconds. To see the THC at work, a
researcher would drip a set amount into the solution from a
syringe, and measure the electrical contraction afterwards. The
effect of the drug is to dampen down the release of neurotransmitters acting on the mouses's muscle cells, resulting in a
weaker twitch.

   One sign of the gathering interest in the cannabinoids – THC
and related substances – was that researchers in different countries got together to form the international society which since
1991 has met every year. Roger Pertwee spoke at the inaugural
meeting on the subject of his reactive mouse tissue.

   'Mechoulam was there when I presented our work on the vas
deferens. The meeting was in Palm Beach: very nice. It was the
time that he was trying to find an indigenous cannabinoid. Then
the next year he sent us something to look at: the stuff from a
pig's brain. It was quite exciting. There was so little you couldn't
see it in the tube; it was just like a smear of Vaseline. We made it

up exactly as if it had been THC, using a particular vehicle which is a type of detergent. We didn't know how much to use in the experiment. Too little and we could have frittered away our material without seeing anything; but it was also worrying to blow the world's entire supply of this stuff at one go. We compromised – and it turned out that we'd got it about right. It was less potent than THC but it produced the same effect, even at low concentrations.'

So the following year's meeting of the International Cannabinoid Society was memorable for reasons other than the sybaritic setting (it was Keystone in the Rocky Mountains – 'We were all sitting out on a veranda,' recalls Pertwee). It was there that the human body's own version of THC was given a name, agreed on by Mecoulam and Pertwee's research groups: Anandamide, from *ananda*, or 'bliss' in Sanskrit, the language in which cannabis was first described as an aid to religious experience around 3,000 years ago.

Anandamide was just the start. In 1993 a team in Cambridge led by Sean Munro found a second receptor for THC, mainly in cells concentrated in organs of the immune system such as the spleen and tonsils. Although it's possible to sketch out some of the functions of the first receptor, now known as CB1, the role of CB2 in the immune system is still unclear. Then in 1995 a team led by Mechoulam found a second endogenous cannabinoid; unlike its predecessor it has not got a melodious given name and remains known as 2-arichidonyl-glycerol, or 2–AG. Geoffrey Guy comments: 'The receptor theory has moved cannabis on from being polarized between paranoid fanatics and fervent believers.' Guy is enthralled by the unfolding discoveries: 'Not only is a receptor system there: it's more all–pervading than one imagines. It's like going into a cave with a candle and when you switch the light on you find drawings all over the walls – here, there, here . . . And if they're everywhere, what's been going on?'

The drug companies are now involved, coming up with new synthetic cannabinoids as well as antagonists to block them. It might even be the antagonists that yield the most useful pharmaceutical drugs: if cannabis is bad for the short-term memory, something that blocks anandamide might be good for it. Or if cannabis famously gives smokers the munchies, an antagonist might help people control their urge to eat sweet things. The French company Sanofi are looking at the prospects of using their CB1 blocker drug as a treatment for schizophrenia, with the rationale that high doses of THC can cause a schizophrenia-like psychosis.

One man, though, was, and remains, horrified by the turn of events: Gabriel Nahas. For Professor Nahas, the high point of studies on THC was the work done in the mid-1980s by Dr David Harvey, an Oxford bio-chemist. 'A big book was written and totally ignored,' he told me.[7] When I first spoke to Dr Nahas he had just got back to his New York home from Montpellier, the location of the 1998 symposium of the International Cannabinoid Research Society. He told me that he'd presented a 'major rebuttal' showing that 'this drug acted on a very fundamental mechanism': a 'membrane of the cell'. 'They went into a new theory about the specific receptor for THC which is just, I'd say, a scientific inaccuracy. This new theory is based on wrong observations which we have discovered in the literature. It's a major scientific scandal, backed by a number of English and American scientists.' Those who attended the conference were confused about Nahas position on the receptors. 'He just won't accept the recent discoveries,' another guest told me. 'He got up and gave a polemic about how THC worked on a cellular level. Among other things he showed slides thirty years old about what happens if you expose bits of assorted rat tissue to massive amounts of THC. They tend to fall apart. But everyone knows there are cannabis receptors.'

In the autumn Nahas staked out his position in a presentation to the British Pharmacological Society written jointly with Dr David Harvey. This took the form of a 'poster', which formed the basis of an article that appeared in a learned journal.[8] It gave an account of the way the receptors might regulate signalling across the membranes of individual nerve and brain cells, and suggested that THC 'deregulates the putative membrane signalling'. In other words, the membrane theory that was in favour in the mid–1980s can co-exist with the new discoveries.

Why does Nahas care so much? The passion of his conviction reminds me of a revolutionary socialist for whom it is vital that the Soviet Union should be classed as having been 'state capitalist' rather than a 'deformed workers' state'. Of course it must be annoying when some pot smokers assume that because a substance resembling THC is found in the brain, THC is in some way 'natural'. No one makes such a claim for heroin or valium, both of which act on specific receptors. Conversely, Nahas is far from alone in insisting that THC gets into cell membranes and 'perturbs' them, as the phrase goes; it's generally accepted that drugs often produce their effects in more than one way.

But given that there's nothing in itself praiseworthy about a drug that acts on a receptor, why should this other mode of action be thought of as especially sinister? For Nahas it 'impairs judgement and the capacity of the brain to distinguish right from wrong, true from false', the cause being 'erroneous signalling'. But why isn't he equally damning about alcohol, which also acts by dissolving in cell membranes, or about the general anaesthetics that are his own professional stock-in-trade?

One answer is that THC is extremely soluble in fat – as indeed is anandamide – and this, for anti-pot campaigners, is its great sin. Nahas: 'What Pertwee is saying is essentially that THC is no more dangerous than the benzodiazepines (i.e. valium) which get out of the body in seven hours. It sticks to the receptors for days, yet it's being compared to a natural ligand which has a very fast turnover of a few minutes or hours.' THC does hang around in the system; unlike anandamide which is eliminated locally in the nervous system, THC disappears into fatty tissue and is slowly metabolized by the liver. This means that drug testing for cannabis gives misleading results; the opposite state of affairs to that portrayed by Trevor Grice when he writes that 'It may be active in the nervous system after it is no longer detectable in the blood.'[9]

Roger Pertwee turns this argument on its head. He argues that pot 'suppresses its own withdrawal syndrome' because of the slow elimination of THC, and that it's this that makes cannabis less addictive than water-soluble drugs like the opiates: morphine and heroin. The consequences of a rapidly eliminated form of cannabis were demonstrated by a disgusting experiment conducted by researchers in Virginia. This gave dogs high doses of THC, followed by the CB1 receptor blocker, and so induced cold turkey-like symptoms: 'trembling, shaking, vomiting, restlessness and diarrhoea'.

The clue to Gabriel Nahas's anger at 'the biggest hoax perpetrated on the scientific community' is that the new consensus allows doctors to see marijuana as a source of medicines. Pharmaceutical researchers want drugs which act on specific receptors so that they can target precisely, to produce an action in the body with a minimum of side-effects. Something that only acts on the nervous system or the immune system is more valuable than something which creates changes throughout the body. General anaesthetics, which act on the membranes of all cells, have a very limited application in relieving, say, the pain of childbirth, a headache or a twisted ankle. The conclusion of his poster on 'Psychoactive Cannabinoids and Membrane Signalling Mechanisms' is that the mechanism of the action of cannabinoids 'appear to limit their suitability for general therapeutic application'. Yet, as one researcher claimed, this mechanism is one that he has asserted, not discovered or demonstrated.

Surprisingly in March 1998 Dr Nahas organized a two-day conference at New York University Medical Center on 'Marijuana and Medicine'. Geoffrey Guy remembers Nahas 'tearing apart' the contributions of speakers with whom he'd disagreed. Roger Pertwee and Raphael Mechoulam were among the speakers, but clearly failed to convince their host, even though when we spoke four months afterwards he paid them a kind of backhanded compliment. 'It's a fantastic cover-up in science which has no precedent, and it's based on the misconceptions of brilliant scientists,' he told me. 'With these facts I'm going to the head of the National Institute of Health. Hundreds of millions of dollars have been spent to find a medical use for THC and millions more are being provided. This nonsense has to be stopped.' After this peroration he complimented me for my interest: 'You have a fantastic theme.'

I was promised a meeting, but he became exasperated with me before it could happen. Unfortunately I asked why marijuana was not having worse consequences in American society – and specifically how sunrise industries of Silicon Valley could have emerged from the weed-infested culture of late-sixties' California. When Steve Jobs, the founder of Apple, attended Reed College in Portland, Oregon, he was a pretty major league freak even by the standards of the West Coast in the early 1970s, and a disciple of the campus LSD guru.[10] Nahas told me that even if Steve Jobs had smoked pot Bill Gates hadn't, and told me an apocryphal anecdote about Jobs telling Gates that he'd be better off if he did. It seemed rather human of Nahas to pass this story on; then his irritation reasserted itself and he accused me of being 'a victim of media brainwashing'. It was a loss, given the absence in modern Britain of real red-blooded anti-cannabis campaigners. There are Peter and Ann Stoker, running the National Drug Prevention Alliance from the converted garage under their bungalow in Slough. Peter is a former civil engineer with many years' experience on projects in the Gulf states. He has a good heart, but it's difficult to engage in argument with someone who tells you that heroin is less harmful than opium, or that THC, unlike herbal cannabis, *doesn't* make you stoned. And Trevor Grice makes some lurid claims in *The Great Brain Robbery*, but as I saw at The Leys School, Cambridge, he can fight shy of defending them in public.

Many think that Gabriel Nahas is wrong. A leading pharmacologist told me: 'He was a scientist who was determined to find out bad things about marijuana – which isn't what you're supposed to do.' But the questions he has raised are interesting ones, even if the answers he claims to have found don't always bear scrutiny. I'm not sure he wasn't right to call for more scientific work in the early 1970s, when legalization really seemed to be on the cards. And his big question is worth more attention than the legalization lobby concede it. Just what does happen to a society when a new intoxicating drug gets accepted on a mass scale?

5

Arouser of Thought

It was Gabriel Nahas's childhood in pre-war Egypt, he tells us in *Keep Off the Grass*, that first turned him against hashish. He writes: 'I know its dangers. I saw them first many years ago in Alexandria.' Apparently as he left for school he'd sometimes see a man lying comatose in the street: a hashish addict, according to his father. (Actually the description would also fit a victim of the heroin epidemic which was current at that time, according to the Egyptian chief of police, Thomas Wentworth Russell Pasha.[1]) Nahas's Uncle Selim, who was a doctor, cautioned him that hashish was 'like a poison' and that he should never use it. 'Oh no' was young Gabriel's reply. He was already aware, he says, of the 'unwritten law' in Egypt, as in other Middle Eastern countries, making hashish taboo among the upper classes. This conflicts with what I've heard about Morocco, but holds good for Egypt (with the exception of some artists and intellectuals – for example, the circle called *al harafish* described in Chapter 3).

Because of his background Nahas is sometimes cited as an authority for the view that 'Hashish addiction has played a major role in reducing the Arab lands to the barren stagnation and oppressive mass poverty that has only been partly alleviated by the oil bonanza.'[2] In fact he is more circumspect, saying that 'the abuse of cannabis, the deceptive weed . . . cannot be excluded'[3] and elsewhere that the appearance of cannabis products 'coincided' with a long period of decline.[4] In Israel Raphael Mechoulam, the discoverer of THC, lives alongside Arab society without being part of it. He told me: 'One of the problems of Muslim society, and Nahas is well aware of it, is that people smoked a lot and were apathetic. It caused a lot of damage.'

When I spoke to Nahas he was not anxious to explore this area. He feels that the pro-marijuana lobby uses his Middle Eastern background to marginalize him, which is fair enough, given America's endemic anti-Arab and anti-Islamic stance. Instead he steered me towards another author, Dr Franz Rosenthal, a professor in Yale's Department of Oriental Studies, who in 1971 had published *The Herb: Hashish versus Medieval Muslim Society*.

This book is a gold-mine. It is the chief source for campaigners who want to put the 'stagnant and desolate' one. But this isn't the point of the book, and it would be a tough one to prove. As one Arab academic put it: 'The West today is a society in which hashish is endemic; so why isn't the West stagnant and desolate?' Franz Rosenthal has told me that his intention was to describe how people in a particular culture responded to the new phenomenon of hashish. His evidence comes from hashish poetry, which imitated the classic Arabian wine songs, and the disputations of Muslim theologians on whether the drug, which was unknown at the time of the Prophet Muhammad, was lawful (*halal*) or, like wine, outlawed (*harām*).

These unfamiliar writings turn out to describe a world that is surprisingly recognizable. Rosenthal sweeps us from the eleventh to the seventeenth century, and from Persia, where according to legend hashish was discovered, to Spain in the far north-west of the Muslim world. At the same time we learn about the culture of hashish in the most precise detail: where cannabis was grown, how hashish was made, how it was taken (always swallowed rather than smoked, before the arrival of tobacco from the New World), and where (the public baths, or *hammam*, was a favourite place), which social classes preferred hashish to wine, and what was the attitude of the authorities at different times.

Modern Western cannabis culture teems with legendary figures like the plant breeder 'Skunk Sam' or 'English Richard'[5] who allegedly brought the art of hashish-making to Morocco in the late 1960s. In a similar spirit the medieval Arabs referred the invention of hashish to Haydar, the leader of a Sufi brotherhood in the mountain region of Khorasan in Iran. Two writers on hashish tell a version of the story: al 'Ukbari, in the thirteenth century, and al Zarkashi, who lived 100 years later. In his work titled *zuhur al 'arish fi ahkam al hashish* (*the Floral Bower of Hashish Lore*) al Zarkashi dates Haydar's discovery to the year 1155. The mystic had been depressed and had felt like getting away from his companions. 'He came across a hashish plant and noticed that its branches were swaying although there was no breeze. He reflected that this must be so because of a secret contained in it. He picked some of it and ate it. When he returned to his companions he told them that the plant contained a secret and ordered them to eat it.' This is a concise version of the story told by al 'Ukbari and they're both almost identical to the story told by chroniclers of the discovery of coffee, which involves a Sufi sheikh (sheikh means religious leader as well as tribal chief), this time called Omar, who was guided to the coffee tree in 1258 by a bird of marvellous plumage, and who like Haydar became regarded as a saint and his tomb as a place of pilgrimage.[6] As Rosenthal points out, the effect of these stories is to put the new drug in a good light by attributing it with a miraculous aura.

Raphael Mechoulam's forensic work shows that cannabis had been used as a medicine in the Middle East at least since Roman times. But its cultural heartland has always been further east: in the mountainous regions that lead up to the Himalayas and stretch across modern Pakistan and Afghanistan. The recreational use of hashish spread west throughout the whole Muslim world at about the time of the Mongol invasions of the thirteenth century. The legal authority Ibn Taymiyah (1263–1328), who was opposed to hashish, linked it with the Mongols, possibly to damn it by association with these terrifying invaders who sacked Baghdad and destroyed the ancient irrigation systems of Mesopotamia – a catastrophe from which the eastern Arab world took centuries to recover. It's possible, Rosenthal suggests, that refugees from the east took the practice with them and that anxiety made people rely on the drug. In Muslim Spain poets began writing about hashish as early as the first part of the fourteenth century – less than 100 years after it was supposed to have arrived in Iraq, at the other end of the Arab world. Rosenthal's sources describe it as being widely used by 1360 in Granada, the last great city of Muslim Andalusia to hold out against the Christian reconquest.

The hashish culture of the medieval Arabs is familiar in many ways. We find descriptions of the well-known signs of being stoned, like the rather seedy-looking reddening of the whites of the eyes. Ibn al Kharrat (1375–1436) writes:

> Our friend is clutching half a pill
> Gleaming as a green pomegranate tree
> We kept him company after he swallowed it
> And an hour later it blossomed in his eye.

And Ibn al 'Afif al Tilimsani (1262–89) describes the munchies using the specific word (*mastūl*) that means high on hashish: 'Stoned people pounce on sweets as greedily as lover on the mouth of his beloved.' The sociology is also familiar. Today cannabis has become universal but still retains an association from the 1960s with students and marginal groups. The essential point about pot in the medieval Arab world is that it was relatively very cheap (showing that however much Ibn Taymiyah and others ruled it *harām*, no effective prohibition was enforced for long). The thirteenth century historian Ibn Abd al Zahir wrote: 'One dirham of hashish buys as much intoxication as one dinar of wine' (a silver dirham being worth only about one-fiftieth of a gold dinar). The governing class and the military élite preferred wine, but hashish was the choice, in Rosenthal's words, of 'Sufis and scholars – a kind of third estate having connection with the military establishment above and the mass of subjects below'. He cites a witty and acerbic scholar, Muslim al Hanafi, whose teaching was unimpaired by his hashish consumption, and whose turban fell off one day in mid-lecture revealing his stash of pills.

Hashish was closely associated with Sufism, or Islamic mysticism – sometimes defined as the love of God as a goal in itself, independent of any desire for reward or fear of punishment. Al Badri (1443–89), the author of the longest single work on hashish, gives a set of supposedly Sufi precepts on the correct ritual, attributed to a probably fictional 'Shaykh Qalandar'. There is a formula for prayer, and advice to take hashish only in the company of other Sufis. Ultimately the hashish taker 'notices the hearts with the eyes and controls the eyes with the heart. He separates from his idea of humanity and joins his idea of divinity'. The Sufi poet al Yanbu'i wrote in the first half of the thirteenth century how the act of eating hashish turned his living room into a place of worship.

Interestingly, it was Yemeni Sufis who first brought coffee to Cairo in 1510 to stay awake during the Sufi ritual of *dhikr*, literally 'remembrance of God', and it was from Cairo that coffee travelled to Venice and the West. Coffee was controversial when it first appeared in the Muslim world, and it was banned repeatedly throughout the sixteenth century. In 1511 the Ottoman Governor of Mecca called the city's two physicians to debate its physical effects. One citizen chipped in, claiming to have experienced a similar sort of drunkenness to wine. For the admission that he had actually tried coffee he was arrested on the spot and sentenced to a beating. The Governor then opted for total prohibition of coffee, and ordered all the coffee houses in Mecca to be closed and their entire stocks burnt.[7]

It's not clear whether experts in Islamic law disapproved of hashish in itself or because it was linked with Sufism. Sufism has always had a subversive tinge, because the claim of a direct experience of God threatens the authority of orthodox theologians, and because the Sufi brotherhoods, the *turuqā*, can provide a forum for dissent. Hashish gave its name to one group, the twelfth-century Assassins, notorious for sectarian terrorism, but even so there's no evidence that the two activities were connected, or in fact, that calling the group 'pot-heads' was anything more than a way of being rude about them.

Just as today, hashish was associated with low life as well as spirituality. Al Badri quoted these lines from Burhan al Din al Mi'mar, with their play on words between *Tinah*, meaning clay, or kaolin, which was sometimes mixed with hashish, and *tinah*, meaning a fig or, as here, an anus.

> Mix your hashish with kaolin till it's just right
> Chew it as you relax on your bed and polish it off
> Then eat all you want – it's nice when you're greedy
> And if you want to make love, be a backdoor lover.

Al Badri gives us access to a range of late medieval attitudes on this subject. One that seems widespread is that hashish is habit forming; he writes: 'One of the properties of hashish is that the user cannot give it up.' Rosenthal repeats the legend of a holy man in sixteenth-century Cairo, Abdallah al Misri al Majdub, who grew hashish which actually cured the habit (though he doesn't say if you had to go on taking this particular hashish to stay cured). This is an unfamiliar issue today, even among anti-

cannabis campaigners; in a society where many more addictive
drugs, legal and illegal, circulate widely it seems rather a remote
problem. (In fact a drugs worker recently suggested that heroin
users appear to smoke cannabis in order to control their habit and
get relief from withdrawal symptoms.[8]) But it's a reminder that
there are pot-heads who aren't anything much else besides, and
that people who smoke all the time need a lot of weed to get
only moderately stoned. It's also possible that eating hashish,
which has stronger effects, is more habit-forming than smoking.

Something even less unfamiliar – at least to non-Muslims – is
the medieval Islamic practice of bolstering an argument by
putting it in the form of a supposed saying of the Prophet
Muhammad. Rosenthal quotes one in which a companion of
the Prophet is supposed to have said: 'I went together with the
Prophet into the countryside. He saw a tree and shook his head. I
asked why he was shaking his head and he replied: "A time will
come upon my nation when they will eat from the leaves of this
tree and get intoxicated, and they will pray when intoxicated." '
What would today be called the marijuana lobby was equally
busy. Dope lovers fabricated traditions of the Prophet favourable
to hashish, as well as writing endless reams of verse – in this
famous instance, quoting the Islamic legal authorities Malik and
al Shafi'i:

It is virginal, not deflowered by rain
Nor has it ever been squeezed by feet or hands
No Christian priest has interfered with the cup containing it
Nor have they given communion from its cask to any
    heretic soul
Nothing has been expressly said by Malik to declare it
    unlawful
Nor is a Koranic penalty for using it prescribed by al Shafi'i.[9]

This didn't cut ice with the authorities. A public park in Cairo called the Garden of Kafur was used as a site for growing cannabis (How did growers establish ownership of individual plants and stop pilfering?) The Sultan of Egypt, Najm ul Din Ayyub, ordered the Governor of Cairo, Musa ibn Yaghmur, to prevent this, and large quantities of harvested plants were gathered and burnt. Then hashish was caught up in a moral purge in the years 1266–7 by the Sultan al Malik al Zahir Baybars, the leader who repulsed the Mongol invasion. Baybars revoked the system of taxed and licensed cultivation as well as closing taverns and smashing storage vessels for wine. One of Baybars' judges[10] wrote:

> Satan has no desire to stay with us
> He prefers to make his home elsewhere and not in the
>   Emir's country
> You have prevented him from obtaining wine and hashish
> You have thus deprived him of his water and fodder.

There were further crackdowns in the following century. One governor not only destroyed the 'accursed shrubs' in various locations around Cairo, but had offenders punished by having their molars extracted. It may have been in response that hashish eaters came to relish cultishness and secrecy. Just as the 'tea' smokers of 1930s' Harlem talked about 'muggles', 'muta' or 'rosa maria',[11] the hashasheen developed a private vocabulary. The Arabs have a passion for language, and a taboo subject sends them into overdrive. (*The Perfumed Garden*, the sixteenth century sex manual, has pages of synonyms for the penis.) The botanical word *qinnab* is simply derived from the Greek *cannabis*; *al hashish* is itself a sort of slang usage – the original Arabic word means grass, mowings or weedy vegetation. Then there are names that describe the little pills in which hashish was eaten before the arrival of smoking from the New World: *al khadra* – 'the green one'; *al ghubaira* – 'the little dust-coloured one'; *al bunduqa* – 'the pellet'. Even more evocative are the names that talk about the experience: *hādim al aqwat* – 'the digester of food'; *nāith al fikr* – 'the arouser of thought'; *luqmat al fikr* – 'the morsel of thought; *bast* – 'relaxation'; *al malūm* – 'the thing we know about', or the name most popular in Turkey: *asrār*, or 'secrets'. Al Badr, who wrote encyclopaedically on the subject, quoted verses punning on one popular name, *al sahīh*, *sahīh* meaning 'perfect' and 'healthy':

> I said to someone who was dying
> Because hashish had sent him to the grave
> 'Did you really die of hectic fever?
> 'He replied: "I died of being healthy." '

Hashish isn't the only word to have lasted down the centuries. The term *maajūn*, meaning 'kneaded' or 'paste', is still very much alive in the far west of the Arab world. When tobacco arrived in the seventeenth century, there was a shift from eating to smoking cannabis. But Morocco is a time capsule: Moroccans wear hooded *jellaba*s, the everyday garment of the late Roman world that also survives in Europe's monasteries; from Muslim Spain the country inherits a style of architecture with patterned surfaces and horseshoe arches and the same quirky version of Arabic script that makes their letter 'q' look like an 'f'. The Moroccans have also preserved the tradition of eating cannabis. Whereas the man in the street smokes the chopped tops of the plants in a small clay pipe, the upper and upper-middle classes enjoy it pounded into *maajūn*, a paste that's placed under the teeth and slowly ingested with glass after glass of hot sweet mint tea. An academic I know came across *maajūn* when he went to an international conference in Rabat and was entertained with a group of colleagues by one of the city's leading families. He told me: 'You can't get it outside a circle of these established wealthy families; it's made in the family and used chiefly through the winter. We happened to be in Rabat but the best is made in Fez. There was a large party of intellectuals. We were invited for dinner and offered either whisky or *maajūn* for those who wanted it. You don't mix it with whisky. We had two in our group who opted for it.' The two bold academics enjoyed their experience and wanted to repeat it, but when they tried to buy *maajūn* in Fez they met with laughter and were told that it wasn't traded, only offered to privileged guests.

The anonymous medieval pot-heads who coined terms like 'secrets' and 'arouser of thought' achieved the near-impossible and conveyed what it's like to be stoned. This is the missing element in much writing on this subject. We don't imagine that the various authors in the long tradition of elegantly written reports – from the Indian Hemp Commission of 1894 to Baroness Wootton in 1967 – actually spliffed up (although Lord Perry, presenting the House of Lords report in late 1998, repeatedly refused to answer reporters who pressed committee members on this point).

This is a problem in writing this kind of book. I hadn't smoked for a while when the idea first came up (in a wine bar in the City with a barrister friend who asked, after two San Miguels, 'Does any one else feel, like me, that maybe it's time for a pipe?'). Was I going to get stoned and write about what it was like? I didn't think so. And then there was the issue of objectivity. By the end of a research period I just might come to conclude that hashish was wreaking the same sort of havoc, say, that gin or opium created in previous centuries. I should not withhold judgment just because I personally happened to like the stuff. Alternatively, if the book should turn into a plea for legalization it would be more credible without a personal axe to grind. Also I intended to interview people who were firmly convinced that dope was a very good or a very bad thing; I wanted to be able honestly to present myself as neutral.

But my downfall came within a few weeks. It happened in extreme circumstances and at the heart of one of the Arab world's old cannabis cultures. The setting was the Hotel Tidiguine in Ketama, the mountain village whose name has become synonymous with Morocco's main export crop, during my July visit to see the *kif* or marijuana plants being harvested.

The Hotel Tidiguine was so strange that I found myself thinking of using it as a setting for a film script. Later I realized that this was because it reminded me of a film that had already been made: Stanley Kubrick's *The Shining*, in which the homicidal action takes place in a huge deserted hotel surrounded by pine forests. The Tidiguine has sixty-eight bedrooms and was built in the 1960s in a modernist Alpine style. It is conveniently close to Mount Tidiguine, 2,448 metres high, whose slopes offer excellent skiing for much of the year. The architect put a tennis court in front, just across the main road to Fez, and the ground-floor rooms look out on to a swimming pool and children's playground.

Today the hotel has lost two of its five stars, the tennis court has become the site of the village's weekly market, the swimming pool is dry and the play equipment is rusting. It remains part of Maroc-Tourist, the state hotel chain (though the official London tourist office only reluctantly conceded its existence), and there are enough staff to keep the place spotless. But I appeared to be the only guest.

Ketama gets a terrible press. Most Moroccan guidebooks advise visitors to stay clear of the whole of the Eastern Rif mountains, where for hundreds of square kilometres *kif* is the only crop. Before I got on the bus from Chefchaouen the hotelier there had refused to put Ketama as my destination on the police registration card. 'Very bad people in Ketama – make you smoke *kif*.'

In London my blood had been chilled by a feature in *High Times* magazine, which described how the road from Fez overlooked gorges which were littered with the wrecked cars of police officers and tourists who had been forced off the road. Later, and fortunately in someone else's car, I saw the local youth driving bumper-to-bumper, rubbing their thumbs and fingers together as if crumbling dope to indicate that they're ready for 'business'. If you accept the invitation, the guidebooks tell you, you are lost. You will be forced, if necessary at knife point, to buy hashish. Then the vendor will tip off the cops in exchange for a reward and you can expect to be stopped at a checkpoint, arrested and left to rot in a squalid jail.

High Times had said that Ketama was literally beyond the law: that once you passed the last police checkpoint you were on your own. The reality seemed to be that there was law but not justice. As I sat drinking coffee outside a café on my first morning (the Tidiguine didn't run to breakfast), a cop joined the other customers, leading two handcuffed boys of about the same age as my own young children. The day before, when Aziz took me out to his farm, he had told me: 'Two years ago they put thousands of people in prison, whether they were guilty or not. It's the king and it's the Americans. The police kill many people with torture. The man in Morocco costs nothing; he's like a dog.'

Aziz had intercepted me at the hotel with practised ease. Rather less than a minute after checking in I was drinking coffee with him in the bar together with two plump, flirtatious girls part of whose living was earned by going round the mountain villages selling useful commodities like plastic tablecloths, deodorant sprays and patent potato-chippers. He listened sadly to my *spiel* about writing a book on hashish, nourishing a hope that I was simply too shy or guarded to admit that I was in town to buy a carload. Later he gave up and left me to be taken in hand by his younger brother Tammam.

I found Tammam a bit scary. He'd spent enough time with English cannabis smugglers to pick up violent tricks, like the ability to send passers-by sprawling with a shrug of his elbows. My second meeting with him was in a doctor's surgery; he was with an elderly French tourist whose leg he'd smashed when he drove into his motorbike. The Frenchman's wife had just arranged for a helicopter to take them out of the Rif. 'It was his fault,' stated Tammam. 'He admitted it.' I would have admitted it too.

On the positive side, Tammam seemed to quite like me. He was intrigued by the Henry James novel I was reading – *What Maisie Knew* – and buttonholed acquaintances to explain the book's premise (the history of a divorce and the couple's subsequent relationships, seen through the eyes of their daughter). On the other hand he hated my habits of trying to speak a little Arabic and asking general questions, and would discourage other dealers from talking to me; I caught the word *jasusi*, which means 'spy'.

I felt I should confront this suspicion and asked: 'Do you get DEA [Drug Enforcement Administration] agents coming up here?'

'Yes,' he said. 'Many DEA, many Interpol.'

'What do they look like?'

Tamam stood rather too close – a habit of his – and stared at me without blinking. 'They look just like you.' He stared some more. 'When we find them, we kill them.'

My original invitation to visit Aziz's facility had by now clearly lapsed, but Tammam had a substitute on offer. The catch was that I had to be presented as a customer rather than a writer. 'Just say you'll come back to buy another time,' Tammam advised. First we were going to meet up for a game of what he called 'snooker-pool' on one of the hotel's many unused tables.

In the event I found Tammam, his friend and a few other young guys sitting round a TV by a hunting-lodge-style fireplace, watching a Spanish soap via satellite. On the screen two young women were having an intense conversation. 'Now they make queer,' Tammam suggested optimistically. Our host-to-be began rolling a spliff, asking me, 'You like to smoke joint?' Given the cover story that had been wished on me I could hardly refuse. I was also conscious of everyone's gaze. Would a DEA agent be allowed to use drugs when on undercover duty? I made a special effort to look appreciative and to inhale as ostentatiously as possible. There was a chorus to the effect that this was the best-quality, number one 'Sputnik'. For a bit I was just smoking a sweetly aromatic cigarette – then the next moment the fact that I was very stoned announced itself with an onslaught of self-consciousness and paranoia. I was being invited to admire the lump of dope. 'How much would a piece like that cost in England?' asked its owner. I told him I hadn't any idea.

Tammam barely blinked. 'In England they don't deal in these small amounts. It's all kilos.'

Me: 'Actually in England it's ounces.'

Tammam: 'In England it's all kilos. This man deals in ten kilos, 100 kilos.'

Me: 'When I first smoked, a piece like this [I indicate its size on my finger] cost one pound. It was called a quid deal.'

Tammam (disgusted): 'That was a long time ago.'

Then we rose to our feet and sloped off to the pool tables. My consciousness was now occupied with the detailed functioning of the muscles governing my posture and movement. The result was that I couldn't walk comfortably or look natural while standing still. Both hands in both trouser pockets seems too nerdy, so I struck a pose with a cue. In consequence, when I handed over the cue to a player it was wet with sweat from my palm. Any hope that my nervousness would go unnoticed was lost when I came to take a shot. Not only did I fail to put the ball in a pocket, I missed it altogether.

My mind went back to London a week or so earlier and a hilarious speech I'd found on the Internet. Its author had been describing the early days of marijuana prohibition in the United States, and in particular the evidence produced at criminal trials by the main expert witness at the time, a pharmacologist who described his own experiences with the weed. In 1938 this man had told a murder trial at Newark, New Jersey, that after two puffs on a marijuana cigarette he had turned into a giant bat. In this guise he had flown around the room for fifteen minutes and then found himself at the bottom of a 200-foot-high ink well. Then I'd enjoyed the mockery of this discredited figure. But now I simply pity a fellow paranoiac. What horrible stuff this is – how right he was to get it banned.

A quarter of an hour later I'm lying on my bed fully dressed, very stoned. (Tammam has sent me away, saying he'll call back later to take me out to the *kif* farm.) Though the idea was that I'd take a nap, I'm awake and rigid with misery. I'm dreading the trip to the middle of nowhere with a bunch of outlaws who suspect I work for their chief tormenter, the American DEA. The fear is mingled with self-pity and sadness. Tammam had urged me for the sake of my three children to stop behaving like a spy. Now I ache at the thought of leaving them. I'm separated from their mother, my wife. Usually I feel angry with Emma, but just now her side of the argument is irresistible.

More immediately, what can I do about Tammam? I rehearse a little speech in which I tell him that I'm unhappy about going out into the countryside unless he has confidence that I'm not a spy, and that if he is harbouring doubts I'd rather decline his offer. But the drawback is that this speech doesn't demonstrate that I'm not a spy – just that I'm a cowardly one. If he wants to kill me, all he has to do is declare his confidence in me and insist that I go through with the visit.

Second plan: immediate flight. But it's getting late and even if a bus is scheduled to stop I'll be at the roadside waiting for it, having made a virtual admission of guilt. Or a taxi? I'd have to get it through the hotel, and the hotel is hand in glove with the hashish business (the staff grow patches of *kif* on the slopes above Ketama and the bar is the social centre of the dope growers and traders, offering a superb band and at least two traditionally costumed prostitutes whose dancing entertains the patrons, as well as attracting customers).

And then, out of the blue, I start feeling better. It's like the effect that P. G. Wodehouse describes of a shot of Jeeves's hangover cure: the sky brightens and the birds start twittering. The reason is that I've discovered what I have to do. Since I arrived my strategy has been to assume a manner of guilelessness that verges on the goofy. I should stay with this, and capitalize on the moral authority I feel through not actually being an under-cover policeman. Currently I'm being deprived of it by Tam-mam's insistence that I pretend to be a big-time dope smuggler. I need to tell him that I'll take no active part in this deception.

Later, as we drove out on the Talata Ketama road though the clouds of dust kicked up from the deforested slopes, I reflected on how tame the situation actually was. Tammam continued to make threatening noises, asking me outright if I worked for the DEA and mentioning that his London friends were armed and would call on me if my story didn't check out. But I don't think he genuinely took me for an undercover agent. The more relaxed I became, the more I came to see him as the counterpart of the useful, but sometimes tiresome, public relations people employed by the Comités Interprofessionels of the French wine regions. He saw himself as official spokesperson for a group of individuals who, left to themselves, could cause all sorts of problems for Ketama. A few years ago a grower had talked too freely to a German magazine; a copy had been seen by the relevant Moroccan embassy and a few weeks later the police came out from Al Hoceima and started making arrests. The more he could persuade me that people in Ketama suspected me of being a spy, the less likely I'd be to talk to local blabbermouths and make inconvenient visits.

(I had another thought while driving to what turned out to be Abdul Hayy's farm. This was that because most visitors in Ketama are there for business rather than tourism, you're not cast in either of the familiar roles of Westerners in Third World countries – exploiter or sucker. There isn't that queasy atmosphere.)

The three or four tokes I took with Tammam and his friends in the lounge of the Hotel Tidiguine were afterwards topped up with the joint that Abdul Hayy rolled with black tobacco out at his farm, and another shared later over a Heineken in the bar with the band and the dancing prostitutes. By the time I was lying in bed I felt splendid, not woozy as if I'd spent the evening drinking, but as if I was in a lucid dream. I was in love with the place, the people, the hotel and the music that came bouncing down the bare walls of the corridors lined with vacant rooms.

Looking back on the Ketama visit, I started to frame the experience in the terminology I was coming across in the Rosenthal book. The phrase 'arouser of thought' seemed specially apt. Being stoned made a bad situation intolerable; then the necessary mental structures to escape it conjured themselves into being. One of these was a quality described by medieval Arab writers on hashish, *diyātha*, translated as 'humility', which helped me off the uncomfortable high ground in my unending internal dialogue with Emma.[12]

Dr Nahas, a man who seems perfectly comfortable in this moral posture, took the road to Ketama in 1972. Like me he went to the bar of the Hotel Tidiguine and like me he was taken to the nearby hamlet of al Azila. The account he wrote a few years afterwards[13] has the surreal strangeness of a foreign TV report on your own country's domestic affairs. He seems to have excluded the possibility that he might learn anything about the Rif from members of the counter-culture. Instead he relied on a colleague of the great anthropologist Claude Lévi-Strauss. He was there in pursuit of an application for a grant for $400,000 from the US National Institute of Mental Health (NIMH) to carry out a field study of 100 pot-smoking and 100 non-pot-smoking Moroccans. His motive was to rebut the famous 'Jamaican Study' by Vera Rubin and Lambros Comitas which had just been carried out for the NIMH, concluding that 'the chronic use of potent cannabis is not toxic to the human mind or body', the central point being that in Jamaica 'Use and expected behaviours are culturally conditioned and controlled by well established tradition'.

I don't know Jamaica, but 500 years after the controversies described in Rosenthal's book, the Rubin and Comitas conclusions fit what I've observed in the Arab world. To some extent there is an inverse correlation between hashish use and the degree of Western control a region has undergone; so Algeria, which was invaded in 1830 and politically united with France, has minimal use of *kif* compared to Morocco, which had a much briefer experience of colonialism. According to the 'stagnant and desolate' thesis, Algeria should be getting some benefits from being free of cannabis. But even before the start of the current savage civil war, it was hard for a visitor to see what these might be.[14]

Nahas was never able to draw any formal conclusions on the

Rif villagers: the NIMH rejected his application. But the research trip did not suggest that these would have been very revealing. He describes how he and his French collaborator met two young Europeans smoking *kif*: one Dutchman and one Frenchman. Nahas declared himself 'amazed' by their presence. Perhaps it's not surprising that the NIMH chose not to fund someone who could be 'amazed' to find hippies in Morocco's top *kif* village in the early 1970s – quite apart from the difficulties of finding 100 non-*kif*-smoking male residents of the tiny hamlet of al Azila.

I shouldn't have been surprised to find my rediscovery of hashish a positive experience. At school I'd gone through the opposite of the academic tailspin that parents fear. After going on strike aged eight when I was sent to a boarding school I rediscovered a sense of motivation nine years later at about the time that I discovered dope. I wouldn't claim that it was cause and effect or that this is generally what happens, but I feel I should mention it, especially as it's at odds with the most common view of cannabis in our culture. Although pot smokers believe it helps with problem-solving and self-reliance, many people see it as a form of escape – rather like a medically prescribed tranquillizer.

It's true that it can be calming as well as stimulating. The brother of a friend smokes to stop 'getting too manic'. This is the image put across in *The Great Brain Robbery*, Trevor Grice's book for teenagers, in a cartoon showing a head warder advising the prison governor on ways of controlling the inmates. Unlimited pot comes a close second to his first proposal of lobotomies all round. The cartoonist thinks of cannabis as resembling the imaginary 'Soma' in Aldous Huxley's *Brave New World* – something that makes people happier without any personal effort. Not everyone thinks this would be a bad thing; my friend Dave, who has never really taken to cannabis, is actually in favour of the idea of a version of Soma. 'People who suffer because of unrequited love have some chemical imbalance in their brain which makes them want to go in for unrequited love. If you can give them a chemical that makes them happy, that's fine by me. Are you saying that it's better to be "authentic" and unhappy than "inauthentic" and happy?'

This is an interesting argument, but it isn't an argument about cannabis.

6

Objects Tilt to the Left

Pot is complicated and unpredictable. People often say that the first joint they smoke doesn't do anything for them, partly because they don't know what to look for. You wouldn't get much guidance from looking at a list of reported effects: euphoria, anxiety, silence, talkativeness, empathy, alienation . . . Dr Freek Polak, a Dutch psychiatrist who smokes pot, told me that it is formally categorized with psychedelic drugs as 'psychodysteptic', an unmemorable word for substances that change your mood but not in a predictable direction (the two other categories being 'psycholeptic', meaning downers like alcohol that depress the central nervous system, and 'analeptic' or 'uppers' like amphetamine or cocaine).

Everyone agrees that circumstances – the state of mind of the user, the dose and the setting – determine how it feels to be stoned. And since no two users are alike, you could abandon any attempt to generalize and stop this chapter here, saying that like sex, or religious ecstasy, or starvation, it is something you can only understand if you've experienced it. It also might be a kindness not to pass on other people's drug experiences, which rank with descriptions of dreams in any league table of uninteresting subjects.

But I'm surprised to discover that there are useful things to say about being stoned. There are common patterns in the diversity of possible thoughts, feelings and experiences when stoned (one of which is a tendency to find common patterns in things).[1]

There seems more of a structure to being stoned than to being drunk – perhaps, as we now know, because the action of pot in the body is fairly specific, through the cannabinoid receptors, rather than through a general 'perturbation' of the cells of the nervous system. My most disturbing discovery when I researched this chapter was that lots of attitudes I hold aren't, as I believed, lessons taught me by life or the result of reflection and introspection; instead they turned out to be part of the shared assumptions of pot smokers, which continued to circulate in my belief system years after the last molecule of actual THC trickled out of my body fats.

This discovery I owe to Charles T. Tart and the research he carried out in the late 1960s while an assistant psychology professor at the University of California. Professor Tart drew up a 224-item questionnaire and circulated 750 copies, mainly to student pot smokers. Most were never returned, perhaps because of the survey's intimidating length. Some respondents were ruled out because they were caught out lying. The survey included fake possible marijuana effects which Professor Tart had invented to catch out insincere or brain-addled respondents, such as 'objects tilt to the left', 'the non-dominant hand becomes unusable', or (my favourite) 'the force of gravity alternates directions'. But 150 marijuana users, in the words of Tart's dedication, 'overcame their fear that this study was a police trap and so gave of their time and experience to make this book possible'. They were all aged between nineteen and thirty; 67 per cent were students; 40 per cent smoked roughly once a week; 35 per cent once a month, and 16 per cent smoked every day.

Tart had to accept from the start that it would not be easy to pin down the nature of marijuana intoxication. He writes:

If you give a strong dose of barbiturates or other sedatives to a person he almost always goes to sleep . . . we describe the state of conscious or lack of it induced by barbiturates as a barbiturate-induced sleep; there's little variability across subjects and our observational process is simple. With a psychoactive drug like marijuana I find the variability across subjects is very high and the observational process adds important systematic bias to what we observe.[2]

Professor Raphael Mechoulam had encountered this variability in the early 1960s, soon after he had isolated THC as the main active ingredient in cannabis. 'When we gave THC for the first time to humans in one case we had a bad trip and all the others we had a good trip. And each one of the people that used it had a different reaction. I think I enjoyed it. I was just sitting there and feeling above everything else. One person became a little anxious; another became a little aggressive. One who happened to be a member of the Israeli cabinet spoke for three hours. I don't think anybody has an idea why one has a good trip; it's the interplay of so many different things.'

In his book Professor Tart tries to untangle some of these interplaying factors. He says that the strength of the drug should be predictable; that people taking it should be feeling calm and confident about using cannabis; that they should be free of repressed emotions, and that they should be among congenial, non-manipulative people. Looking through these preconditions for a good experience I feel amazed to have got through my days in Ketama with little more than a rather ropy hour and a half.

A veteran weed smoker makes the same point about the stuff's protean, unpredictable quality. Actually the 'Paki black' he sold in the late 1960s would have failed Professor Tart's first criterion of predictable strength, seeing that it was made of nothing more potent than egg white, Potter's Asthma Powder and patchouli oil. The gnome-like, beret-wearing Karl McCulloch is a broadcaster, poet, novelist and former conman. These days he's repentant about the 'bum shit' he sold to tourists in Piccadilly Circus for £14 an ounce. 'I was always aware that I was a prick,' he reflects, though he emphasizes that at the time his drugs of choice had been alcohol and downers rather than cannabis.

Karl, a communist son of red Clydesiders, had been introduced to 'tea' ten years earlier by an acquaintance from a Bayswater club called the 'Artist and Palette' where patrons were entertained by a naked girl, ostensibly posing for life drawing. 'It was run by a man with a Rasputin beard and his alcoholic wife. I was mixing with the middle classes. There was an American I knew as Beatnik Jack: a guy in his twenties who knew Kerouac and the beat poets, or claimed to. When he got on the phone he'd say, "Hi, buttercups – this is God" – I was really impressed by that. He took me to a West Indian place in Notting Hill, a small café where we scored from a man with a hat and I had my first marijuana joint. I remember saying, "When does it happen? When does it happen?" and being convinced that nothing was happening.'

For years Karl was 'an occasional smoker of dope but it was peripheral to the drink. It was after I stopped drinking that it became central.' By the mid-1970s his alcoholism had become life-threatening. A doctor at the Middlesex Hospital gave him an emergency referral to a pscyhiatric hospital, where he began the journey back to recovery. 'When I went to Alcoholics Anonymous I carried on smoking dope. I went to AA for five years, but I didn't talk about it. I just talked about the fact that I wasn't drinking. Basically I lived a seriously dishonest life.'

Drug-taking is forbidden to AA members. Yet despite flouting this fundamental rule Karl put his life back together. He went to college to learn clerical skills, then acquired a job with an insurance company, a flat and a mortgage – and after work enjoyed a deepening relationship with the weed. He took early retirement after a heart attack and now lives in a small, immaculate council flat in Stratford decorated with pictures of his jazz heroes. The particular quality he finds in pot is that it is not a predictable experience. 'I enjoy being stoned. It makes me think deep thoughts. It makes me enjoy music more. I've smoked every day for twenty years, with few exceptions, and every day it's a surprise.'

But some things do happen predictably. Charles Tart's Californians overwhelmingly agreed with the statements: 'I enjoy eating very much and eat a lot,' 'I find it very easy to go to sleep at my normal bedtime,' 'My memory span for conversations is somewhat shortened so that I may forget what the conversation is about even before it's ended.' Professor Tart distinguished between 'drug' effects and socially-learned effects, and concluded that these very widely reported signs are the pure effects of the drug.

As mentioned earlier, researchers now think it likely that cannabis has two methods of action. One resembles the effect of alcohol or general anaesthetics: a general disruption of the nervous system caused by THC dissolving in cell walls and 'perturbing' them. The other results from the chemical similarity of THC to the body's two naturally-produced cannabinoids: anandamide and 2-AG (the difference being that the body's own cannabinoids are constantly produced and constantly removed, near the cells whose receptors they 'switch on'. THC is removed by the liver, more slowly and at a more distant location).

What Tart calls the obviously 'drug' effects of cannabis could be those that work through the body's cannabinoid receptors. The effects of cannabis are close to the functions of the endogenous cannabinoids. Raphael Mechoulam lists some known functions of anandamide: 'It's been found to be involved in sleep; it's been found to be involved in short-term memory; it's definitely to do with pain.' The cannabinoids sometimes overlap with other control systems. Mechoulam has found that 2-AG, for example, is an alternative method to nitrous oxide of reducing blood pressure. What's more relevant is the discovery that the cannabinoids, both the natural ones and THC, can apparently trigger the opioid system, whose receptors are activated by both the natural opioids (enkephalin and endorphin) and by heroin and morphine. Roger Pertwee adds that anandamide helps stimulate the appetite, especially for sugary foods; to me his most interesting suggestion is that anandamide, by limiting short-term memory, performs an essential role in preventing the brain from getting clogged up with trivialities.

Of course this account of the purpose of short-term memory loss sounds all wrong if, like me, you spent your adolescence reading and re-reading *Doors of Perception*, Aldous Huxley's 1954 account of taking mescaline. Psychedelic drugs aren't supposed to be filters, but the exact reverse: something that loosens the grip of the brain's natural screening mechanism, and so connects us to thoughts, perceptions, memories and sensations that would otherwise be sifted out. My unifying theory is that it's the more prosaic and functional thoughts that get lost when you're stoned, leaving room for the more lurid stuff normally lurking beyond the reach of consciousness.

Fear, which invariably gets called 'paranoia', is the most common bad consequence of smoking cannabis, normally stopping some way short of the fully dramatized hallucinations of a bad LSD trip. It's the downside of the unpredictability that makes Freek Polak classify pot as 'psychodysteptic', and which means that despite his plainly addictive personality, Karl McCullogh doesn't feel at risk from dope. 'It isn't like any other drug. The reason cannabis isn't addictive is that it doesn't necessarily improve things. It enhances perception – but that can be a bad perception. So if you're feeling low it's really pointless taking cannabis. I do think it increased the paranoia after my heart attack.' (On the other hand many MS patients, who have plenty to worry about, find that cannabis gives them more equanimity.)

Pro-cannabis experts claim that inexperienced smokers are more at risk. Dr Freek Polak says that unfamiliarity in itself is unsettling: 'When you become aware that the way you think or the way you see the world is changing or has changed – that can be a frightening experience in itself.' In *Hashish!* Robert C. Clarke says that feelings of anxiety or even panic are 'rarely a strong effect' for experienced users. But even if you've been smoking on and off you can get into trouble if you break too many of Professor Tart's suggestions for ensuring a good experience.

I remember being petrified with fear during my first visit to the Rif in the mid-1970s. A young guy had met me and my then girlfriend in Chefchaoen and invited us out to his farm, where we'd stayed one or maybe two nights. The views over the hills were exhilarating, and it was fascinating to see how hashish was made, with an oldish colleague permanently stoned from beating powder from dried plants over a sieve. But it was a claustrophobic social situation: we were imprisoned in our role as guests; our host didn't want to talk or go for a walk or do anything except smoke relentlessly. So I sat mutely beside my girlfriend accepting joints which soon tipped us from being ill at ease to feeling grossly anxious.

The set-up wasn't ideal, but the main thing that made us miserable was simply excess. There is such a thing as too much cannabis, even for enthusiasts. Two of the peoples of the Congo, the Kassai and Balaba, this century formed a cannabis cult called the Beni Riamba, using the herb as a medicine and a symbol of peace, but also as a means of punishing criminals by forcing them to smoke to the point of unconsciousness.[3] On the face of it you'd expect long-term cannabis smokers like Karl McCulloch to be immune from this problem and be paranoia-free. Yet in the world of what might be called 'cannabis professionals' – people who sell pot, or raise seeds, or write on the subject – it's surprisingly common to hear that so-and-so is chronically 'paranoid'. An acquaintance lived for several months in Amsterdam with friends who, unlike her, all smoked a lot of pot. 'There was always this paranoia under the surface,' she told me. In Amsterdam I also heard a lot about the paranoia of various cannabis celebrities: how one wouldn't venture from home for fear of DEA agents, another was so given to feelings of persecution that he felt he was insane to risk further anxiety in search of journalistic exclusives, and so on . . . In fairness, though, people who make their living from selling or writing about an illegal substance have good reason to feel threatened. Although Howard Marks tells me that he is not troubled by paranoia, I would not like to have been in his shoes during the months in which the Drug Enforcement Administration was closing the net around his smuggling operation.

Of course, 'paranoia' is a word which in psychiatry means something more precise than a well-founded fear of prison. The Royal College of Psychiatrists reported to the House of Lords committee that the phrase 'cannabis psychosis' should be avoided, because of its lack of precision. Instead they describe a 'toxic confusional state', with confusion and memory impairment and an 'acute functional psychosis', resembling the symptoms of acute schizophrenia. Both of these were to be distinguished from true psychosis in that they cleared up within a week of abstaining from cannabis.

As well as being a pro-legalization activist, Dr Polak has spent many years treating emergency psychiatric admissions to Dutch hospitals. 'There used to be a large general hospital near the Vondelpark – it's now been removed to the south-east part of town. But the Emergency Room got very experienced with these cases: many tourists, but also Dutch people who first tried it. If you have people who are very frightened that they're going mad combined with the specific experiences of cannabis you can have something that looks like an acute psychosis. The classic medical approach was to give them heavy sedation and even anti-psychotic drugs, or to hospitalize them. But all over the world this approach has been replaced by simply reassuring them. You hope they have a friend or a confidant with them and say that if they remain quiet for half an hour it will get better, or if it's bad you offer a little tranquillizer.

'A very small percentage of these cases are really psychotic, and it may even prove to be the beginning of schizophrenia. Probably no one gets schizophrenic because of this, and they would have become schizophrenic anyway. We have no way of knowing that. What is reassuring is that the incidence of schizophrenia – that is, the number of new cases each year – has been getting somewhat lower for the past few years in Holland. It certainly isn't increasing, and given the large number of young people trying marijuana I think that is significant.'

If fear is one of the nastiest consequences of smoking pot, its effect in enhancing sex must be one of the nicest. This was the bait that landed Jack Herer, the best-selling author of *The Emperor Wears No Clothes*. Jack, now in his fifties, is the chief guru of the 'hempists', who see the cannabis plant as the world's most important fuel, food and fibre crop. He gave me an interview in Amsterdam's Cannabis College, funded by various coffee shops and sited in an elegant house on the main canal in the red light district. He was exhausted after a week of late nights and early mornings, and was further distracted by acolytes who were busy with a vaporizer – the technique of volatilizing THC from pot with an electrical heat gun, as used for stripping paint. The vaporizer left him racked with coughing, unsure of my name and with a tendency to lose his thread – but he was also funny, warm and articulate. His first experiments with pot had centred, he told me, on the stuff's ability, noted by medieval Muslims, to 'open the gates of desire' (still a reason for hashish's popularity with working-class Egyptian men before they go home to their wives).

This is Herer's story. 'I'd just got divorced from my first wife. She had started smoking two years earlier and she begged me to smoke because she said it would loosen me up, because I was too uptight. I refused. I told her she was doing a dastardly thing. We had three little children; how could she smoke marijuana? I was a real asshole.

'At the time I considered myself a Goldwater conservative. I was totally conventional-looking. Everything I wore was probably polyester. When I heard people talking about the ruin of the environment with plastics and non-biodegradable materials I thought they were full of shit. I thought they were a bunch of intellectual posers who lived in an ivory tower.

'After my divorce I moved into a big building divided up into apartments, and a girl I met there and fell in love with was a pot smoker and she worked on me for months to get me to smoke. Finally that girl got me stoned. She put earphones on me and I heard music in colour. I could close my eyes and I could see each note coming out. I'd never before used my imagination in such complete synchronicity where everything was flowing and running and moving. It was like a curtain painted in my head. The next thing I knew I was waltzing to the music.

'I smoked some more. It was the best marijuana – Acapulco Gold for $25 an ounce. Now it would be $350 an ounce, if you could find it. The first time you're stoned it's really like an acid trip: breathing in and breathing out, I was really so stoned, everything went into slow motion, everything sounded like the world got slow.

'She took me into the bedroom stoned and we smoked some more of this great pot and we made love – and it's probably the first time in my life that I can say I was totally conscious of another being. Who knew you could get totally lost in a little piece of skin? You could get lost for hours, or days, in and out, going in three dimensions in your mind through every possibility that could exist between a man and a woman. This was the most incredible love experience, the most incredible orgasm I'd ever experienced. I'd been married for eight years and I'd had three kids, and I'd had orgasms all my life, but nothing like this. I can remember we went into the kitchen after we'd finished making love, and the first question I asked was, "Why is this against the law?" '

The top-of-the-range marijuana seems to have given Jack Herer a range of sensations equalled only by a lucky minority of Charles Tart's respondents. Whereas he experienced full-blown 'synaesthesia', the item suggesting 'Sounds have colours or visual images associated with them, synchronized with them' had divided them a few months earlier: (43 per cent experienced it never or rarely; 33 per cent found it happened 'sometimes'; 16 per cent 'very often', and only 7 per cent 'usually'). But the Californian students agreed about the sex stuff, with all but a few finding that their orgasms were more pleasurable, and that their sense of touch was 'more exciting and sensual' when stoned.

Again the slowed-down sense of time is something almost everyone who smokes pot seems to share. Even more told Professor Tart that 'When I walk some place my experience of distance covered is quite changed – e.g. not being aware of the space between, just seeming to suddenly be there – or, conversely, feeling that it takes an immense number of steps to cover a distance.' Long ago, this special property rescued a July walking holiday with three friends on Skye. Past midsummer the weather is often wet, but this year was, we heard, exceptional. Sodden fleeces were coming away from the sheep, which had been too wet to be sheared. Any foot placed on soft ground was gripped by suction, and any footprint immediately filled with water. The highest daytime temperature was 14°C, not an untypical December temperature in London. But we happily walked up to twenty miles a day through the soft rain, fortified with chocolate, cheese, Famous Grouse whisky and some exceptional grass.

Jack Herer was lucky in his choice of companion for his first marijuana experience. But what's also striking about his story is that pot was the catalyst for a complete transformation in his life. He went on to write a best-selling guide to evaluating the quality of grass, then discovered environmentalism and finally the belief in hemp's planet-saving qualities. It would help us make sense of cannabis if the 'drug' effects were the straightforwardly physical ones, in the same way that slurred speech and sleepiness are obvious effects of alcohol and barbiturates respectively. The changes in outlook, thought and perception could then be labelled as 'cultural', or at least shelved to await some further advance in our understanding of the physiology of cannabis and the cannabinoids.

But the Tart survey reveals that one of the first signs of being stoned is that people start to look at the world in a new and distinctive way. A big majority of the respondents agreed with the statement: 'I can see patterns, forms, figures, meaningful designs, in visual material that doesn't have any particular form when I'm straight, that's just a meaningless series of shapes.' This is an effect that's shared by both cannabis and full-blown psychedelic drugs such as LSD. It is characteristic of being stoned or tripping, just as after-images following moving objects are the particular signature of an LSD trip.

The finding comes in Tart's first section, which deals with visual changes. It's true that a love of intricate and repetitive designs goes with cannabis[4] – but the tendency to see similarities, structures and meanings is not confined to the optic nerves. Stoned pattern-detection and pattern-making can engross all the senses and every field of thought. In *The Electric Kool Aid Acid Test*, Tom Wolfe's work of 'new journalism' about the hippies, its hero, the novelist Ken Kesey, is asked whether two things are connected. 'Of course they are,' he replies. 'What are they again?' I find that when I'm stoned I take a great pleasure in transport networks – canals, railway lines, even London buses – mainly because they link places together. One of the first manifestations of the belief that 'It's all connected' is as so-called 'paranoia', i.e. 'That's the second police car I've seen in half a mile – I must be being followed'; or, 'People are failing to react to me in a friendly way – they were probably criticizing me before I came in.'

The late-sixties' drug culture was obsessed with habits, compulsions, conventions: everything that was summed up in the phrase 'people's games'. Overwhelmingly, Tart's students found that 'insights about myself, my personality, *the games I play* come to mind when I'm stoned and seem very meaningful.' The games in question could be being played by others: 'I have feelings of deep insight into other people, how they tick, *what their games are*, when stoned (regardless of whether they check out later).' Most reported a sense of unity with other stoned people, but were repelled by everyday social structures, and agreed that: 'I find it very hard to play *ordinary social games* when I'm stoned.' In a Robert Crumb cartoon of the period[5] a smug hippie pleads with an indifferent world for 'no more ego games' ('There', he can't help adding self-importantly, 'isn't that better?'). Ken Kesey's hippie followers, as recorded by Tom Wolfe, are forever banging on about 'cops and robbers games' or 'mind games'. The Byrds moaned, 'I can't play the game of life to win'; John Lennon wrote a song about 'mind games' . . .

This sort of pop insight doesn't come ready-wrapped in gummed-together Rizlas. The sixties saw the popularization and merging of Marxism, Psychoanalysis and Structuralism – the schools of thought which aim to reveal the hidden structures of society, the mind and culture. But there's a world of difference between wrestling with a system of theory and reacting with spontaneous amusement to the highly patterned behaviour of a ticket collector or a pretentious host. A chief attraction of cannabis is the idea that everyone can puff on a spliff and discover the joys of deconstruction and analysis. 'Governments don't like this stuff,' I'm often assured, 'because they don't like people thinking for themselves.' This is *al asrār* – 'the secrets' – as described by medieval Turkish Sufis.

While I like the way that cannabis is creating a common ground for people from different cultures, I feel more ambivalent about the 'insights' it creates. I think of it rather like a photographic developer, revealing latent patterns and images: as Baudelaire said when criticizing hashish, it shows nothing to the user that isn't already there. What it does bring up are new connections. These aren't 'real' in the sense of being factual – but this doesn't mean that they aren't powerful or important.

Modern biblical scholars like Thomas Thompson of Copenhagen University believe that few of the stories in the Old Testament are historical – not those of Abraham and Moses, nor those of Saul, David or Solomon either. Instead he argues convincingly that they are drawn from a range of cultures, from Greece to Babylon, and are used by the authors of the Bible to express their various doubts and certainties.[6] Since the time of slavery, black people in exile in America and the West Indies have seen these universal stories as reflecting their own experience. The most comprehensive work of re-imagining them has been achieved by the ganga-smoking Jamaican rural labourers and shanty-town dwellers who have reclaimed the Old Testament and the Book of Revelation as a sacred prophecy of justice for the black diaspora.

Ganga can't create such a world view, but it can help a people to weave something striking out of their history and culture. It can probably help scientists put together ideas in new ways – I can think of two contemporaries who run labs who are confirmed pot-heads. But you don't have to have rigorously tested facts to want to draw conclusions from them. One morning at Exodus my over-confident, upper-middle-class tones attracted the attention of a member of the collective who wandered over to pass on Bob Marley's much-quoted remark that there is no fool like an educated fool. On the other hand, 'educated fools' don't believe, as this guy did, that the moon landings never took place, and were shot in a terrestrial television studio.[7] You could argue that pot's pattern-reinforcing quality is safest in the hands of artists. It's noticeable that musicians, studio engineers and film editors all work well stoned, whereas journalists sometimes find it more difficult (although since I started this book I keep turning up pot-smoking novelists). One possible difference is that the factual writers are responsible for the truthfulness of their raw material, not just for structuring it.

It's reasonable to be worried by the way cannabis blurs the distinction between pattern-recognition and pattern-making. But how much does it actually matter? No one should live their life under a burden of delusions, but a period without being stoned – which would seem a sensible idea in any case – should give time to undertake some quality control. At least pot rewards people for thinking, which is more than you can say for alcohol.

But there is something I find pernicious: a sort of know-it-all quality, which I'm perhaps especially prone to, deriving from a sense of having privileged insights. It's maddening when the insights are shallow, second-hand or half-baked, and depressing when the subjects believe that having achieved a higher level of consciousness, life has nothing left to teach them.

Other observers make just this point. During the 1950s the anthropologist Roberto Williams-Garcia studied a small Indian group near the Gulf of Mexico and its ritual use of cannabis. A group member in his twenties told Williams-Garcia that 'La Santa Rosa' could not be treated as something to be passively consumed. He said: 'It is not necessary that it play with you. It is necessary that you play with it. And those who can't restrain themselves, those who are of a mind that has problems, they have trouble. This type collapses. If one controls oneself one learns new things about the psychological processes.'[8]

In recent times the most notable product of stoned thinking has been the theory that the cannabis plant itself can offer almost everything that mankind needs. You could argue that this is the ultimate example of a narrowing vision, shrinking till it sees nothing except the pile of dope in its immediate view. Or, like Anita Roddick of The Body Shop, Willie Nelson, and a legion of hemp activists, you could be excited and inspired.

7

The Religion of Hemp

In 1973, when Jack Herer was thirty-three and an author on marijuana, he took an LSD trip with his friend and business partner, a head shop-owner called 'Captain Ed' Adair. 'He and I lived together sometimes when our wives or our girlfriends threw us out,' he told me in the course of conversation in Amsterdam's Cannabis College. They had decided to campaign for marijuana legalization and to do all they could to tell America that they believed it to be 'good and fine'.

After the publication of his book on marijuana connoisseurship, Jack had been approached by a number of readers telling him about an angle he hadn't covered: the fact that marijuana was formerly used to make paper. 'I used to look at the little pot and wonder how they used that to make paper. They said, "Did you know they used to use this to make clothing or sheets or pillowcases, or that 'canvas' is the Dutch pronunciation of Cannabis?" I just got absolutely "How come I've been smoking four years, I've become a writer on marijuana, and I never know it could be used like this." '

He started going into libraries and teasing out information about the other use of cannabis as hemp, the fibre crop that had been cultivated in America until the mid-1950s and is still grown on a big scale in China, Eastern Europe and some former Soviet republics. He found old textbooks that praised hemp as a rotation crop and a US Department of Agriculture report from 1916 which argued that hemp could replace wood pulp as the raw material for American paper. The more research he did, the more uses he discovered for this versatile plant.

Then, as Jack and Captain Ed were sitting talking, stoned on acid, an idea descended on the pair simultaneously, and with the force of revelation. 'Boom! In a millionth of a second it came to us that marijuana could save the world. It sounds so ridiculous, but as we came down from the acid we knew we were still right. It had been right there in front of our faces: so far in front of our faces that we couldn't see it. In this one night, in this one-millionth of a second, we were able to realize that it was the number one paper fibre fuel, fuel and food. It's the only single source that grows without pesticides and herbicides. It wasn't only greater than the other sources – it was greater than all the three million other sources on earth.'

Since the last hemp farmer went out of business its cultivation had become outlawed in the United States. In 1993 state narcotics officers used army reserves and the National Guard to root up 9.3 million wild descendants of cultivated hemp plants in the single state of Wisconsin. This is despite the fact that hemp strains of cannabis have too little THC to be worth smoking, and the same remains true of their wild descendants. For Jack Herer, his new awareness of hemp's potential made the ban 'seem so ludicrous, so ridiculous'.

This thought bubbled away in his mind for a few years. Then in 1980 he wrote a four-page booklet on marijuana prohibition entitled 'The Emperor Wears No Clothes'. The title comes from the Hans Christian Andersen story of the naked potentate who has been tricked into believing that he's magnificently clothed, and it reflects the author's conviction that his opponents were straw men, and that marijuana prohibition was a house of cards which would collapse once the facts were known. In 1985 the booklet re-emerged as a full-length book, published by Herer. It's now in its eleventh edition, having so far sold an astonishing 600,000 copies.

Since then 'hemp shops' have opened in almost every American city, selling hemp clothing, cosmetics, foodstuffs and drinks. Calvin Klein's 1998 Spring/Summer collection featured a silk and hemp fabric. In 1996 Adidas launched a shoe called 'The Hemp' to draw attention to the uppers made from hemp fabric, and kept it on the market despite pressure from the White House's Office of National Drug Control Policy.[1]

Anita Roddick of The Body Shop is a fan of *The Emperor*. The chain's big launch of 1998 was its skin moisturizers based on hemp oil, which is rich in essential fatty acids, with leaflets in the shops cleverly headed 'Hemp – the Great Smear Campaign'. These repeated Jack Herer's chief theme: that 'Hemp played a vital role in world commerce for over 8,000 years up until the 1930s when a number of US-based industries competed by allegedly launching a smear campaign linking "industrial grade" hemp to the drug marijuana.'

The seeds that make the Body Shop's skin oil are grown in France, which together with Spain grows the bulk of Europe's hemp crop. With the help of European Union subsidies this has ballooned over the last decade, with over 54,000 acres under cultivation – a ten-fold increase in the course of a decade. Germany and Britain now allow its cultivation. There's also a European Union hemp breeding programme, with French, British and Dutch partners, chiefly directed to the dour goal of eliminating THC from hemp. Germany also has an annual trade fair – 'Cannabusiness' – which its organizer Frank Zander launched as a personal response to reading *The Emperor*. Its theme is 'Both Dope and Rope', with pot-smoking paraphernalia, textiles, cosmetics, hemp-flavoured foods from beer to chocolate, and papers on show under a single roof.

But Herer's biggest achievement has been to turn the tables on his opponents. As his English admirer, the former Rob Christopher, now Free-Rob Cannabis, says, 'It isn't cannabis that's the crime; it's cannabis prohibition.' Allan St-Pierre of the NORML foundation told me that defence attorneys in marijuana cases these days like to go to court in suits made of the finest hemp fabric. They then allow the jurors to appreciate the quality of the cloth and say something like, 'Why ladies and gentlemen, my client isn't guilty of growing anything that I wouldn't wear myself.'

The Emperor manages to make hemp look as American as apple pie. Herer says that the first and second drafts of the Declaration of Independence, of 28 June and 2 July 1776, were written on hemp paper, recycled like most paper of the time from worn-out sails and ropes sold by shipowners. The first legal regulation of cannabis had come 154 years earlier, when Jamestown colony in Virginia made it mandatory for farmers to grow hemp – an example followed in Massachusetts, Connecticut and the Chesapeake colonies. All naval powers at this time were as dependent on hemp for sails and ropes as they were on oaks for the hulls of ships, and many countries had such laws. Jack Herer calculates that the sailing frigate the USS *Constitution*, restored in 1927, carried sixty tons of hemp, not just as canvas and rigging, but in the form of flags, maps, logs, bibles and uniforms.

It's this sort of obsessively conducted calculation that gives *The Emperor* its flavour. It doesn't look like any other book, partly because of the high proportion of photographically reproduced primary sources. There are postage stamps from Italy and North Borneo celebrating their countries' hemp industries. A German World War II 'Humorous Hemp Primer' (*Die lustige Hanffbibel*), reproduced and translated in all its thirty-two pages, foreshadows later claims for the plant's extraordinary versatility: 'the fibre strand, the smooth seed, the woody part and the narrow leaf. Every part is dedicated to serve the four-year plan.' There are reproductions of classic jazz 78 labels: 'Weed Smoker's Dream' by the Harlem Hamfats; 'Reefer Man' by Cab Calloway and his

Orchestra, 'Marahuana' by the Royal Castilians. The 1998 edition carries advertisements for hemp stores and other products and services. (My favourite is for a book called *Talks with Trees – a Plant Psychic's Interviews with Vegetables, Flowers and Trees*, by Leslie Cabarga. Ms Cabarga offers to answer such riddles as 'what a giant redwood tree thinks about the destruction of ancient forests' and 'how does garlic feel about being stir-fried'.)

High Times magazine's description of *The Emperor* as 'the bible of the hemp movement' has stuck. It's apt not least because of Herer's tireless promotional touring, on a scale to rival the missionary journeys of Saint Paul. When I met him in Amsterdam he was reeling from the excess baggage charges incurred in bringing over a stack of the books. This included a de luxe all-hemp *Emperor*; this bristly hardback tome sells for $100, but includes a large contribution to Herer's organization Help End Marijuana Prohibition which campaigns to change the law and support those in prison. On another occasion, when campaigning for the 1986 Legalize Cannabis Initiative in Oregon, he handed out no fewer than 60,000 copies to voters. The copies went out in three waves, and each time support for the Initiative grew: 'We gained overwhelming numbers. So we knew we could get people educated, because people respond to education.'

Jack Herer was a pot lover before he discovered hemp, and you could argue that *The Emperor's* main impact has been as a campaigning tool for legalization activists. But you don't have to get high to develop an all–encompassing vision of a plant's virtues and potential applications. One man Jack Herer reminded me of, though physically unlike him, being very elderly, English, and conventionally dressed, was the late Lawrence Hills, the gardening writer who founded the Henry Doubleday Research Association, which is the main British centre for organic gardening. Hills sounded like a hempist when he talked about the blue-flowered, hairy-leaved herb, comfrey. Apparently it was the only plant which contained Vitamin B12, and so could give complete animal-free nourishment to vegans. It had other unique healing properties and was essential in organic gardening, both in compost and, when quickly rotted and strained, to create an all-purpose plant liquid pick-me-up. But although I hadn't known it at the time, Hills's enthusiasm masked severe setbacks. New work had just been published suggesting that the Vitamin B12 had only been detected because of contamination of laboratory samples. Then there was a second, more severe blow: animal tests found tumours in the livers of rats fed on comfrey, and official warnings went out against making comfrey tea.

Lawrence Hills had to put up with being labelled a crank. But today plenty of conventional people are interested in unconventional crops. Over-production has caused farm-gate prices to sag, and the European Union is keen to encourage farmers to experiment with crops that won't add to the food mountains. In response Britain's fields have turned yellow with oil-seed rape and blue with flax. Meanwhile BP and Shell have started programmes to find plant substitutes for both fossil fuel energy and petroleum-based plastic compounds.

Here history is repeating itself. One aim of the New Deal Democrat administrations of America in the 1930s was to help farmers who had been plunged into poverty by a price collapse. The Agriculture Adjustment Act of 1933 authorized what today's European Union would call setaside payments. The historian David P. West has made a study of this period in his monograph *Fiber Wars*[2]. He describes the social price paid by the mainly black agricultural labour force for the decision to reduce the acreage under cultivation: one side-effect was the great migration to the northern cities to look for factory jobs.

There was also a programme which in 1938 established four US Department of Agriculture laboratories with a brief to discover uses for farm surpluses as industrial raw materials. This initiative was ultimately inspired by William Jay Hale, the Dow corporation chemist whom David West credits with predicting the rise of synthetic fabrics. Hale wanted to see a new partnership between agriculture and the chemical industry which he christened 'chemurgy'. Because of its high cellulose content hemp was a favourite crop of the National Farm Chemurgic Council, which had been founded in 1935; Henry Ford responded with a prototype of a car whose plastic body was reinforced with hemp fibre.

England now has a reborn hemp industry, though it has some way to go to fulfil the American dreams of the 1930s and 1940s. In 1993 an East Anglian agricultural seed company started a subsidiary to try to take part of the niche market for upmarket horse-bedding from the French. France, while fervently anti-pot, has an established hemp industry which, among other things, supplies the raw material for cigarette papers, and which was sending the chopped 'hurds' – the woody centres of the plant's stems – to English race-horse owners. At that time no cannabis was legally grown in Britain despite a European Union subsidy of £225 per acre and an agricultural tradition which has scattered the country with place-names such as Hampstead or Hemel Hempstead. It didn't take much pressure from the new company, Hemcore, to get licences from the Home Office, subject to certain conditions: the use of ultra-low THC strains developed in France, planted well away from main roads.

Even so, some pilfering goes on. One farmer told me of losing scores of kilos: 'We don't really mind as the word soon gets around that it's useless to smoke.' But when I first saw a muddy English field sprouting a towering crop of mature hemp I could see why people would think that it's worth trying (this was soon after I'd returned from seeing the *kif* harvest in Morocco). It isn't a question of 'a physical similarity to the plant marijuana', as The Body Shop said in its press release announcing its hemp moist-urizers. These are true *Cannabis sativa* plants, with the unmistak-able leaves and a smell, the farmer told me, that he soon came to recognize in local pubs. The authorities can be confused as well: John Hobson, one of Hemcore's directors, told me about a police motorcyclist in Oxfordshire who had reported what he thought was the bust of the decade after coming across a field of maturing cannabis.

John Hobson works in a side office of Harlow Agricultural Merchants – motto: 'Small enough to care – big enough to serve' – under a poster advertising the 'unbeatable performance of Muscat Winter Barley'. It's difficult to imagine him sharing a platform with the charismatic, ponytailed Jack Herer (let alone a spliff). But they're equally committed to the revival of hemp. Where Herer looks for evidence to back his case that hemp is a miracle plant, John Hobson is searching for new markets for the 10,000 acres projected to be grown in 1999 (a more than six-fold increase since 1993). One of his hottest leads is with German car manufacturers, who are committed on environmental grounds to replace fibre glass with vegetable fibres in the composite materials used in car bodies. Even when hemp farmers aren't actually hempists they are their natural allies, if only for market-ing reasons. At the moment most of the clothes sold in hemp stores are made from imported Chinese cloth, but there's no reason why the British growers shouldn't get some of the action, especially as the US DEA still refuses to relax the ban in America, on the grounds that it would be easy to use THC-free plants to disguise marijuana.

Ed Rosenthal of all people is on record as supporting this claim. He's the author of America's best-selling 'how to grow pot' manuals and writes that 'Farmers who gross perhaps $1,500 an acre on hemp would have a terrific incentive to grow one or two extremely similar-looking plants and double their gross.' He describes this as a 'sore point, well known but not discussed by hempsters. They must think that no one else has thought of it.'[3] The answer, I've heard, is legal hemp planted very close so as to favour the development of a single long stem. Plants grown for high-THC plants tend to be shorter, with a different growing habit, and would stick out like a sore thumb in aerial reconnaissance.

But Ed Rosenthal has plunged much deeper into controversy over *The Emperor*. Jack Herer doesn't just claim that hemp is a versatile crop, he also believes that it can save the world by halting the greenhouse effect. He calculates that if 6 per cent of the agricultural land in America was used to grow hemp, this could provide all the country's power requirements as what is called an energy or 'biomass' crop, mainly through being burnt in power stations. Although this releases carbon dioxide, the main greenhouse gas, no more is returned to the atmosphere than the plant locked up through photosynthesis when it was growing. So the process is what is technically called 'carbon-neutral' and doesn't add to the greenhouse effect.

But here Jack Herer parts company with the advisers to Europe's emerging hemp industry. Dr Mike Bullard of the Agricultural Development Advisory Service, who is the co-ordinator for the European Hemp Breeding Programme, says: 'Hemp isn't a credible biomass crop; it isn't that it wouldn't work – the question is why you'd grow it when you can get higher yields from other crops. You'd be looking at a perennial, not an annual plant. Here coppice for biomass is going from strength to strength.' In Britain the main effort is going into willows which are regularly 'coppiced' or cut back to the ground. The trees respond with a thicket of shoots which are harvested every few years and which when dried are being used in various experimental power stations. One advantage of willows is that they can be grown on land that's too boggy for food crops.

In America Ed Rosenthal came to the same conclusion as Mike Bullard. He told me: 'I don't think that hemp will work as a biomass crop. The fibre is worth so much money and the pulp is worth so much money, but biomass is the lower denominator. Where I do think hemp is going to be really big is as a fibre crop, for paper and as a construction material.' By going into print with this conclusion he triggered one of the most public rows the American legalization movement has witnessed.

In an anthology he edited and introduced in 1994 called *Hemp Today*, Rosenthal does a line-by-line analysis of the hemp-for-biomass argument and finds it wanting. First he suggests that trees, as used in Britain's biomass experiment, are more suitable than annuals, which need to be sown and harvested each year, requiring the repeated use of tractors. In any case, the first candidate for burning in power stations would be plant-derived material that currently goes for landfill, such as waste wood and paper;[4] next he points out that except in the richest soils hemp has high fertilizer requirements; then he unpicks Herer's figure of '6 per cent of America's land surface'. It can't be prime farmland, but to put uncultivated land under the plough would create great environmental pressures. (This is apparent in Morocco where tree-felling to plant *kif* is causing very obvious damage to the ecology of the Rif mountains; the cannabis plant's long tap-roots contribute to the erosion of the hillsides. *The Emperor* observes that hemp is the one energy crop that can be grown 'from the Arctic to the Equator'. But even if this is so, asks Rosenthal – so what? Farmers only need to know how crops will do on their own farms; the question of how it performs in a completely different climate isn't really of interest, and anyway it's hardly ecologically sensible to blanket the globe with a single-crop species. Rosenthal adds a table showing the biomass

yields of a wide range of crops, from alfalfa (8 tons per acre per
year) to switchgrass (7.2 tons). The 3.5 to 5 tons per acre he
quoted for hemp looked average, at best.

Confronted with this polemic, Jack Herer failed to appreciate,
according to Rosenthal, that 'my complaint is really a technical
complaint. Maybe the market will decide that I'm wrong. He felt
that it was a personal attack on him.' When the two men were
booked to appear at a legalized marijuana rally in San Francisco,
Rosenthal says, he found Herer was passing out pamphlets
denouncing him. 'A couple of people tried to stop him; I went
to help hand them out. Now when I give a speech I tell people:
"Jack wants to save the planet; I just want to get you high." ' The
irony, according to Rosenthal, is that he helped bring *The Emperor*
into existence. 'Jack earns a lot of money but he isn't a good
caretaker for the money he earns. So when he said I "wasn't hip to
hemp", I financed the book.' And in fact the joint introduction to
its 1990–98 editions contains a dedication 'to my selfless landlords
Ed and Esther who extended me so much leeway in deferred
payments so that this project, which they also believed in, would
not cease or bog down because of my lack of funds.' Ed
Rosenthal adds: 'You have to understand why this got blown
out of all proportion was that *High Times* magazine was using it to
sell issues. It never got to the point where Jack and I weren't
buddies or where we weren't speaking.'

But perhaps Jack Herer was right to see an attack on the biomass
argument as an attack on the central case put by *The Emperor*.
The trouble is that biomass is not just a technical issue. In 1998
students in the Gallery Studies department at the University
of Essex mounted an exhibition on the subject. Dominique
Rogers, who edited the catalogue and wrote two articles,
concluded: 'The great quality of hemp is its ability to grow
anywhere, very fast. Even if it were used only as a replacement

for fibreglass it would totally justify its existence. As an entertainment it is not as bad as alcohol. As a medicine it has great potential. What more do we want?' The answer, obviously, is to save the world, and the world is not going to be saved by hemp moisturizers, training shoes or even composite materials for the car industry.

After their LSD vision in 1973, Jack Herer and Captain Ed Adair's next conclusion was, according to Herer, that if they were right, anybody putting 'any other type of argument was ignorant or evil'. In time this turned into the other major strand in *The Emperor's New Clothes*: the 'conspiracy against marijuana' (which we'll come back to in Chapter 11). This is similar (suspiciously similar?) to the true story used as the background to the plot of *Who Framed Roger Rabbit?*: the alliance of General Motors, Standard Oil and the Firestone tyre company which bought up and then closed down the popular and efficient streetcar system in Los Angeles, replacing it with what's become a polluting and congested freeway network. For the streetcars substitute America's hemp industry, and the conspirators in this scenario include the Du Pont company, with its investment in synthetics from petrochemicals, the Hearst newspaper empire, which was campaigning against reefer-smoking racial minorities, and the law enforcement establishment, whose empire-building had been disrupted by the ending of Prohibition. You don't prove a wider conspiracy just by listing the people who benefited, any more than you convict a murderer on motive alone, but by naming the yellow press, the narcs and the oil business as the conspirators, Herer turns cannabis/hemp into a symbol of opposition to three of the most powerful, and least popular, forces in America. If a plant that anyone can grow anywhere could provide so many of our needs, from clothing to food, to warmth, light and transport, individuals and communities could reclaim power from the oil and pharmaceutical corporations.

There's an echo of the 'Doctrine of Signatures' first propounded in the seventeenth century by the German mystic Jakob Boehme that God has expressly created herbs as medicines, marking them to guide people to their appropriate use.[5] If you're 'hip to hemp' you can invoke a natural order against the arrogance of power – in reaching this state you will have turned to new information sources and away from the mass media.

If the hempists sometimes sound like religious believers, their faith turns on something that's already rich with cultural resonances. In the past hemp often played a part in the folk rituals of Eastern European village life, and still does for the 7,500,000-strong Hmong people who live in the south of the Chinese province of Yunan, near the Vietnamese border. Robert C. Clarke, the author of *Hashish!*, encountered a hemp culture that had nothing to do with the drug use of the plant in one of the valleys of this mountainous region, where people live at an altitude of 10,000 metres. 'I was there with my Chinese girlfriend to study their use of hemp; they have an ancient *batik* tradition. One thing I'd been interested in doing was going to a funeral, because of the ancestor worship thing. What I saw was a totally hempen funeral and it totally blew my mind.

'In the home of the deceased they put the corpse on a stretcher tied with hemp ropes; and this is a really important part of the tradition that they should be hemp – most of their ropes these days are nylon, but they go and make them or get them from neighbours. Over the body they lay a hemp shroud. Down the inside wall opposite the corpse they have banners thirty centimetres wide made from undyed hemp cloth hanging vertically. They have this long involved ceremony to send the body off to the afterlife, which can take days. When they sacrifice animals they have a length of hemp bark or twine which goes from the neck of the animal: a chicken or a goose which is traditional. They put it in the dead person's hand and the animal is usually sacrificed just outside the front door so that the dead person can lead the sacrificed animal to the afterlife.'

There was even more hemp. The corpse, shrouded in hemp, rested on more hemp cloths. Villagers came in at intervals to 'feed' the corpse, pulling back the shroud to do so; these mourners wore hemp slippers. Robert Clarke thinks the importance of hemp is partly that it decomposes readily, and for the Hmong people it's as important that the corpse decomposes in order to reach the afterlife as it was for the Ancient Egyptians that it should remain free of decay.

Why do they do it? Clarke had been interested in seeing a funeral because he had heard that hemp had previously had a ritual importance in funerals among the Han Chinese, the country's dominant ethnic group. More recently, though, silk has become the favoured material in mainstream Chinese culture, replacing hemp which has associations of rural poverty. The Hmong were a semi-nomadic people and hemp was the only fibre plant they grew. 'Most of these people have grown up weaving hemp. Now it's going out of fashion but people keep a bit in their house for funerary reasons, like a ball of bark to make the sandals. The whole notion is that after the elders have died they feel their children will never be able to find them unless they're wearing hempen sandals. They also put a ball of string in the dead person's hand because when the dead person travels over the mountains to the afterlife they meet demons and dragons, and they throw this ball of hemp into the mouths of the demons to stop them eating them.'

Of course, hemp isn't unique in having such rich cultural associations. Peoples often seem to develop cults around the animals or plants they depend on for their survival – whether the herdsmen of northern India with their cows or the Mediterranean peoples turning their staples of bread and wine into the body and blood of Christ. Hemp is today being reinterpreted into a role that goes beyond its undoubted practical and ecological merits. The hempists are indeed at the cutting edge of debate when they talk about a future economy based on plants rather than fossil fuels; how many people, other than farmers, would find themselves gripped by a detailed discussion of biomass yields – or have even heard of biomass? But I feel awkward with hempists in the way I do with religious people. In order not to disagree with 'Hemp can save the world' I have to paraphrase it into: 'a rediscovery of the potential uses of plants will save the world', which feels as unsatisfactory as when modern churchmen explain away the Bible.

Jack Herer is at least lucky that it was his friend Ed Rosenthal who scaled his claims down to size rather than a less sympathetic critic. As Rosenthal told me: 'I think you need people like Jack and people like me.'

And the hemp revival is still in its earliest days. It looks likely that as in the 1940s and the era of chemurgy it is major industries like car manufacturers who will be most interested in hemp fibre as a commercial crop; but the ecological and spiritual associations that cluster round this crop will add value to niche products made from the oil, the fibre and the seeds. John Hobson of Hemcore observes: 'People want to turn towards natural things and away from chemical products. When we got started all we were thinking about was horse bedding; it's got bigger than we ever imagined.'

8

Strains and Stresses

Hemp is big at least in the sense that it encourages hempists to think big. Various people told me that hemp milk was so nutritious, with such an extraordinary range of fatty acids and trace elements, that it was a kind of elixir or cure-all. You germinate the seeds (which don't have any THC and so don't make you stoned), then grind them in a pestle and mortar or coffee grinder, dilute the paste with water till it's the consistency of milk, and strain it through muslin. It doesn't taste either good or bad – though certainly better than soya milk – but the possibility that it's doing you good puts a bounce in your step, like reading an upbeat newspaper horoscope. Hemp seeds, though, aren't big business. When I bought my £2-worth, I told the guy who sold them to me that one of his customers had recommended him to me. He was crestfallen to realize that he knew right away which one it must have been, and said: 'Shows how many customers I've got.'

But one branch of the business really is a commercial success: the one selling seeds that are bought so that they can be grown into potent cannabis plants. These seeds are legally produced in Holland and are on sale in Britain, though they're banned in America, and other EU countries such as Germany are cracking down. The Dutch seed industry is the nearest thing there is yet to an international, above-ground cannabis trade, and it's the *raison d'être* of the world's most visible cannabis event, the Cannabis Cup, in which seed firms are the main competitors.

In a way it's surprising to see significant money being made from a plant that needs hardly any attention and grows like a weed. The added value comes from the selective breeding that created varieties such as 'skunk'; but the pioneer cannabis breeders nearly all did it for love, not money. A case in point is David, still awaiting trial for his growing operation in a north London rented house. This had yielded him twenty-seven kilos of high-quality sinsemilla buds worth more than £50,000, grown from 'Dutch varieties, which I grew more or less for commercial reasons rather than the love of the thing. What I want to do is to produce my own thing.' The money-raising exercise had been forced on David by a family crisis. His real passions were the charas fields of Kulu and his work creating a seed line of his own, using breeding material that had been supplied free by other enthusiasts. He recognized that a prison sentence – for which he was allowing between six and eighteen months – would interrupt his programme: 'But the seeds should last for one to five years, so I'll be able to carry on with my experiments.'

Another commercial opportunity is the trade in the equipment for indoor cultivation: fans and lights. These put professionalism within everyone's reach – something I lacked when I tried growing seeds indoors in my girlfriend's house at Oxford, round the corner from Leckford Road (a street which figures in the personal histories of Bill Clinton, Howard Marks and Tony Blair). I lined the cupboard under the stairs with silver foil, covered the floor with seedlings in pots, and overhead hung an ultra-violet tube and some sun-lamps, calculating that between them they'd take care of the full spectrum. It looked and felt purposeful; some people were reminded of a disco, but it could have been some weird experiment in the university's science area, or something rigged up for an episode of *Star Trek*. Amidst the heat, the diffused, unearthly light and a hot electrical smell the plants shot up, but they had no strength or side growth. After a time I felt guilty about their treatment and took them, three at a time, to the garden of another house where they soon expired.

No one now would get it so wrong. The main source of advice in the 1970s was Nick Saunders' *Alternative London*, recommending readers to try planting budgie seeds. You were likely to do this anyway if you saved marijuana seeds as low-THC hemp seeds were used to bulk up the weight. But these days there's any amount of advice on tap. Mel Franks and Ed Rosenthal, joint authors of the original *Marijuana Grower's Guide*, have now gone separate ways, Mel Franks to publish successive editions of the now 'de luxe' *Marijuana Grower's Guide*, Ed Rosenthal to write the *Marijuana Grower's Handbook* and to publish 'Ask Ed', his monthly column of growing tips in *High Times* magazine. These manuals protect themselves from prosecution with statements denying that their authors recommend breaking the law, and they're a publishing phenomenon, with sales running into hundreds of thousands.

David lent me most of his impressive library. He was one of the first people to buy Robert C. Clarke's newly published *Hashish!*, parting with more than £20 for the edition that was withdrawn immediately because the colour photographs fell out as soon as the book was opened. Rob Clarke has never written a grow-manual, but he's been a seminal figure since he published *Marijuana Botany* in 1981. This provided the science behind modern cannabis breeding and cultivation (though he dislikes some high-tech aspects, such as hydroponics, on environmentalist grounds). In particular he argued for 'clones', that is, genetically identical plants raised from cuttings; today every serious grower works this way.

Since 1987 he has lived in Amsterdam in an inner suburb called De Pijp, which despite being only half an hour on foot from the centre only manages about as much charm as the

average south London high street. I met Clarke and his neighbour, the journalist Annie Rieken, in their local branch of the
Green House coffee shop. This was where Rob had written
Hashish! over several years, passing the emerging manuscript to
Annie at regular intervals, 'so', she said, 'that I could take out all
the "howevers" '. I had a copy on me, which turned out to give
them their first sight of the reissued edition in which the photos
stayed glued in; they moaned about the difficulty of making
photographs of hashish look interesting. A photo at the end of
the preface is captioned, 'Few Westerners have ever experienced
the pleasures of smoking hashish of the highest quality, such as
this rubbed Manali'. But this rare product of the Kulu district, as
Rob and Annie pointed out, actually looks on the page like
nothing so much as a flounder, or some other flat fish. My
girlfriend Pauline made me go and buy some pot to show
solidarity, and with equal sensitivity told me to stop smoking it
when I began losing my thread.

It seems logical that Holland should have become the world
centre of cannabis breeding and research. There's Dutch horti-
culture, which mass-produces flower bulbs for export and, with
the help of cheap North Sea gas to heat the greenhouses, huge
quantities of tasteless tomatoes. The business in weed and hashish
follows a precedent set by the wine trade; the port of Amsterdam
was one of the main import and distribution centres for northern
Europe. Plus, of course, there's decriminalization, which continues the civic tradition of the Dutch republic. This is the
opposite of a cultural melting-pot: instead, Holland's history was
of a kind of social apartheid, with its people divided between
separate religious communities agreeing to tolerate each other's
beliefs, however much they disliked or disapproved of them.

Rob Clarke has a modest-sized flat decorated with hemp
textiles and a couple of cannabis plants for decoration – Chinese
varieties grown for their edible seeds. 'It's more comfortable here

to study cannabis,' he told me. 'People in the business are relaxed and willing to talk.' But he sees Holland as a secondary centre rather than the origin of the revolution in cannabis breeding. He saw the start of that when he was still a student of botany at the University of California, Santa Cruz in the Bay Area of San Francisco.

'Before college,' he says, 'I was a real straight kid. A Christian. I was a member of all kinds of things: I was a Young Republican – and also a member of Students for a Democratic Society, which sounds confusing. I was just curious about things. I smoked my first joint in a lounge in a dorm at a first meeting of my dorm mates. One of the activities, in addition to drinking Californian wine and beer, was smoking pot. I didn't really get high – I'd already been drinking – but I was much more interested in the ritual.' Even so, it transformed Robert Clarke's life, giving him more travel and adventure than his conventional contemporaries but less money, 'plus my parents don't think it's been a great idea'. At college he lost his virginity, took LSD, wrote a ground-breaking dissertation on the botany and ecology of cannabis, 'which is how I ended up meeting a lot of people and how I got all the information to write *Marijuana Botany*'.

In the mid-1970s America was seeing a boom in home-grown marijuana, from both back-to-the-land hippie families and returning Vietnam veterans. The basis of Robert Clarke's re-search was field trips to out-of-the-way places: Indiana, Arkansas, the Ozark mountains of Kentucky. 'It was mostly people who were growing for their own consumption. At that time there weren't a lot of people going out to make a bunch of money; it was Ma and Pa growing enough to sell some and make their life easier. It mostly started with a bunch of hippie drop-outs, organic vegetable growers.'

These first-time growers were less set in their ways than their counterparts in regions where they had been growing cannabis for generations. The Americans soon discovered sinsemilla; the best Mexican marijuana farmers boost potency by uprooting the male plants and harvesting the females without letting them set seed.[1] Meanwhile people returning from the hippie trail brought seed from varieties that had never been seen in the New World. The most famous hybrid that resulted was 'skunk', whose parentage included the pungent *indica* varieties from Afghanistan. A Californian–Afghan connection was first opened up in 1968 by the underground society of bikers-turned-psychedelic drug dealers called the Brotherhood of Eternal Love. Glen Lynd, a founder member, travelled to Kandahar and developed a lucrative connection with the Tokhi brothers who owned a rug shop there. A kilo of Afghan hashish which cost $20 in Kandahar could resell for $21,000 in California. A single shipment in an adapted van raised $400,000 for the Brotherhood to spend on distributing free LSD. Meanwhile, the community of growers felt sufficiently relaxed to inaugurate competitions for the best pot, held in the autumn as a kind of harvest festival celebration.

Sooner or later, real cannabis enthusiasts tend to want to grow and breed their own plants, mugging up in the process on some botany. The father of taxonomy, the Swede Carolus Linnaeus, only recognized one species, *Cannabis sativa*, meaning 'grown as a crop', which he named in 1753. But in 1783 Jean Lamarck recognized *C. indica* ('Indian Cannabis') as a separate species, joined in 1924 by *C. ruderalis* ('Cannabis for rope'), named by the Soviet botanist Nicolai Vavilov. *C. indica* is chiefly found in Afghanistan, where it makes the classic Afghan hashish. We can speculate that the compact, broad-leaved 'skunky'-smelling plants have evolved into their distinctive form through selective breeding for hashish making. The heartland of *C. ruderalis* is Eastern Europe and it may be the culmination of breeding for fibre. More usually, though, *indica* and *ruderalis* are regarded today as cultivars of a single highly variable species, *C. sativa*.[2] Another suggestion is simply to classify cannabis according to the three forms in which it is encountered: wild plants, cultivated plants and cultivated plants which have gone wild and become weeds. In general, in temperate countries cannabis has been a fibre crop, whereas in hotter regions it has been grown for its THC. (No one is sure exactly why cannabis plants secrete THC; Roger Pertwee thinks it may be a form of pest repellent, which works by impairing insects' control over their movements.) In China where the plant's seeds are valued as a food these can be huge – almost the size of coffee beans – as a result of selective breeding. But the plant's role can change from one use to another.

David, who has a biology A-level, likes to discuss the differences between *Cannabis sativa, indica* and *ruderalis* forms. But he learned most from practical experience, 'basically by watching the plants in India', and it's this that inspired his first efforts at growing his own in England.

'In 1992 I'd got some plants from India and I thought, "Fuck it – I'll have a go." I'd got access to a bit of derelict land, but I started them off in my father's greenhouse to give them a start. My reason was that previously I'd tried growing them directly into the soil and they'd always been killed off by the rabbits. So I grew about eight plants: three females, three males, one hermaphrodite, and one died. Although they were from India they matured fully out of doors and set seeds. They had the smell and the aroma and it was better to smoke than the sort of herb you'd buy in a pub. And that's when I thought, "You can do this." '

The next move was to introduce some other genes to the Indian plants. David appealed to overseas friends for likely seed and was sent a promising strain from California. 'I grew four plants in the greenhouse, and I'll never forget what happened next. They'd germinated, with just two baby leaves, and a bloody slug got in. All there was left was one green stalk. But it actually grew – I couldn't believe it. It actually grew leaves, so I crossed that one Californian with an Indian male. A month and a half later I had some fully mature seeds which were planted and re-crossed with themselves and I also bred in some New Zealand pollen. The Indian and the New Zealand plants were both very high-yielding, and the Californian was quality but not quantity. It was also a bit faster-maturing than the Indian and the New Zealand was very fast-maturing.

'I've now got this huge collection of seeds; I call them "London Travel Zones". I've grown from it and it's as good as anything you'd get from Holland – and it grows outdoors. As an example, I gave some to a friend who's not a full-time smoker – just a couple of joints over a weekend. He asked if I had some smoke. I told him, "I have this stuff. I grew it myself down in my garden, but don't let it fool you: it's as strong as everything else.' He ended up not saying anything for a couple of hours; it really wiped him – in fact it had quite a negative effect on him; but it shows I've obviously got fairly high THC.'

People like David have been at work all over the developed world, and the result, especially when it's grown under artificially controlled light, can be cannabis so strong as to become an issue in the legalization debate. Trevor Grice says that a modern joint 'could be anywhere between five and fifty times stronger than its 1960s' predecessor' (this could be one of those statistics you're not meant to linger over: the longer I ponder it the less precise it seems to get). Heather Ashton, Emeritus Professor of Clinical Psychopharmacology in Newcastle University's Psychology Department, nails her colours more firmly to the mast, saying that a joint in the 1970s would typically contain 10 mg of THC as opposed to 60–150mg today.[3] Lynn Zimmer and John

Morgan's *Marijuana Myths, Marijuana Facts*, a scholarly book by two long-term supporters of marijuana law reform, cuts this argument down to size, pointing out that the early 1970s' data is based on unrepresentative, ultra-low THC samples.

However, it's undeniable that sinsemilla buds on sale in a Dutch coffee shop will be more potent than old-fashioned grass. In Britain Afro-Caribbean smokers show some resistance to the new style, which they think of as less natural than Jamaican-grown 'greens'. Darren, a young black dealer, remembers his first encounter with modern weed with mixed feelings: 'The first time I ever smoked home-grown skunk it was directly from the person growing it. I said, "Guys, I'm not smoking any more." I had to go out in the middle of the day, the streets were busy, and I couldn't quite handle it. I've been smoking for ten years and I can pretty much conduct myself as normal, but I felt like a novice – completely out of control. I didn't feel safe.'

It may be the Rasta-tinged ideology that makes the Exodus collective prefer big but relatively mild 'logs' as smoked in Jamaica. 'There's a stigma against high THC levels,' Glenn Jenkins told me. 'It's the equivalent of Special Brew. To me it starts straying into Monsanto territory and it would weaken our stance against that sort of activity.'

'You don't know whether thirty years down the line it's going to turn out that these plants are doing you some sort of damage,' added Mick Anthony.

But as well as their outdoor seed strain, Exodus members grow what they call 'Cheese', which is a mutation of the famous Skunk No. 1. Guy, a dreadlocked former blacksmith, showed me his small hydroponic growing room, with ten short bushy plants coming into flower under powerful sodium lamps. 'It knocks you stupid,' he said. 'It isn't a weed for every day.' The justification is that this variety works as a cure for hard drugs. 'The thing is, that with this amount of drugs in society, and a culture of drug-taking which is pretty blasé, you need somthing to cut all the way through all that. You can be a smackhead or a rockhead, smoke a big fat joint and find you can't get out of your seat even for your next rock.'

In Amsterdam Dr Freek Polak links the craze for ultra-strong pot with the fact that it's illegal. 'During Prohibition people drank less beer and wine and more gin and whisky, because when you're dealing with an illegal substance you don't waste your time on the weak stuff. As far as I'm concerned it's an argument for legalization.' Robert Clarke is unrepentant that his work has helped make cannabis stronger: 'The more potent it is, the less you smoke to obtain a certain level of stoniness, and the less you smoke, the better it is for you.'

The main way that stronger cannabis has spread around the world is via the Dutch seed business, which for example supplied the material for David's ill-fated growing operation. An Australian from a Dutch immigrant family known only by his first name, Nevil, is the legendary founder of this business. He brought the new Californian varieties to Amsterdam after coming across a copy of *The Marijuana Grower's Guide* by Mel Frank and Ed Rosenthal. 'Nevil really started everything,' according to Steve Hager, the editor of *High Times*. It was research for an article on Nevil that brought Hager to Amsterdam in 1987. The city bowled him over and he struck up a rapport with the Dutch cannabis breeders: 'We were like lost brothers finding each other,' he told me. Hager set up the first Cannabis Cup the following year.

Nevil didn't show up at the Cannabis Cup Expo in 1998. I heard that he keeps a low profile, and that he has been targeted by the American DEA after earlier publicity over the (illegal) export of his high-potency seeds to the United States. Although out of sight, his presence was still felt. People were talking about his change of partners, leaving Ben Dronkers' Sensi Seed Company for Arjan's Green House. After the awards Arjan and his partners posed for publicity shots with the tableful of cups they'd won, and a slight, short-haired man joined them briefly. I never found out if this was the living legend.

As well as discovering Amsterdam in 1987, Steve Hager returned with great story about Nevil. Nevil apparently learned the laws of breeding with the classification of dominant, recessive and intermediate traits when he was a seven-year-old, living in Perth in western Australia. The reason was that he had a passion for parakeets and so sat at the feet of one of the country's top parakeet breeders. 'He was a quadriplegic and he was incredibly intelligent,' Nevil told Steve Hager.

But as a young man, Nevil went classically off the rails; he smoked pot at school, then began dealing, then moved on to other drugs: barbiturates, then morphine, then heroin. 'I knew cannabis wasn't harmful,' he said. 'I concluded the harmful effect of other drugs must be exaggerated as well.' He ended up jumping bail while awaiting a court hearing, heading first for Thailand, then Holland. It was as a patient on a Dutch rehab programme that Nevil hit on the idea of becoming a marijuana grower. There were Government funds available to get addicts into useful work, and he got a grant to set up an indoor growing chamber. Only in Holland, as Hager commented in his *High Times* article.

But he soon discovered there was no market for home-grown marijuana (I've heard Dutch-grown pot of that period described as 'spinach'). Instead, Nevil decided to try to make hash oil, the THC-rich gunge that the Moroccans make by dissolving low-grade hashish in highly inflammable liquids. One day these caught a spark from a thermostat and erupted into flames. It was while he was recovering from first- and second-degree burns that Nevil decided to go back to marijuana. Perhaps he could find buyers if he used better seeds – skunk, for example. It was when he tried and failed to buy some that he realized first, that this was an unmet need and second, that in Holland he could have a legal business producing and selling high-potency cannabis seeds.

There's not anything very exciting about the ordinary kind of seed merchant, but the cannabis seed business still depends on fresh discoveries from wildly exotic places. At the Cannabis Cup expo I met Scott, a burly young New Zealander, talking on the phone to his colleague Nevil (it was on the Green House stand where the previous day Howard Marks had been the visiting celebrity). Scott told me that he had been travelling for eighteen years, especially to the region where Afghanistan and Pakistan border the Indian state of Himalchal Pradesh, and to Brazil, and would like to make further trips, to Madagascar and Assam in eastern India: 'I know of some particular strains of *sativas* out there.' The *High Times* article reported Nevil's trips to Pakistan, where he sent a party over to Afghanistan to bring back seeds from Mazar i Sharif, and to the borders of Russia and Hungary (for *Cannabis ruderalis* with its clockwork-like flowering habit).

Another thing that makes this seed business unique is its prices. The most expensive seeds sold by the Green House Seed Company are 175 guilders (around £50) for thirteen. I thought this was steep. Scott shrugged: 'The work that Nevil and I do we don't really get paid for. If you make something really good hopefully people don't mind paying for it.'

Over the past year or so the buzz about medical cannabis has given an extra edge to the work of plant breeders. Until 1998 the only source of government-approved marijuana was the University of Mississippi, which grows a mixture of plants outdoors to create two standard strengths of moderately potent joints.[4] These are supplied to the eight remaining glaucoma patients licensed to get medical pot under a federal programme (which was closed to new patients in 1992) and to research groups looking at subjects such as marijuana toxicity.

Geoffrey Guy has to do better than the University of Mississippi. You could argue that the House of Lords committee has already endangered his £10 million investment by recommending that patients should be allowed to buy cannabis, irrespective of quality, on production of a doctor's prescription. But he believes that by producing special strains he can make himself indispensable.

There is a dimension to cannabis connoisseurship that's missing with wine. The level of alcohol in wine is important: too little, it can taste thin; too much, and wine can seem 'hot' or unbalanced. But few people discuss the different kinds of high you get from different drinks, even though it's possible that these could be fractionally different according to balance of the different alcohols: ethanol (by far the largest), methanol, the iso-amyl alcohols, and so on. Cannabis users, by contrast, talk in the first instance about the quality of the high and later, if at all, about taste. This doesn't mean, of course, that they talk in detail about the sixty different chemically related substances – the cannabinoids – which are found uniquely in cannabis, two of which, taken on their own, make you stoned (THC and THCV, a rarer cannabinoid found mainly in Thai and South East Asian plants). However, pot smokers almost universally agree that different kinds of cannabis produce a different feeling, and every different plant, if it is not a clone, will have a slightly different blend of cannabinoids (what's called its 'cannabinoid profile').

The cannabinoid which most interests pot connoisseurs, after THC, is CBD or cannabidiol. It isn't formally classed as psychoactive but it alters the action of THC. In *Hashish!* Rob Clarke suggests that cannabis that's heavy in CBD takes longer to have an effect, and that the high is less euphoric and lasts longer, and that there is less tendency to sleepiness. The simplest way of classifying pot, after generally 'weak' or 'strong', is by the ratio of THC and CBD.

While recreational users are interested in the different highs created by different cannabinoid profiles, Geoffrey Guy wants to discover exactly what impact they have on the body. He has formidable resources in this quest, which he described over the phone, as he didn't think it would be within the spirit of his Home Office licence to let me see them in person.

'The glasshouse was used in a pesticide and fungicide testing programme and it's designed to grow plants in absolutely standard conditions. Therefore we control all aspects: light, daylight length, light intensity, heat, humidity, carbon dioxide . . . my botanists say they've been very pleased; we've had a very high yield rate on our cloning. Something near 100 per cent took root. We planted the seeds from Holland in August and we've taken hundreds of clones from those original plants. We're now about to do the analysis on the clones, which are now ten weeks old, so that by the time they get to maturity we'll have a full analytical and chemical breakdown. We've done thousands of analyses.'

A set of photos followed the next day from Geoffrey's PR agency. There was a forest of indoor-grown cannabis, tied to bamboo stakes in big plastic pots in a mixture of soil-free compost and white grains of Perlite. The first-generation plants towered in the background. These looked all wrong as plants intended to produce weed; a visitor to Exodus saw the pictures in a newspaper and said, 'This geezer doesn't know what he's doing.' Seed-grown plants waste time and energy on growing bushy; the modern approach, as advocated by Rob Clarke, is to make cuttings which will turn into compact, high-yielding plants. And in fact in other pictures there were recognizable clones – only a foot high, but with the developed growth habit of mature plants.

It might have been a routine assignment for a *High Times* photographer, but actually it all looked different. Geoffrey was emphasizing his respectability with a white coat and an expression of intense, almost pained seriousness. And the photos had apparently been taken neither by, nor for a cannabis connoisseur. Amsterdam's seed companies go in for shots of engorged fruiting buds of an almost pornographic voluptuousness. But here all the attention was on the plants' familiar multi-fingered leaves which are barely worth smoking.

The seeds came from HortaPharm, the Dutch company which, unlike Maripharm, did hold a licence to develop medical strains for a period, before the Dutch Government pulled the plug on this kind of activity, at least for the time being. HortaPharm's Dutch and expatriate American researchers had been after very high levels of THC, but, said Geoffrey Guy, 'Because they had a love and a passion for the botany and the agronomy they equally included all different varieties of cannabis – hundreds or thousands of samples.'

Not everyone is convinced that this kind of effort is worthwhile. One sceptic is Scott Imler of the Los Angeles Cannabis Research Center who simply concentrates on giving patients high-THC marijuana, and who takes a jaded view of the value of cannabis breeding: 'There are a lot of pot growers in California, and I'm sure in Amsterdam, who don't think medical marijuana can exist without them. They're trying to spin marijuana connoisseurship into this notion that different strains produce different therapeutic functions. There's some truth to this theory, but the reason it's being promulgated is to provide work for the breeders rather than to provide relief to patients.'

But Geoffrey Guy believes there is still much to be learned about the Cinderella cannabinoids: the obscure ones which are not psychoactive in themselves but have some other as yet undefined action, or which modify THC in some partly understood way. He argues that there's no point in reinventing THC, since synthesized THC is already a medicine, licensed for AIDS and cancer patients in the United States where it is marketed in gelatine capsules under the trade name Marinol. So an early task was to sift through the thousands of seedlings to find clones naturally high in a single cannabinoid. 'Our programme is to have clone lines whose cannabinoid production will be either exclusively THC or exclusively CBD. Then we've got others which have no THC but which produce high concentrations of CBC, CBG or THCV: those are the other cannabinoids of interest. We'll establish in the clinical trials which are most beneficial for different conditions. We can then go back to our clone library to breed plants which will specifically produce these ratios and use those clones for the mother plant of that line of production. That will also give us very secure plant registration rights.'

There are already reasons to be interested in the other cannabinoids. Both THC and CBD look as if they can prevent brain damage after strokes, according to research carried out by the British-born neuropharmacologist Aidan Hampson at the US National Institute of Mental Health lab in Bethesda, Maryland.[5] Aidan Hampson explained to me how the brain is harmed in a stroke – which is not, as I'd imagined, mostly through bursting blood vessels doing physical damage. Instead, there is a kind of chain reaction in which dying brain cells, deprived of blood and hence starved of oxygen, spew out their full load of neurotransmitters, including the highly excitatory substance glutinate. 'It's just saying to the neighbouring cells "Fire! fire! fire!",' he explained. The stimulation inflicted on these neighbouring cells far exceeds their fuel supply, and they collapse and die, and in turn release their full complement of glutinate. (The process only stops when cells have access to an alternative blood vessel to the one originally damaged.)

But the havoc wreaked by a stroke is not caused by the glutinate on its own. Cells which are unexpectedly fired up by this substance need oxygen, which with sugar forms the body's essential fuel. But one effect of trying to find oxygen in a low-oxygen environment is to create the highly destructive oxygen-based compounds called 'free radicals'. Aidan Hampson likens these to firebrands, or fireships, which destroy all they touch. The urgent need is for anti-oxidants which bind to the free radicals and put them out, to continue the analogy. Vitamins C and E are powerful anti-oxidants, but are of no use in a stroke as they don't cross the blood–brain barrier. But the cannabinoids achieve this with ease, as any pot smoker can testify.

Aidan Hampson's team was only just moving from work using rats' brain cells to seeing whether cannabinoids help live rats recover from simulated strokes. He was some way from publishing this second programme in a scientific journal, but was optimistic that an anti-stroke medicine could be developed which, unlike the main drug in use at present, would offer no risk to a recovering patient.

When Geoffrey Guy put together his written submission to the House of Lords committee in 1998 he listed other properties of the more obscure cannabinoids. He suggested that CBD in isolation might be a sedative and in high doses might also be anti-epileptic and anti-psychotic, that CBD, CBG, CBC, CBNA and CBG had pain-relieving properties and that the first four were also anti-bacterial and anti-fungal agents.

To evaluate these properties Geoffrey Guy has created an Aladdin's cave for HortaPharm's botanists, who had been left facing an uncertain future. 'Our success has been very much down to the help from HortaPharm,' he acknowledges. 'If they hadn't existed I'd have had to deal with non-legal entities. As it is, the plants are grown from stock as part of a research programme by the only people in the world licensed at that time. For them it's the fruition of many years' work.'

The pay-off should come in a variety of ways. GW Pharmaceuticals will have plant breeders' rights in certain strains of proven medical desirability. Even when these strains are high-THC ones they may be more attractive to offer patients than synthetic THC on its own. There is more to cannabis than cannabinoids: one American researcher reports that the plants' essential oils have sedative and painkilling properties and that one in particular called 1.8-cineole enhances the flow of blood through the brain and stimulates brain activity.[6]

Part of the problem with Marinol, the synthetic THC, may be that it has to be swallowed. When smoked, cannabinoids go straight into the bloodstream, but when they're eaten they go to the liver, where most of THC gets converted into another substance, 11-hydroxy-THC, which produces a high that is slower to arrive, but more intense, much longer-lasting and less predictable.[7] Geoffrey Guy's preferred method is inhalers, like those prescribed for people with asthma, which he's convinced should be filled with extracts from real cannabis plants rather than with synthesized single cannabinoids.

This is his real passion. Whole-plant medicines are not the easiest cause to take up in an industry in which licenses are granted on the criteria of consistency, safety and efficacy *in that order of priorities*. In choosing cannabis, though, he has picked his ground carefully. A synergy has been demonstrated between different cannabinoids. Researchers in the early 1980s administered THC to subjects, made them anxious by getting them to speak in public, then used CBD to calm their nerves.[8] The CBD worked, not by blocking the effect of the THC, but by a helpful 'antagonism of effects between the two cannabinoids'. Dr Guy sums up his ambition: 'I hope what we will show is cannabis as a template or as an example of the whole-plant approach: that the whole is greater than the sum of its parts.'

Geoffrey Guy has created an extraordinary business. If he doesn't lose his shirt he will be in a position to relieve the sick, vindicate his theory about whole-plant medicines and even make a second fortune. The Dutch cannabis seed industry has come to inhabit a more familiar commercial world, though one in which, because of its grey legal status, everyday standards of consumer protection don't necessarily apply.

One question is whether their customers get what they think they've paid for. The vagaries of Holland's drugs law mean that a company can grow cannabis plants to produce seeds, and its associated coffee shop can sell weed carrying the same brand-name. But it doesn't mean that companies are allowed to grow cannabis plants to sell as pot. Every day huge amounts of material are put on bonfires or dumped on compost heaps. As well as keeping the seed companies within the law, this is good practice as smokers today demand sinsemilla – unfertilized rather than seed-bearing buds. I was told that surprisingly little of the weed bought by the coffee shops is actually grown in Holland. More and more of it is contracted out to producers in Poland, where labour costs and bribes to police and customs officials both come at bargain-basement prices.

If seeds are advertised as being from a particular strain, will the weed you grow be the same as the one you can buy in a coffee shop under the same name? This is what the seed companies claim; if you go to Sensi Seeds, next door to the company's Cannabis Museum, they will suggest a trip to the Sensi's Museum Coffee Shop to check out your intended purchase. The Green House, as another seed company-cum-coffee shop, offers the same opportunity to 'try before you buy'.

But Annie Rieken, who works for the Cannabis College information service sponsored by several coffee shops, questions whether this is always a revealing exercise. She points out that customers have no way of knowing whether the plants you grow from seeds will really resemble the stuff you buy in the seed company's coffee shop. It may be grown from the seeds on sale to the public; but in Holland it may well be grown from cuttings taken from the mother plants, which can be guaranteed to be genetically identical to the award-winning big-name varieties. As Robert Clarke pointed out to me, the difficulty with cannabis is that the plant is dioecious, with the male and female organs generally carried on separate plants, unlike most familiar flowers and vegetables. Because cannabis has to rely on another plant's pollen if it's to set seed, there will always be a tendency for the sought-after qualities to be lost. The greatest tribute to clonally identical cuttings is that people will go to the trouble and danger to smuggle these out of Holland rather than taking the easier and legally safer option of carrying seeds.

Apart from promoting their brands in coffee shops, the Dutch seed companies sell by means of glossy catalogues with photos of the top varieties, with massive colas or fruiting tops to emphasize the size of their yields. The pictures will be used by distributors in countries like the United Kingdom or Canada where it's legal to sell cannabis seeds. In the catalogues these look like regular flower or vegetable seeds, with two differences: the jaw-dropping prices and the fact that the plants illustrated aren't grown from the seed they advertise; instead, they're the seed mothers. This would be an odd way to sell petunias, let alone cannabis, which, as we've seen, is especially prone to variation because it's dioecious and can't fertilize itself. The seed-grown plants will be like photocopies of the originals, and seeds produced from any second generation will be like photocopies of photocopies.

This isn't just a theoretical problem. An expert grower at the Exodus Collective told me that a certain Dutch firm had supplied dud seed to someone he knew, and as a result he'd never used them again. 'This geezer bought some Northern Lights from them and got a female and a male, and from the female he got 200 plants. The smell and the taste were perfect but the buzz didn't work.' It isn't that cannabis can't come reasonably true from seed: the necessary conditions are clonally identical mother and father plants to produce what horticulturalists call F1 hybrids, and measures have to be taken to stop rogue pollen drifting in. While Holland permits trading in cannabis seeds, it doesn't apply the stringent regulations that the European Union enforces on normal seed companies. As and when cannabis moves further into the mainstream, we could expect photos of what seed-grown plants really look like, and a warning that what you grow may differ substantially from the stuff that impressed the Cannabis Cup judges.

I also wonder if commercial pressures aren't skewing the story of cannabis to give Amsterdam, where the money is made, too much emphasis. So much original breeding work was carried out by growers in California and the American north-west who had every reason to be shy of publicity. Even today, as David has found, growers around the world are as happy to trade seeds as to buy and sell them. Most of the genetic material travelled around the world in the 1970s, not because of plant-hunting expeditions among Kalashnikov-toting tribesmen, but simply because the United States had become a huge importer of marijuana; in the days before sinsemilla, this meant that large quantities of viable seed arrived with the fruiting heads of cannabis.

One figure who has stayed out of the limelight is the American named 'Skunk Sam' who brought seeds of this variety to Holland, collaborated for a time with Ben Dronkers of Sensi

Seeds, and has since disappeared from view. Skunk is so famous that it's become a generic term for modern high-potency weed; one reason is that this *Cannabis sativa–indica* hybrid really will come pretty true from seed. Like the other benchmark varieties, it comes from the United States. It was bred in the 1970s in Santa Cruz, the wine-growing region south of San Francisco. Others are Haze, also from Santa Cruz, which is a mix of *C. sativa* strains including genes from Thailand and Columbia, valued for a 'delicious taste' and a 'clear', 'bell-like' high. Northern Lights comes from Washington State, which is too cold for cannabis to ripen outdoors; it was the first variety specifically bred to be raised under grow-lamps. All three were bred by enthusiasts like David with his outdoor seed strain; like David's, their work has been anonymous and not very lavishly rewarded.

But hype and commercialism are a lesser evil than falling victim to the War on Drugs, and American pot-heads see Amsterdam as a welcome sanctuary. Rob Clarke recalls the culling of the back-to-nature marijuana farmers he knew from his college days. 'Law enforcement started getting heavy at the end of the seventies,' he told me. 'They were afraid of the money; it had become too easy to make too much too fast. There were people getting involved who were scary, who were just into it for the business. One morning the authorities woke up and said, "These fuckers are going to buy the state of California." ' The drop-outs either gave up the fight or become victims of the clamp-down. Under 'Operation Green Merchant', launched in 1989, federal agents investigated purchases of gardening equipment to get leads on suspected cultivators. Several died in shoot-outs in raids; less dramatically, the clamp-down blighted the whole of the counter-culture. 'So many people's family life was destroyed by prison,' said Clarke. 'That's the real tragic side of it.'

But American refugees enjoyed a moment of comic relief

when America's current 'drug czar', retired general Barry McCaffrey, went on a European fact-finding tour in the autumn of 1998. McCaffrey first visited Sweden, whose hardline policies have achieved dramatic reductions in the number of young people trying cannabis. In this congenial setting, McCaffrey declared that Holland's liberal policies were a 'disaster' resulting, among other things, in a murder rate much higher than America's. When the Dutch pointed out that the figures were actually the other way round, his press spokesman in America issued a correction, saying that the figure should have referred to attempted murders, in which the Dutch were far outstripping the United States. The gloss put on the statistics was that the Dutch were too stoned even to get their murders together properly. (Needless to say, a second retraction duly followed, admitting a big American lead in homicide generally.)

McCaffrey refused to visit a coffee shop during his gaffe-haunted stay in Holland. He would have been most likely to run into his countrymen at the Green House, where I met Rob and Annie, and which is well known to readers of *High Times* because of Nevil, who is now part of the business, and Arjan, its boss. The month before the Cannabis Cup Arjan had given me a quick interview in his office above the most recently opened coffee shop – Green House Centraal on a canal in the red light district. He is responsible for its look: swirling abstract mosaics, table tops decorated with slices of fossils, organic shapes to evoke without pastiche something of the spirit of Art Nouveau. There's no trace of the cannabis tat – naff Bob Marley posters and giant marijuana leaves – that is the routine coffee-shop style in this touristy part of town. Everyone is spookily good-looking, from the young women who serve behind the bar (the coffee and the Dutch and Belgian beers are irreproach-able), to the long-haired young guy at the far end, facing away from the street, who offers you the long menu of different kinds of pot (but only one of hashish), to the boss, Arjan, aged thirty-two, a Nordic hunk well over six foot, with shaggily-cut blond hair and frowning intelligence. Arjan will soon join his rival Ben Dronkers of Sensi Seeds as one of pot's first legitimate million-aires – always supposing that he isn't one already.

Arjan told me that he was the first coffee-shop owner to have come into the business through pot rather than as a club or bar owner. 'I started growing when I was eighteen and I was a grower for seven or eight years. At one point I couldn't sell my pot to any more of the coffee shops: they didn't want to pay the prices. It was more expensive because it had a different taste – not stronger, but a different high.' His first coffee shop, the one in De Pijp, was, he said, 'directly a big success. A totally different story to any other coffee shop.' Arjan gives credit to his dynamic partner Brenda, who takes care of the food and drink buying and aspects of the business not involving cannabis, which she doesn't smoke. In fact Arjan makes a point of not being stoned during the day, though he claims to relax with half a joint in front of BBC2's *Newsnight* 'most evenings'. 'When I don't smoke I work too much; I have to smoke.'

One novelty was the decor: a break with the old coffee shops 'where you can't look in – where it's a bit sleazy-looking'. But the Green House's main point of difference had been the pot. It was part of the move away from imported hashish, mainly Moroccan, and towards locally grown high-potency weed, much of it exclusive: Master Kush, Early Pearl, White Widow, White Skunk . . . Its rival Sensi Seeds had a coffee shop which could offer Northern Lights, No 5 X Haze and Jack Herer, bred at Cannabis Castle, the country home of the company's owner Ben Dronkers, before Nevil jumped ship. The question for the 1998 Cannabis Cup was whether any effective challenge would come to the Green House now that Nevil had thrown in his lot with Arjan's formidable empire.

In October hundreds of Americans were already starting to arrive. In 1998, as for several previous years, Annie Riekey was working as the local fixer; her column of tips in *High Times* pleaded that her compatriots should 'be patient. Dutch service is particularly unhurried compared to the States and many Americans seem loud and impatient by Dutch standards.' I was intrigued by the way she provided a bridgehead for the Americans, and wanted to come back and see her liaising with the coffee-shop owners in the week before the Cup. In the event I didn't come back till half-way through the week of the Cup, which in retrospect was a good thing. If I'd dogged Annie's footsteps I'd have annoyed and embarrassed her, given the backstage politics of the 1998 Cannabis Cup.

9

Cup Fever

Perhaps because it's so cramped, the Hotel Ostade is a place where you get into conversations with the other guests. Just after I met Cicely at breakfast and learned at first hand about MS and medical cannabis, I struck up with Danielle, who'd directed her to the Green House on the previous day. Danielle, a French-woman who works in a hemp shop in Germany, showed me the two pieces of body language that for her sum up the annual experience of the Cannabis Cup. One is the patting of pockets and the fumbling in bags that goes on endlessly as people reassure themselves that they have the necessary equipment to spliff up. The other is the sequence of smiles and placatory gestures triggered in unaggressive people when they're crowded together in a confined space. (For most of the time this is a complex of bars and function rooms called the Pax Party House, located in De Pijp, Amsterdam's unglamorous underbelly. Visitors enter under a sign with sixties-style graphics of male and female diners-and-dancers in black tie and evening dress (non ironic) and a notice in Dutch, saying 'For all your party requirements'.)

Inside the Pax Party House a well-spoken young English-woman, pale, with braided hair and lots of earrings, is anxious that I should meet a friend who has something special to tell the world. He has a hat, a beard and glasses and turns out to be an ex-*Daily Mirror* sub-editor, a contributor to *International Times* and PR man who now lives in Amsterdam and has just launched the first issue of *Coffeehouse Culture*. 'We've got something new to say about the cannabis experience,' he tells me with a kind of mild fanaticism. 'If you look at the coffee-shop experience you can really see a society evolving to a higher level that seems to be a product of the increased consciousness that cannabis produces. I sat in a coffee shop, a real Amsterdam coffee shop, and somebody left behind their bag of grass: really fine grass. Thirty people sat on that table. When it closed the bag was still there. And I saw the same thing happen six times.'

I wonder whether this story doesn't have more to say about short-term memory loss than a new morality. 'I suffer short-term memory loss,' he volunteers. 'I can explain the short-term memory loss. We are using expanding consciousness; there's a lot going on in our brains; there's a lot of activity; we are using more of our minds.' This is a bit unclear but what he meant was that something has to give to make way for these increased mental powers.

A more mainstream figure in the context of the Cup is 'Eagle Bill', the cannabis shaman, a middle-aged American with blazing eyes, a smile and a headband, who is giving all and sundry toots on his vaporizer; this is a vast piece of kit, with the smoke passing through a glass bowl the size of a Japanese lampshade, but which he sells at little more than cost price. He tells me with un-selfconscious saintliness: 'I'm a happy person. I've always held on to good things. Negative things will eat your heart out. Anybody who grows the cannabis plant is my friend.' Eagle Bill shows up later at Arjan's press conference and photocall and sets up his equipment in the coffee shop. 'Let's all go get vaporized,' said one of the happy crowd to no one in particular.

Written down, this reads like the bilious observations of some CIA-funded intellectual. But the sight of lots of stoned people being nice to each other does evoke a particular range of cultural stereotypes: Moonies . . . lobotomy cases . . . victims of alien abduction. . . . However, fortunately or unfortunately, the social conventions of cannabis use don't always disguise more familiar human traits.

The Cannabis Cup has a routine centred on the Pax Party House. Every day the exhibitors must tear themselves from their hotel beds and brave the dank and grey streets to be at their stands by 11 a.m. The expo includes hemp clothing, pipes and paraphernalia, kitschy calendars and posters (naked chicks festooned with cannabis leaves), bookstalls, including some heartbreaking stuff on the victims of the War on Drugs, and the stands of the big coffee shops. Green House has gone for glossy closeups of their prize-winning plants, plus some examples of the real thing in pots under the dazzle of grow-lamps. Sensi Seeds have celebrities: Jack Herer the hemp guru, a friendly, vulpine man who's signing all-hemp special editions of *The Emperor Wears No Clothes* to raise funds for legalization; beside him there's the less assured figure of Laurence Cherniak selling his Cannabis Playing Cards. Where the seed merchants went for plant material, Cherniak has been to record the world's cannabis cultures and to take photographs. And on the far right there's Eagle Bill.

Every day buses come to offer free tours of coffee shops and the seed companies' facilities. The top floor is one of the locations where Council is held towards the end of each day, open to all judges (the round trip from the States confers the status of judge, or a judge's pass can be bought locally. Annie gave me one of the laminated passes, worn round the neck, which I've since passed on to my thirteen-year-old son who, catching on fast, puts it round his neck, holds a piece of dried (THC-free) hemp and says, 'Free the weed!'). Because I missed the start of the week I never went to Council, but it's described in the official programme: 'Council is a group-mind process; cannabis is a facilitator for group communication. Judges have a responsibility to share their visions, heart-songs and sorrows. Tears at Council are purifications of tremendous persecution.

Council's primary objective is to discuss candidates for the Cannabis Cup and assist the balloting process. The judges say "Ho!" when they agree with the speaker; thusly, Council flows toward consensus.' (I suggested, to no one's amusement, that it must sound like a class for trainee Santas.) There are bars on each floor, so that judges can refresh themselves with draught Heineken and graze on the Dutch staple diet of chips with mayonnaise.

Meanwhile there is a stream of unofficial events. The coffee shops throw parties with plenty of free pot. The French contingent feel a little beleaguered in Amsterdam: unlike the Dutch and Americans they don't share a mastery of the English language. Moreover, the French Government has made itself unpopular by harassing the Dutch over their liberal soft drugs policy and causing a recent tightening of the regulations on coffee shops; a popular postcard on sale in the city says 'Fuck the French'. The writer Michka and her fellow French activists have responded by organizing a 'French Cannabis Embassy' which throws a party at Cannabis College, with poetry, a sampling (*une dégustation*) of French-grown pot, and the presence of Gilbert Shelton, the cartoonist creator of the Fabulous Furry Freak Brothers who now, along with Robert Crumb (Fritz the Cat and Mr Natural), is domiciled in France.

The climax of the week is the awards ceremony held at Amsterdam's legendary concert venue De Melkweg (The Milky Way). It's hardly necessary to observe that this is much more fun compared to an equivalent wine event, say London's International Wine Challenge. Where the Wine Challenge dinner has black ties, awful food, dreary speeches and backbiting about how the results are a fix, this has loud live music, pot, delicious Dutch and Belgian beers – and endless backbiting about how the results are a fix. The programme includes an anti-War on Drugs sketch with the theme of 'The Emperor Wears No Clothes', a hemp fashion show, a performance by the legendary John Sinclair and his band, another band with 'Rocker T', and finally the presentation of the large number of awards by a series of celebrity judges.

I'm sure it's not just the weed that shrouds the evening with unanswered questions. What exactly is John Sinclair legendary for? Why are the Americans in the audience so much older than the Dutch minority? And is it prejudiced of me to feel that English white Rastas carry it off better than their American counterparts?

If there's a theme it's America's white middle classes paying tribute to black culture. John Sinclair lovingly recites Bo Diddley's 'Who Do You Love' – '*I've got twenty-seven miles of barbed wire. I've got a cobra snake for a neck-tie. I've got a brand new house on the roadside, made from rattlesnake hide.*' Robin Ludwig does note-perfect versions of the accoustic guitar-playing and singing of Robert Johnson, the awesome Bluesman who died, probably poisoned, in 1938 aged twenty-seven. The Cannabis Cup band play dub reggae in the style of 1976, with instruments dropping out of the mix or being given a spacey prominence in the style of 'King Tubby Meets Rockers Uptown'. That record, like all dub, was created in post-production from the backing to Jacob Miller's 'Who Say Jah No Dread' sessions; what we're hearing now is a live approximation of something that happened in a Kingston studio event a quarter of a century ago.

The academic tone is not coincidental. Steve Hager explained the next day that he wanted to demonstrate that cannabis forms part of a real culture. Hence his innovation of the last two years: the Cannabis Hall of Fame, which currently houses Bob Marley, Louis Armstrong and Mez Mezzrow. To try to make this kind of association strikes me as pushing at an open door. Is there any recreational drug that doesn't have cultural associations, whether cocaine and Hollywood, booze and literature or coffee and *sachertorte?* Cannabis is hardly separable from its ritual use as many different people's Holy Herb.

In 1997 the organizers flew in Rita Marley from Jamaica to perform on the main stage and to witness the induction of her late husband into the Hall of Fame. This year, though, there was lots of black culture but very few black people. Nor were there representatives from the huge tracts of the globe where cannabis is the main recreational drug. Amsterdam has a substantial Moroccan population which is catered for by one or two rather depressing-looking coffee shops – which, unsurprisingly, were not contestants at the Cannabis Cup. The nearest we come to a nod to Islamic culture happens the next day at the Hemp Hotel. Rob Clarke illustrates a short talk on his book *Hashish!* with an extraordinary sequence of 16-mm film, illustrating Afghan holy men smoking a water-pipe. The sight of these wizened old guys coughing as they take huge lungfuls of smoke provokes laughter, not unfriendly, among the watching Americans. But a Turkish dealer is stung by this depiction of fellow Muslims and walks out.

The Cannabis Cup does embody the notion, which I find very seductive, of helping to define a new world cannabis culture, in which fifty-something Americans would open their hearts and minds to something less familiar than the dear old Grateful Dead. I suggested to Steve Hager that he book the house band at the Hotel Tidighine, and he asked to hear a cassette, though not with marked enthusiasm. (Since then I have been puzzling over how to organize it, considering that the hotel is barely connected to Morocco's telephone network.)

It's wonderful to see such reverence shown for the culture of America's oppressed people, but I'm confused by the fact that it doesn't involve actually mixing with them. The atmosphere is different – and more stale – than in the racially mixed audiences in mid-seventies London when roots reggae first came over in the form of Burning Spear or The Mighty Diamonds. In the

Melkweg there are no references at all to post-hip hop black music; what is being celebrated might as well be extinct. And this makes it a bit two-dimensional. Reggae is insurrectionary, sexy, witty . . . if it had amounted to no more than the hemp fashion show models' chant of 'Hemp Hemp Hooray', wouldn't it have sunk without a trace? Of course there should be a sense of history – but being stuck in a rut is a poor advertisement for pot, and the retreat from the present is all the odder considering the current popularity of cannabis.

You can make a sort of parallel with the seed business, which Steve Hager sees as a gathering-in of endangered varieties at threat from the War on Drugs or, in Afghanistan, the Taliban's preference for the more lucrative opium. People in the West these days appreciate the qualities of Afghan-derived *Cannabis indica* without the need for any actual Afghans to be involved. Pot is getting less international; the Dutch Drug Policy Foundation sees the best bet for legalization as a system by which the coffee shops are supplied by a small number of local Dutch suppliers. With hydroponics, grow-lamps and a breeding programme, the Europeans and Americans can do without Morocco, Thailand and Afghanistan. Until now at any rate the Third World has remained the only source for hashish – it will soon, in Rob Clarke's view, be challenged by Switzerland, given the scale of outdoor planting there.

One man at the awards ceremony made a brief reference to 'something with more tradition' in the tide of bioweed, Nederhash and hydro cannabis. It was Laurence Cherniak, author of *The Great Books of Hashish*, as the 'celebrity judge' called on to make the presentation for the best imported hashish. When he stepped out on to the stage of the Melkweg I felt like cheering, and by the time his moment in the spotlight was over I had not been disappointed. Cherniak provides refreshing proof that cannabis is not going to turn us all into egoless, good-vibey citizens of some Brave New World. He is strange.

Laurence Cherniak has done incredible things. Rob Clarke's hashish book is a piece of coffee-shop scholarship, collating the accounts of others, apart from his trip to Ketama in the 1980s. But Cherniak really has been everywhere, sat down with remote peoples in three continents, survived Afghanistan and the Bekaa Valley, taken irreplaceable photographs and is a source quoted by many others, including Clarke. And yet . . . why, for example, does volume 2 of his cannabis book, which includes opium, have to contain a stomach-turning photo of a bungled and bloody injection in the back of someone's hand?

For a long time I was eager to hear the story of how Cherniak set out on his adventures, and I traced an e-mail address through which I asked him if we could have a chat on the phone. Our correspondence became very drawn out. This was partly, it seemed, because he was pretending to be his own secretary or amanuensis negotiating terms on which 'Mr Cherniak' would be willing to talk to me. This became a game of Snakes and Ladders. I fell back some way by misspelling his first name, then made it up by mentioning that this book would be illustrated, which let me in for some arm-twisting to include his forthcoming Cannabis Playing Cards (I was ready to submit, but Bloomsbury decided against illustrations). Eventually an e-mail told me that Mr Cherniak was pleased by my 'kind and gentle responses', suggesting that a live interview might at last be on the cards – but by then I had got distracted by other concerns.

Cherniak turned out to be a small, trim figure with neat brown hair of an even tint. Like the fictional Troy McLure of The Simpsons, with his catchphrase of 'You may remember me from such public information films as . . .', he appealed to the audience for recognition, going one step further by asking anyone who had heard of him to put their hands up . . . a gambit that somewhat backfired. He gamely undertook a little promotion for his photography and research, panicked when he couldn't read the names of the winners, turned petulant when the Number 3 team didn't immediately appear ('Oh, *please* come up') and showed a novel turn of phrase in dismissing them ('So – Aloha !').

I finally met him in person with Jack Herer the next day at Cannabis College. He had noticed a silk-screen image above a mantelpiece of a hugely magnified cannabis resin gland and was indignant about breach of copyright. Herer was more concerned about the image's resemblance to an erect penis, reassuring him: 'I'm just glad nobody else ever took a picture that looked like that.' I introduced myself; he said: 'So, we meet at last,' looked meaningfully at me, took my hand and then gave it a curious wrench, as if trying to dislocate my arm. I promised to interview him, but in the end had to run for my plane. Of course, Laurence Cherniak is not unique among authors, or even cannabis authors, in having a well-developed ego. Rob Clarke had been fuming the previous day at having to illustrate part of his talk 'with a bunch of Cherniak's photographs'.

Laurence Cherniak's stage appearance had been a pleasurable but brief interlude in the main business of the awards ceremony, which was giving cups to the Green House. Most of the Dutch at the Melkweg stood at the back, recognizable by their fashionable clothes, short hair and fresh faces. But Arjan and his posse were in front of me at the side of the stage to minimize delays as, on almost every possible occasion, they bounded up to take first prize.

My first inkling that not everyone was content with this state of affairs came when the owner of De Rokerij coffee shop, on accepting a second prize, pleaded: 'Come on everyone, no protests any more! Just have fun!' Then there was Arjan's acceptance speech when he went to collect the top trophy.

He said: 'There was a lot of controversy around the cups – why we always win the cups, but we have to work very hard . . . We hope that next year we have more coffee shops entering. For us it's good for the whole industry that the whole industry enters, and that even more Americans come over for the Cup. When we heard that a few people didn't want to enter we were really, really sorry. We hope they enter more next year.'

The consensus was that the Green House had won a hollow victory. Their chief rival, De Dampkring (The Atmosphere), had pulled out after winning the Cannabis Cup in '96 and '97, circulating leaflets describing the event as a 'commercial circus'. Next day I saw Steve Hager for the first time at his press conference in the saloon-style Emerald Room of the Pax Party House (the different rooms are named after different gems). He was a slightly built guy in his forties with a young face and greying hair. He wanted to talk about his technical coup in putting the awards ceremony on the Internet. 'It's going to transform our whole way of dealing with this issue. Once people see this on TV the whole Reefer Madness campaign is just going to melt away.' But a British journalist researching a feature for *Sky* magazine had previously been briefed by someone from De Dampkring and wasn't going to give Hager an easy ride. One thing that had infuriated De Dampkring had been that they didn't feel that their victories in the two previous years had sufficiently diverted *High Times* from its editorial love-in with Arjan.

Hager: 'When people win they get coverage. You don't read about all the teams who *tried* to get to the Superbowl. He's consistently won more cups than anybody else so he gets more . . .'

Guy from *Sky*: 'The guy was saying it isn't like that. Last year's winner withdrew . . .'

Hager: 'Dampkring are probably back next year. They pulled a big publicity stunt and got a lot of attention for themselves and didn't have to worry about losing.'

Guy from *Sky*: 'They told me that they bought the cup last year. They had to spend 40,000 guilders ($20,000) to win the cup.'

(The *Sky* reporter was amazed by the amount of free samples going around. Later that day he and his girlfriend were trying without success to smoke their way through a mound of free weed they had either to smoke or leave behind. I took a bit, then lost it, and panicked going through Gatwick customs that it was somewhere in my luggage.)

The money spent isn't surprising when you consider the number of Americans paying $200, plus travel and accommodation, to serve as judges: nearly 2,500 in 1998. The samples themselves are a major investment (the sixteen out of Amsterdam's 356 coffee shops that enter the Cup have to submit four to each judge), if the coffee-shop owners absorb the cost, as they are urged to by the *High Times* organisers. But that's only the start of it. Eya from the Blue Bird, which also pulled out in 1998, described it as 'an advertising campaign': 'Last year the Green House put on a whole media show, dancing girls, girls standing handing out free samples, free joints'. The parties are one investment; there're also the shuttle buses and the free merchandizing (stickers, T-shirts, bags and caps). Staff are sent out to the Pax Party House to mingle with the judges, light a joint with them and bend their ear on the qualities of their employers' product. One of the most important weapons is a laminated plastic tag, similar to those that *High Times* gives to the judges, which carries the name and address of your coffee shop and entitles the bearer to free or discount drinks and smokes. 'It isn't a cannabis competition,' one observer told me. 'It's a beauty contest for the coffee shops.' And Arjan's personality is worth a lot of votes: 'He's charismatic and capable. A lot of the Americans are socially insecure – they spend their whole life in hiding because of American culture – and he's smiling and shaking their hands and saying, "I remember you from last year."' Apparently Arjan is a rich kid, the son of a senior Shell executive, and stands out among the usual drop-outs and bad boys who are the more usual kind of coffee shop proprietor.

De Dampkring is run by a couple of traditional coffee-shop types who field Eric, their shop manager, to inquisitive journalists. The story, as told by Eric, is that they went in for the competition one year because the response of their Dutch customers told them that they were on to a winner with their weed. Gamblers are supposed to be hooked by their first experience of winning; these first-timers found themselves drawn into a superpower-style confrontation with Arjan, with correspondingly escalating budgets. Then they realized they were in over their heads.

'The American people come here and have a very nice week but they don't see how it drags some coffee shops apart,' said Eric. 'During the competition last year we saw people from other coffee shops tearing our posters, because they're envious. We want to make the competition worth nothing. The herb in many of the coffee shops is quite similar – we buy from the same grower. It's really not about the quality of the stuff. The difference only is how you bring it to the customer. We have a coffee shop fifty-two weeks of the year and fifty-one weeks are for the Amsterdammers. *High Times* wants us to focus only on the Cannabis Cup.'

But De Dampkring were not aloof from all PR activity during the 1998 Cannabis Cup. They achieved a propaganda masterstroke by leafleting the Pax Party House on the first day. Then they supplied free Afghan hashish to be smoked in the vast four-tube Egyptian hookah of the Hemp Hotel, which offered the opportunity to take a puff at this monster in a nightly prize draw.

The evening after the awards ceremony this was offered to all-comers; if De Dampkring had gone to see how their gift was being received, they would surely have been gratified to find the air thick not just with fragrant fumes but with dissent.

Sometimes I couldn't quite understand what people were talking about (was it the hashish affecting me or them?). A guy called 'Lulu' from Paradise Seeds said of the hookah, 'This is a prostitute. I want to fuck this prostitute.' (Wild guess − a reference to Dampkring's PR budget?) Less obliquely, and with all the passion of a disappointed Cannabis Cup entrant, he denounced the Cup, *High Times* and the Green House: 'It's McDonalds.' There was surprise that Green House were both winners of the Cannabis Cup for one kind of pot, and runners-up for another. Rob Clarke asked whether the winner in a swimming race could say, 'One hand touched the end of the pool, so I'm first, and then my other hand touched it, so I'm runner-up.' He also cast aspersions at one of the Green House entries − 'Fucking compost, man' − suggesting it had a fungal infection from incorrect drying.

Two months after the eleventh *High Times* Cannabis Cup the first ever Coupe CannaSuisse was held in Berne, 400 miles south of Amsterdam. Five hundred tickets were sold, each with six numbered but anonymous samples of Swiss weed attached. The judges had three weeks to compare their merits before the award ceremony, which followed a legalization forum with the head of the Swiss federal police. According to Sabine Lord, one of the organizers: 'The argument in Switzerland, right across the political parties, isn't about whether we should legalize but how we should legalize.' The Swiss regularly hold referenda, or *votations*. A bid to legalize all drugs had just been defeated, but there were plans for a separate vote in 1999 on cannabis alone.

In Amsterdam Switzerland had seemed to be that year's hot

topic. I'd particularly noticed the French supporting their fellow Europeans by smoking hashish from German Switzerland, which was black like Afghan or Pakistani. The Swiss were making hashish because they had so much weed; it transpired that they were growing field upon field of high-THC cannabis in the open air. As a plant with a long history of cultivation it had been accepted, being legally protected by the Swiss constitution. It was also legal to sell ganga as the stuffing for 'aromatherapy pillows'. You only broke the law if you slit the pillow open and smoked its contents. Really.

Michka gave me the phone number of Bernard Rappaz, an organic fruit and wine grower from the wine village of Saxon, in the Valais, the mountain valley formed by the Rhône before it enters Lake Geneva. Bernard told me that cannabis did well on the same south-facing slopes that made good vineyards, where many farmers were now ripping out their vines because of over-production. He had first planted cannabis in 1993 and now had twenty hectares, or nearly fifty acres, dedicated to it. This would be a lot by the standards of an English farmer growing hemp for fibre, let alone for someone growing real weed. In the early years he had marketed it as a *tisane* or infusion, and later had pressed the seeds to make hemp oil. Even though this has no THC content the police had confiscated the crop in the early years. Now he sells it for various purposes, including high-THC medical marijuana.

'It's quite funny,' he said. 'It all originally comes from seeds from grass I was buying on the street in Amsterdam, in Dam Square in 1971, which came from all different countries. Each year I'd sow the seed and keep the best, and now I've created a stable variety which I call Walliser Queen which is perfect in Swiss conditions. It has these extraordinarily large buds and a very distinctive taste, rather like blond tobacco. We used to show it in Holland at the Cannabis Cup, but we couldn't last year because of the rule that only Dutch companies could enter.'

When I spoke to him, Bernard was basking in Wallister Queen's triumph in the CannaSuisse blind tasting. 'I'm a wine maker in the first instance – I trained in Burgundy – and the whole basis of judging wine is blind tasting. The Cannabis Cup is nice, *c'est folklorique, c'est amusant*, and it publicizes cannabis. Of course it's very commercial: millions of dollars are at stake for whichever seed company wins.'

Steve Hager stayed behind in Amsterdam after the 1998 Cup and did a round of urgent lobbying – to some apparent effect. There is a lot of goodwill for the idea of the Cannabis Cup and for the ideal behind it, which Hager expresses as communicating to the world that cannabis has a genuine if under-recognized culture. 'The people here are basically trying to show that they're the best agriculturists in the world,' he told the press conference on its last day. 'These are highly intelligent, creative people that come here, yet we have this image all around the world that we're a Cheech and Chong joke.[1] We are trying to show that this is not a Cheech and Chong joke. This is a serious agricultural competition; the judges here take the competition very seriously, and they're dedicated to finding the best cannabis, and I believe they've found the best cannabis.'

But the way the Swiss go about their new competition shows the Cannabis Cup in an unflattering light. The problems did not begin with this year's walkout. How can anyone judge sixty-five different kinds of cannabis in inside a week? How can this mind-boggling task be farmed out to people whose only qualification is that they'll pay to do it? And how can any comparative sampling be done on a basis other than 'blind tasting', in which a product is judged entirely on its own merits, without knowledge of its provenance? Bernard Rappaz is absolutely right: no wine competition, however flaky, would dream of letting the judges see the labels.

High Times disassociate themselves from the freebies, the parties and the razzmatazz. But they all played an important part in the event as it took place in 1998 incarnation. At times the organizers reminded me of a certain obscure English wine journalist who has pulled off the trick of getting paid both by the broadcasters who air his material and by the wine producers he recommends. Any reforms to the Cannabis Cup would remove some of its financial underpinning. It would make the competition more genuine if the numbers of judges were cut, their qualifications examined, and the assessment period extended over weeks, so that they were not too ripped to know what they were smoking. There could still be a large number of 'guests' and maybe a separate Guests' Cup.

But this would make the Dutch less anxious to hand out free pot and issue party invitations. Blind tasting, too, would lessen the party atmosphere: what would be the point in building a name if the sampling was anonymous? And if Dutch guilders didn't pay for this 'week of sublime indulgence', as *High Times* advertise it, it would have to be American dollars, making the excursion either more expensive or less profitable.

Steve Hager said one of the truest things heard during the whole week when he insisted to reporters that 'Cannabis *is* a business – it's one of the world's biggest businesses.' The things about the Cup I had puzzled over make sense if it's seen in business terms rather than as a purely cultural exercise. Having more than 2,000 people assess sixty-four different samples in under a week is not the most scientific way of running a competition, but the 'customers', many of whom come back year after year, clearly feel they've had their money's worth.

I think that there are business reasons too why the culture on offer at the Cannabis Cup has rather a fossilized feel to it.

(Another possibility, which had worried me for a bit, was that pot stops people being interested in new things. Otherwise, why would a young man be seen wandering round the press conference with a guitar playing 'That's it for the Other One' by the Grateful Dead, off their 1968 album *Anthem of the Sun*) The proceedings must be pitched to appeal to the people most likely to spend between $850 and $2,000 on a round trip from the United States. In America the people who see pot as central to their identity belong to the generation targeted by the War on Drugs – the culture that was driven out into the cold. Eric at De Dampkring described the difference between the valued American visitors and his Dutch customers as being that the Dutch are just ordinary people who go for a joint after work instead of a drink. Lucky Dutch.

10

Pot of Gold

There's something exhilarating about seeing such a vast international business as cannabis, as Steve Hager quite rightly described it, that's beyond the control of any one interest group. This is unlike tobacco or oil or bananas – and quite unlike heroin, a trade that was carved up between the Sicilian and American mafia in a historic deal in the Hotel Grande Albergo e delle Palme in Palermo in October 1957. However you dress cannabis up, in religious, medical or counter-cultural clothes, it keeps outgrowing them. As a global business it's now worth at least £100 billion a year – a pot of gold that attracts the most diverse people. The fact that it's illegal means that not just growers and merchants make a living from cannabis, but customs and police officers, gangsters, drug workers, seed merchants and grow-manual authors as well.

It's a business that has increased in complexity as it's grown, with a tendency to add new activities rather than making old ones redundant. Medical cannabis expertise is an exception – a skill that disappeared and is being rediscovered. It was a doctor who first brought cannabis to the Western world, the first of three transforming events in its recent history. The trials of cannabis in India in the 1830s gave Dr William Brooke O'Shaughnessy the material for his definitive paper in 1842 for the *Transactions of the Medical and Physical Society of Calcutta* on 'The preparations of the Indian hemp, or gunjah (*Cannabis indica*); their effects on the animal system in health, and their utility in the treatment of tetanus and other convulsive diseases'.

Within a few years a London pharmacist, Peter Squire of Oxford Street, had developed an extract and tincture of cannabis under O'Shaughnessy's direction. At the same time nurserymen in suburban Mitcham who had developed a trade in pharmaceutical opium poppy-heads tried with limited success to grow a crop. Victorian doctors prescribed cannabis for conditions including muscle spasms, rheumatism and the convulsions of tetanus, rabies and epilepsy. Cannabis cigarettes were sold in 1887 at 1s 9d a packet for 'immediate relief in all cases of Asthma, Nervous Coughs, Hoarseness, Loss of Voice, Facial Neuralgia and Sleeplessness'.[1]

The next paradigm shift took place in France. Dr Jacques Joseph Moreau of the Bicêtre hospital in Paris pioneered the 'recreational' use of hashish by founding the Club des Haschischins held at the Hôtel Lauzun in Paris and attended by Charles Baudelaire[2] and Théophile Gautier, the author who coined the aesthete's slogan 'art for art's sake', and who wrote a fabulous and much-quoted description of a trip created by eating hashish. Moreau, who in 1845 published 'Du haschisch et de l'aliénation mentale', advocated it as a form of psychiatric medication.

But the fundamental fact about cannabis in our times is that it's against the law. This change in its status took place in the first half of this century, and there's no consensus about why it happened; I go into the arguments at length in the next chapter. Banning cannabis created enforcement agencies and authorities; but the prohibtion never secured universal public support and for more than thirty years there have been campaigns to remove it. In an offer to referee the tussle between the two lobbies, researchers have prised substantial sums from funding bodies.

And for much of the past thirty years another huge change has seemed imminent: legalization and regulation. This would stand to reverse the trend towards greater complexity in the market. It's so cheap and easy to grow cannabis, at any rate in reasonably warm places, that all sorts of people can make a living from it. But if it became a legal commodity like any other, the winner would stand to take all (the sight of the Green House scooping the pool in the Cannabis Cup offers a kind of foretaste).

This is a prospect that worries the dealers. Andy says that if he was Home Secretary rather than an underworld dealer, 'I'd legalize everything because it would fuck the dealers up. It would be the end of crime because no one would have any reason to steal. I'd have certain chemists or certain things you could only get in certain areas. But you couldn't do it because it would be a bit like ethnic cleansing.'

There's some comfort for people like Andy. Zelda, the former queen of the Back Beat Club, said, 'I'd still buy it from a dealer. I want to support him and I want the best in quality – and I don't want to pay taxes.' Someone who'd be grateful for the patronage is Darren, the twenty-five-year-old son of what he calls 'a typical West Indian couple', who came over on the *Empire Windrush* (the first boat to transport Jamaican migrants to Britain), and now work respectively on the buses and in nursing. Darren started dealing while he was doing a college course in electronics: 'I didn't have any money and it's a way of making money. All you need is a bunch of friends who smoke. You don't have to tout for customers. It's amazing how the business can take off. If everybody could set up a business like that we'd all be entrepreneurs.'

And he believes it's a business that would be destroyed by legalization. 'The fact of the matter is that I'd really feel it and a lot of other people, my friends, would feel it. We would stand to lose so much – we'd be forced to move on to harder stuff.' Already he sees under-achieving contemporaries finding a sort of salvation in crack-dealing: 'It can bring you everything you wanted – everything you thought you'd never be able to get because of your lack of education. You can literally be that guy with the nice house and the nice car and 2.5 kids without having to go to university or work a nine-to-five job.'

Legalization wouldn't put the enforcement agencies out of business; the one DEA agent I know is kept fully stretched monitoring doctors and dentists suspected of over-prescribing legal drugs. And the makers of drug-testing kits would still be in business, making equipment for employers and traffic police; legalization might stimulate them into devising a more accurate test for cannabis than the current one, which detects tiny traces in the body which persist for days or even weeks after smoking a single joint.

But some large businesses do appear jittery about the competition they'd face after legalization of cannabis. The pharmaceutical, alcohol and tobacco industries featured in an investigation carried out into the funding of the anti-drugs charity Partnership for a Drug-Free America. This group was responsible for a TV ad which has entered America's collective consciousness, with an image of an egg being broken into a frying pan. 'This is your brain on drugs,' the commentary went. 'Any questions?' Questions were asked in 1987 after the Partnership put out a TV ad apparently depicting the brain wave of a fourteen-year-old smoking pot. The image turned out to have been taken from the readout of a coma patient.

In a feature for the journal *The Nation*,[3] the American journalist Cynthia Cotts established that between 1988 and 1991 the Partnership had accepted $5.4 million in contributions from legal drugs manufacturers, including $1,100,000 from the J. Seward Johnson Sr Charitable Trusts, $150,000 from Du Pont, the company that's a honey-pot for cannabis conspiracy theorists, $120,000 from the Proctor and Gamble Fund, $110,000 each from the Brisol-Myers Squibb Foundation and Johnson and Johson, and $100,00 from SmithKline Beecham. Tobacco and alcohol companies also did their bit for the partnership: An-heuser-Busch, the makers of Budweiser, contributed $150,000, with the same sum coming from Philip Morris, the makers of Marlboro and RJR Reynold (Winston) and $100,000 from American Brands (Jim Beam whisky and Lucky Strike cigar-ettes).

But these industries like to back both horses. There have been reports of cigarette companies in France using the name Marley as a trade-mark or, in Britain, researching the idea of putting tiny amounts of weed into cigarettes to give them an extra selling edge. Even more innocuously, Brown and Wil-liamson, the makers of the Kool brand, were found in February 1999 to have carried out research in the mid-seventies into a cigarette which tasted of pot but was actually a blend of Virginia and Turkish tobacco with alfalfa leaves.[4] A wine PR man I know began his career in the pharmaceutical industry; his first assignment was to work with the creator of Lemsip on a new cannabis pill. My retired neighbour's verdict is 'give it to Imperial Tobacco or ICI and take it away from the dealers'. Imperial Tobacco already make a useful amount of money out of cannabis-smoking through their recent acquisition of Rizla cigarette papers (which coinciden-tally are largely made of French-grown hemp). They employ FFI, a specialist youth-oriented PR firm which also works for Evian and Holsten. This company successfully pitched the idea of taking a Rizla tent – the 'Rizla Experience' – to pop festivals, offering coffee and fruit juices. Sandra Hussey of FFI gamely tries to put a respectable spin on this: 'People who smoke roll-ups are expressing their individuality.' Has Ms Hussey ever seen someone make a tobacco cigarette with Rizla King Size, which has just under 10 per cent of the market? 'Yes, I actually did once.' She asks to pass when I inquire whether she feels more comfortable about people smoking cigarettes or joints with her client's product.

The only people openly to draw up plans for marketing cannabis have been the legalization campaigners. In 1980 the Legalize Cannabis Campaign (LCC) put out a working document on 'The Legal Marketing of Cannabis in Britain', reprinted several times during the 1980s. The LCC wanted to keep cannabis out of the hands of traditional capitalist enterprises like those dominating the markets for spirits and tobacco; it thought these would irresponsibly stimulate demand through advertising and would standardize a low-quality product. Instead the campaigners wanted a new kind of cannabis industry which would pioneer producers' and consumers' co-operatives while clamping down on the black market. The document gives no quarter to the idea that people should want or be allowed to make money out of cannabis and has a strong flavour of the Left in the late 1970s/early 1980s.

This isn't surprising as legalizing cannabis had to compete with other single-action campaigns of the day. Tim Malyon, the journalist who founded the LCC, had to fight for attention with Ronald Reagan and the revival of the cold war. He remembers: 'The anti-nuclear movement took off in a big way, which was fine: I supported that myself. But it meant that the focus for campaigning became an anti-nuclear focus. We had a problem with the student unions – with the Young Socialists: "Nobody will need to take drugs when the revolution comes." The soft left, the broad left was in favour, but the further left, the SWP, took the same line as the Young Socialists. You could argue that the cannabis laws are a bit like the old "sus" laws, that that's how the police were using them, but they weren't interested, basically.'

Each of Britain's legalization campaigns has been the mirror of its times (though a thread connecting them has been the contrast between a lucrative commodity and a cash-strapped pressure group). First off was Soma in 1967, set up as both a research and campaigning organization. Unlike modern activists who emphasize the natural, holistic aspects of cannabis and the environmental benefits of hemp, Soma played up its intellectual and scientific credentials. The letterhead featured such luminaries as Francis Crick, the discoverer of DNA, and the psychiatric guru R. D. Laing. Synthetic THC was all the rage, and one of the attractions of membership was the chance to take part in experiments using the drug, which was still legal. Unfortunately THC was also ruinously expensive, something that Soma's research officer, Don Aitken, believes helped sink the group financially. Soma was anyway soon eclipsed by Release, with its focus on legal rights, funded with donations from George Harrison and an underground 'community tax' from clubs like UFO and Middle Earth. But Release too hit the rocks financially in 1974, and after it was bailed out with a Home Office grant to fund its charitable work it stopped being a frontline campaigning organization. This function was taken over briefly by CARO (the Cannabis Action Reform Organization), set up by Nicholas Saunders, the publisher of *Alternative London* and, later, Ecstasy guru, before the founding in 1978 of the Legalize Cannabis Campaign.

The LCC, born in the era of two-tone and Rock against Racism, recognized that cannabis legalization was an issue that extended beyond a core constituency of white hippies. Tim Malyon was inspired by a case of institutional sadism. When he was working for the Release in the late 1970s, he came into contact with a Nigerian serving time for a heroin offence, a jazz musician and former merchant seaman named Frankie Macauley, who'd become addicted after being treated for a work-related injury. Malyon got to know Macauley after his release: 'He was a small, quite athletic guy, and he had a really bubbly character to him. If you were pissed off and you met Frankie he'd have you laughing quickly, even if he was in trouble.'

By the time he left prison Frankie Macauley was no longer addicted; in order to stay well away from heroin he gave up jazz and began a new career as a drugs worker. According to Malyon, 'He was a brilliant drugs worker. We're talking about the late 1970s when barbiturates were the main drug, and he was one of the very few drug workers who could cope with severely addicted barbiturate users. He set up a rehab specifically for them; but he continued to smoke cannabis. The police knew where he lived and they raided him and busted him and he got a conditional sentence. They raided again and he was sent down and went into Brixton prison. And they raided and busted him again and he did a long period in jail for that.

'It was because he was black, and it was because he had a record for heroin possession, and because he was a really easy target. The rehab he was running closed and it just kind of broke him. He died not long afterwards. He was a very dear friend of mine.'

The LCC started in apparently propitious times. Tim Malyon recalls: 'There was a period during the late seventies, early eighties, when a lot of states in America were decriminalized. We had good contacts with NORML, which had been started by Hugh Hefner, and things were definitely flowing in a pro-cannabis way.' Reggae provided a natural constituency, as did the punk bands, despite the anti-pot rhetoric of some of them. Later the campaign organized the first international legalization conference, in Amsterdam. Its rebel credentials were strengthened when *New Musical Express*, under pressure from its publisher IPC, refused to carry one of their advertisements. 'Although it was a little incident it got us a huge amount of publicity,' says Malyon.

'We were functioning as a really together campaigning organization. We were selling T-shirts and badges and doing all these gigs.
We had three full-time staff and, in conjunction with NORML,
we ran this Amsterdam conference.'

But in America the pro-cannabis tide halted and then, with
Ronald Reagan at the White House, began to flow strongly in
the other direction. Matthew Atha took up the reins when Tim
Malyon quit as the LCC's organizer in 1983. 'The people that
had started it were expecting quick legalization,' Matthew Atha
believes. 'There was a bit of money from the benefits in the early
eighties, but then a lot of people dropped out. A lot of the
people were cranks and hippies who couldn't get together a
Smokey Bears' Picnic in bloody Jamaica. If people are stoned all
the time it does make them less efficient; but then there are some
people who can use it like tea or coffee. It always used to be a
rule at LCC that nobody smoked till the business was done.'

The LCC staggered on into the 1990s. Its last days proved – as
if proof were needed – that dope doesn't transform unregenerate
human nature. There was new blood: a young Rob Christopher, who had inherited money through his Austrian grandfather's distilling business. In his later incarnation as Free-Rob
Cannabis (he changed his name by deed poll) he liked to tell
people, 'My wealth comes from drug-dealing, but bad drugs, not
good drugs.' Rob was given to enthusiasms: at the time of the
Gulf War it had been the Territorial Army. Now it was pot. He
opened a House of Hemp in Bethnal Green in East London,
roughly along the lines of Sensi Seeds' Hemp Museum in
Amsterdam, and after he joined the LCC in 1994 this was
the logical place for the campaign to meet.

Rob had mixed feelings about the way things were going.
'Things started to happen a little bit. Meetings were held
regularly – but at the end of the day nothing was being
achieved, other than things being discussed.' Another LCC

member recalls his impact on this moribund organization: 'I think the problem was that he was over-enthusiastic, which isn't a failing. There were people who'd been in it for so long they'd tried everything and weren't any longer prepared to try anything. If he said, "Let's have a disco," they'd say, "We've done discos." If he said, "Let's have a rally," they'd say, "We've already tried that." '

But according to Rob, it was paranoia that finally fractured the campaign after he joined with a fellow-spirit in calling for a high-profile 'cannabis conference'. He told me: 'It was put about that we were M15 agents.' Rob had asked for access to membership records, to 'know what the state of the membership was, and to inform people about his conference'. Did LCC members really think he was a spook, or was it simply that his youth, money and brashness put their noses out of joint? In any case, the campaign crumbled under the clash of egos. When Rob decided to put his money into opening a hemp shop in Glastonbury and setting up a cannabis information club, the LCC found it was trading while insolvent and folded. (However it survives in Scotland. The Edinburgh organizer, Linda Hendry, managed to salvage a north-of-the-border membership list before the London office finally closed.) I diagnosed classic smoker's paranoia – a suggestion Rob found in rather poor taste. 'The paranoia goes with people who don't have trust and there had been a lot of bad shit going down. In those days people used to get sent to prison.'

Actually people still get sent to prison, especially if, like David, they have been caught in the aftermath of a large growing operation. The muddle and indecision of the activists are not shared by people who are aiming to make real money from cannabis, which David had to do for family reasons. He became what the law regards as a serious drugs trafficker as a means of getting his brother out of an Indian jail without telling his parents or asking for their help. The brother had been caught with two and a half kilos of charas when police had boarded his bus for a random check. The minimum sentence was ten years, under tough anti-cannabis laws introduced in 1987 under pressure from the Americans (making both brothers in effect victims of America's War on Drugs).

I interviewed David a few days before he was due to be sentenced at one of the notoriously unsympathetic Outer London Crown Courts. When I went over to his house I took him two bottles of wine: a Chablis, to drink right away, and a slow-maturing Bandol. Though I didn't spell it out, my theory was that the longer the sentence, the better the wine he would be drinking when he got out. He told me that setting up the big growing operation had been a simple decision, when he realized that he needed funds to bribe the witnesses at his brother's trial.

'You imagine your brother or sister in an Indian jail – although the Indian prison experiences were remarkably civilized – more civilized than an English jail. But there was no way I was going to tell the old man, after working all these years. If he'd heard about it he'd have come out there, they'd have smelt big money and taken the lot.'

Because he's hippyish-looking and in his twenties, David reckoned that he would pay a maximum of £20,000: in the event this was an over-estimate by £5,000 of the actual cost of fees for the lawyers and bribes for the witnesses. Then he went shopping. He needed a house, a set of sodium lights and some reliable ganga plants. Some of the lights – ten 40-watt lamps – came from a police auction of seized property and cost £30 apiece. 'It was a whole growing system: they still had fingerprint dust on them.' The cuttings came from mother plants grown from Dutch seeds (Misty, Shiva Shanti and Kriss Kross). The £3,000-worth of electricity was supplied free by London Electricity, thanks to a by-pass of the pre-digital metering system.

David said the idea wasn't theft, but to avoid a tell-tale electricity bill.

Cannabis thrives in an environment that's utterly different from a family's normal living conditions. During the period in which their energies go into putting on growth, the young plants like to be in a blinding light twenty-four hours a day. Even in the high-ceilinged, five-bedroomed house David chose, the heat produced by the lamps will become overwhelming, so the windows must be kept open. Fans must be placed in sequence to whirl the air cyclonically round the room, not just for ventilation, but to toughen the plants' stems. Once this strange world has been created it must be hidden. Drawn curtains are not enough to hide such strong lights; they have to be reinforced on the inside with plastic sheeting, slashed for ventilation (the light that leaks will scatter on the inside of the curtains and look like ordinary domestic lighting).

In October 1996 David settled in on a spare bit of the ground floor for the five-month duration. 'I'd purposely moved away from the area where my mates hang out, otherwise people would want to do dope tourism. People start talking and soon you've got PC Plod or a load of gangsters tearing the door down.[5] At that time I had my college degree to finish and my brother was still in India. I was smoking a lot – I'd brought back a half-kilo of charas – and I was worried and paranoid. One morning I woke up and there were lots of builders in the back garden, but that didn't come to anything. The good thing about London is that nobody gives a fuck. The landlord was a black guy, African, and he was very moody; but I'd changed all the locks and I knew he couldn't get in.'

For most of the growing period David's luck held. Then in the spring, by the time the plants were in nine-inch pots and the lights were giving a twelve-hour day and night flowering cycle, the landlord started insisting on his right of entry. He needed a surveyor's report on the property for a remortgage. 'Luckily I was ready to harvest, though if we'd have waited we could probably have got another two kilos.'

Even so, the 100 plants turned in an impressive twenty-seven kilos of top-class material. David had had a previous spell in a friend's grow-room; armed with this experience he dried the plants, trimmed the leaves off the buds, found customers and basked in compliments. By July he had started selling the stuff, but his attention was turning from business to his personal passion. The trimmed leaves and other remains of the plant had enough well-dried resin glands to make a little high-quality sieved hashish. He had left one house and was waiting to move into another, and was using a stay at a friend's flat as an opportunity to get to work with a sieve.

Just after 7 a.m. one Thursday morning, David was roused from the sofa where he was sleeping by the sound of nine police smashing down a door (not, as it happened, the right one. 'Don't worry, mate,' one of them reassured him. 'We're the police.' The prosecution would later tell the Crown Court judge that they had found a strong smell of cannabis in the flat and, after a search, just over six kilos of cannabis. David is sure he had more like ten, including some good-quality bud and a small bag of hashish powder. One of the cops, he says, put his nose in this bag and asked, 'What's this, sarge?' But they hadn't found the big growing operation that David thinks they had been expecting. One of the team had been 'a really nice cop, or maybe he was a bloke from the customs. He was saying, "You wouldn't believe the big hydro growing operation I just did." '

This officer soon left, leaving what turned out to be a bunch of police from the Burglary Squad to take their prisoner to the police station. David had mixed relations with them. At one point, he says, he goaded the sergeant into shouting, 'You're lucky you're English, you fucking hippie,' before colleagues hustled the man out of the room. 'The copper was implying that if I was black I'd get a good kicking,' David said. 'My black mates are getting searched all the time.' But he was also lucky to be charged with six kilos rather than twenty-two. Four kilos never turned up on the charge sheet – a certain leakage is often reported of seized drugs in police care. There was a further twelve kilos of bud at another house. David had the keys on him when he was searched, but the police failed to follow up the lead. If they had done so, and if he had been facing an American court, he would have gone to jail for a long time – a mandatory minimum of five years without parole, under the 1984 Sentencing Reform Act.

But in Britain, it seems to be conventionally agreed among many law enforcement officers that pot isn't a real crime. The angry detective sergeant also told David that his wife smoked to relieve her PMT. Later, at one of David's court appearances, he would be flanked in the dock by two hired security guards, who'd surreptitiously ask him, 'Was it skunk, mate?' in appreciative tones. They're members of the same culture as the young customs man who questioned me on my return from Morocco and who grinned and said 'Magic!' when I told him I was writing about cannabis.

While David awaited sentence in the summer of 1998, other forces were gathering. From the United States, Canada and Australia and half a dozen European countries, activists, lawyers and doctors were flying to London to discuss, not the rights and wrongs of legalizing cannabis, but how to go about it.

11

Conspiracies

A properly funded, professionally organized cannabis legalization campaign is not part of the British political landscape. But this phenomenon made a brief appearance amid the lakes and lawns of Regent's Park on the weekend of 5 September 1998, when the financier George Soros paid for a conference on 'Regulating Cannabis', capitalizing on a widespread feeling that change was at last in sight.

Everyone was at Regent's College: the moving spirits behind the Dutch coffee shops and the Californian medical marijuana movement; the men in suits from the American pressure groups – the National Association for the Reform of Marijuana Laws, the Drug Policy Foundation and Soros's own Lindesmith Center. Plus there were Glenn Jenkins and Mick Anthony from Exodus; Geoffrey Guy; the drugs charity Release, who were the joint organizers; Tim Malyon and Don Aitken, who has been in one of the UK's five cannabis campaigns (there were both mark one and mark two versions of the Legalize Cannabis Campaign). There was almost a full complement of the people whose books sit on shelves hand-labelled 'Scumbags' in gothic script in the Slough home of Peter and Ann Stoker of the National Drugs Prevention Alliance (only the psychiatrist Lester Grinspoon of Harvard Medical School, author of *Marijuana Reconsidered* and *Marijuana, Forbidden Medicine*, was missing). The delegates were refreshed with satay and spring rolls between sessions and the speakers ended the day over dinner at the Groucho Club.

Yet in spite of that year's events – the *Independent on Sunday* campaign in Britain, the victory of the American states referenda on medical marijuana, spreading decriminalization in Europe – the mood was less upbeat than the words of the key speakers. The leading campaigners also brought with them the experience of disappointment, after years of political battles, at seeing legalized pot turn from a sure thing to a lost cause. I guessed they had all met up at many such events.

Lester Grinspoon, whose unseen presence hovered over the proceedings, had written in 1977 that given the increasingly 'sensible' terms of the marijuana debate, 'It is likely that within a decade marijuana will be sold in the United States as a legal intoxicant.' This prophecy looked entirely reasonable in the mid-1970s. At that time eleven states had removed all penalties for minor possession offences, and in 1978 President Carter backed decriminalization.

But public opinion, which is making younger activists feel so optimistic, doesn't inevitably move in a single direction. It was also in 1978 that the first poll for a decade appeared to show a fall in the number of adults supporting legalization. In an article published in 1993 in the magazine Reason,[1] Jacob Sullum quotes the Gallup figures as 28 per cent in 1977, falling to 25 per cent in 1978 and plunging to around 16 per cent by the late 1980s. At the same time marijuana use among teenagers began declining, from peaks recorded in 1978 and 1979.[2]

Activists and libertarians point with justified horror at the repression of the 1980s 'War on Drugs' – paraquat-spraying on marijuana crops, DEA narcs on the nation's campuses, forfeiture, interminable minimum sentences – but this could not have been initiated with public support. What's more, the mood began to change before the big spending public information programmes of the Reagan era designed to promote the 'Just Say No' message: as Jacob Sullum points out, people were simply scared by the speed of the change – use among high-school students had reached an all-time high in 1979 when more than 60 per cent of leavers had tried marijuana.

This can be a hard fact to swallow. All activists tend to believe so much in their message that they require the existence of a malign and all-powerful force to explain the fact that the world has not yet been converted. For me, the fascination of the Release-Lindesmith conference lay not only in the platform speakers, but in the leaflets offered to delegates, stacked on tables near the registration area. These were my first introduction to the great cannabis conspiracy theories. I heard for the first time about Henry Ford's hemp car, that the diesel engine was originally designed to run on hemp-seed oil. It may even have been there that I first came across the phrase 'decorticating machine': essential if you're to keep your end up in a hemp conversation. The essential point is that America's first federal law against cannabis was passed 'to secure the financial profits of DuPont and other petrochemical and timber interests who were threatened by new technical developments using the hemp plant' (the decorticating machine, in fact). This law created a job for life for FBI man Harry Anslinger, J. Edgar Hoover's former head of Prohibition enforcement, who carved out a fresh empire with the new Federal Bureau of Narcotics, subsequently rechristened by Richard Nixon the Drug Enforcement Administration (of which the pill-popping Elvis Presley was an early honorary badge-holder). Cannabis prohibition therefore unites big business, federal spooks and the destruction of the environment, not to mention the Moral Majority and fundamentalist Conservatives. With enemies like these, how can the legalization activists go wrong?

But is it actually true? The history of the legal control of drugs offers some solid landmarks in a shifting sea of 'interesting if true' factoids.[3]

In Britain, sales even of outright poisons were not controlled before the Arsenic Act of 1851; then the Pharmacy Act of 1868 specified that opium and laudanum must be sold in a container labelled 'poison' – a sort of equivalent of the health warning on cigarettes – while allowing the unrestricted sale of many opium-based patent medicines. There was no outright ban on consciousness-altering drugs before the Defence of the Realm Act of 1916, and cannabis was not made illegal until the Dangerous Drugs Act of 1925.

So cannabis stayed legal in Britain (and America) throughout the nineteenth century. It had arrived as a consequence of European imperialism, which gave Britain and France dominance over countries where hashish use was long established. The novelist and historian of cannabis A. D. Harvey describes the first systematic use of hashish by the British in India in the 1770s when the Muslim ruler Hyder Ali captured some English and Scots soldiers serving with the British East India company; they were circumcized and given *maajūn* to deaden the pain of the operation. They were kept under guard for the next ten years and occasionally given more *maajūn*. Later one of the prisoners recalled: 'This opiate is made, either into liquid or solid, with sugar, from the boang tree, the produce of which they smoke with tobacco. It causes the most astonishing sensations. In the course of a few years we were in the habit of smoking it freely to drown our troubles and we well knew its effects.'[4]

Jack Herer's *The Emperor Wears No Clothes* gives the impression that cannabis was welcomed and accepted everywhere before the 1930s' 'conspiracy' to make it illegal. The picture is more complicated. When Napoleon invaded Egypt the French imposed a ban on hashish, although, like the Mameluk sultans' earlier prohibitions, it was generally disregarded.[5] Hashish may have been widely smoked in Egypt at the time, but respectable people disapproved. The orientalist Edward Lane, who lived in Cairo for a quarter of a century to study Islam, called it a 'pernicious and degrading custom' and notes that 'the term hashshash is a term of obloquy. Noisy and riotous people are called hashshasheen.'[6]

Although cannabis was a side issue, the last century saw the start of campaigns to restrict the availability of opium, then the most important and widely used drug. It's true that Victorian authors could sound startlingly casual about what we would call hard drug use – the classic example being Sherlock Holmes's practice of fighting boredom by injecting himself with his favourite '7 per cent solution' of cocaine. But the rise of controls on drugs came in response to a long campaign. It began with resistance to the Opium Wars fought by Britain in 1839–42 and 1856–8 to browbeat the Chinese Government into accepting imports of the drug from British India. A Society for the Suppression of the Opium Trade was founded in 1876, with Lord Shaftesbury, the philanthropist commemorated by the statue of Eros in Piccadilly Circus, becoming its president four years later.

Opium, at once painkiller, child-quietener and 'recreational drug', was central to Victorian people's lives. Victoria Berridge and Griffith Edwards, authors of *Opium and the People – Opiate Use in Nineteenth-century England*, describe the 'anti-opiumists' as an élite group, lacking the mass base of the earlier campaigns against the Corn Laws or slavery, but which, with doctors well represented in its ranks, managed to establish a distinction between legitimate medical drugs and drugs taken out of 'viciousness' or 'curiosity' – a distinction that's still central in the medical cannabis debate.

For modern activists, the crowning glory of the nineteenth century was the finding of the Indian Hemp Drugs Commission of 1895 that 'moderate use . . . is attended by practically no ill effects'. But the Commission's very existence is testimony to concerns about cannabis. In a Parliamentary Question in 1891, Mark Steward MP asked whether the Secretary of State for India had seen newspaper reports that 'the lunatic asylums of Bengal are full of ganga smokers'.[7] The Government line in 1891 was to restate the policy of the viceroy nearly twenty years before that while the intention was to reduce the use of these 'noxious' preparations, it would be impractical to ban them because of the offence caused to some groups' religious feelings. A new Liberal Government set up the Hemp Commission which 'demolished', according to Berridge and Edwards, the suggestion that cannabis caused insanity, including in its many pages J. M. Campbell's poetic 'Note on the Religion of Hemp'.[8] Cannabis wasn't the only drug exonerated in 1895; that year also saw the publication of the report of a long-called-for Royal Commission on Opium which infuriated the anti-opium movement with its finding that the drug was used in India 'for the most part without injurious consequences'.

But the issue wasn't closed. In Egypt the superintendent of the Cairo asylum, a Dr Warnock, published a report on 'hashish insanity'[9] the same year, which drew opposite conclusions from those of the Hemp Commission. The Egyptian authorities – who were in effect a branch of the British colonial service – finally got their point of view across at the second international Opium Conference, held in 1924–5 in Geneva. Dr El Guindy told the delegates that 'acute hashishism' caused delirium and insanity, which in the long term led to 'physical and mental deterioration'. Although the British abstained in the vote they fulfilled their obligation to the League of Nations by including cannabis in a new Dangerous Drugs Act.

While the ruling circles in Egypt regarded hashish as a vice, they saw it as different in kind from heroin, which was just then beginning to devastate the lives of the poor. In his memoirs

Egyptian Service 1902–1944, the police chief Sir Thomas Wentworth Russell Pasha recalled: 'I did a lot of night-time prowling
in those days and knew by heart my way around the slums where
the roughs and the cackling laughter of the hashish dens were by
now giving way to the emaciated shadows of heroin addicts
slinking around the offal bins.' Professor Sabry Hafez of London
University's School of Oriental and African Studies believes that
the main reason for the official dislike of hashish-smoking was its
cultural link with subversion and disrespect for authority.

Mexico rapidly turned the Geneva conferences into domestic
law and made marijuana illegal from December 1925. The
United States did not; the American delegation walked out
from Geneva to protest at the convention's failure to outlaw
opium production and to bring in a ban on heroin that would
have included medical use. 'Otherwise,' says the historian Dr
David Musto, 'I'm sure that we would have had prohibition of
cannabis in 1925.' Instead there was a succession of prohibitions
by individual states, but no federal US ban on marijuana until the
Marihuana Tax Act of 1937.

And here comes the conspiracy. Many people believe, as I have
described earlier, that marijuana prohibition came about because
synthetic fibre manufacturers wanted to eliminate hemp as a
competitor. The theory has the effect of discrediting and
ridiculing the persecution of marijuana smokers, which is something I would also like to see happen. And it's true that a small
and struggling hemp industry in the mid-West was further
shackled by the bureaucratic attentions post-1937 of the Federal
Bureau of Narcotics. But it's hard to swallow the grand cabal,
involving the Hearst newspaper group's investment in forestry
for paper and DuPont, supposedly concerned by the development of a decorticating machine for stripping hemp fibre from
the plant stems which would have transformed the hemp

industry. Jack Herer, the chief architect of the conspiracy theory, is zealous about tracking down documentary sources. He offers a passage from DuPont's 1937 annual report which warns shareholders that the company cannot accurately predict its future tax liabilities, in part because 'The revenue raising power of government may be converted into an instrument for forcing acceptance of sudden new ideas of industrial and social reorganization.' How stoned do you have to be to mistake that for a smoking gun? Try as I may I cannot squeeze from this phrase any suggestion that DuPont cared about decorticators or even regarded hemp as a serious competitor.

Professor Richard Bonnie of the law faculty of the University of Virginia was together with his colleague Professor Charles Whitebread given access to all the files, open and closed, of the predecessor of the Drug Enforcement Administration – the Federal Bureau of Narcotics. Together they wrote a frequently hilarious book called *The Marihuana Conviction – the Legal History of Drugs in the United States*, which is currently being reprinted by the pro-legalization Lindesmith Center and is quoted at length by Jack Herer. Professor Bonnie wrote the book before the conspiracy theory was developed but told me, 'I would be sceptical about it. Based on what I know it would surprise me.' The Wisconsin plant breeder and hemp enthusiast David West has documented the damage that red tape did to America's small hemp industry after the 1937 Act came into force. He originally took the DuPont conspiracy theory on trust – for no real reason, he said, other than that it had had such an airing in the media. But he changed his mind after a detailed study of the American fibre industry of the period. 'The notion that the Treasury Department could be involved in promoting DuPont's interests begs credulity,' he said.

David West's monograph in Ed Rosenthal's *Hemp Today* makes it clear that American corporations do fight dirty and

engage in conspiracies; DuPont helped secretly fund a body in
the mid-1930s called the Farmers' Independence Council,
which campaigned against farm subsidies. (Rather as companies including DuPont and drinks and tobacco firms would
more than half a century later bankroll the Coalition for a
Drug-free America.) But hemp does not emerge as any kind of
competitor to DuPont. West shows it to have been 'pinched
between cotton, flax and . . . tropical imports' and starved of
federal support. If anything, the greatest enemy of hemp was
its close relative the flax industry, whose leaders railed against
wartime subsidies for 'this narcotic [dope] plant'. Flax died
around the same time as hemp, with no accusations of foul
play.

What is certain is that Americans in the 1920s and 1930s were
in the grip of moral panic about 'dope'. The right to be
intoxicated had after all been suspended during Prohibition,
and marijuana, if taken in sufficient quantity, produces all the
effects of being stoned. It's obvious from the contemporary
evidence that no American legislator had the least knowledge of
marijuana or interest in its toxicity or addictiveness when
compared to heroin or cocaine. The fact that it was favoured
by Mexican immigrant workers and black jazz musicians was
enough to condemn it. A total of two questions were asked –
both by a republican senator from upstate New York – in the
brief hearing which led to the criminalization of marijuana. The
first was: 'Mr Speaker, what is this bill about?' To which the
Speaker replied: 'I don't know. It has something to do with a
thing called marijuana. I think it's a narcotic of some kind.' As
Professor Bonnie points out, the story of how marijuana came to
be prohibited is sufficiently powerful without invoking a conspiracy.

In the Bonnie–Whitebread history the funniest part of all
describes the ignorance of the authorities of the drug they'd just

banned. Commissioner Harry Anslinger, who had previously been in charge of enforcing alcohol prohibition for the FBI, found just one expert, Dr James C. Munch, of the Pharmacology Department of Temple University in Pennsylvania, to agree about the perils of marijuana: thirty-nine out of the forty-two he invited to a specialist conference on the drug politely disclaimed any knowledge of the subject, and the representative of the American Medical Association refused to accept that marijuana was dangerous. In the absence of fresh information Commissioner Anslinger reasserted the claim, which had been circulating in the American press for a decade or more, that 'Marihuana is a dangerous drug which produces in its users insanity, criminality and death.'

Criminal lawyers pricked up their ears at this. A new defence strategy began appearing at murder trials in the late 1930s and early 1940s: not guilty by reason of insanity caused by marijuana use. In one case the defence did not even try to show that a double police murderer had actually smoked marijuana – only that a bag of weed in his room had given off 'homicidal vibrations' causing the accused to kill dogs, cats and finally the two policemen. The jury bought it, as they did in the other marijuana defences of the period, and the legend of 'reefer madness' became entrenched in American culture.

After researching the history of marijuana prohibition in the United States, Professor Charles Whitebread reached an awesomely simple conclusion. He told the Californian Judges Association at their 1995 annual conference: 'The iron law of prohibitions – all of them – is that they are passed by an identifiable US to control the conduct of an identifiable THEM.'[10] He put this case hilariously and compellingly – citing, for example, Britain's selective ban on gin between 1840 and 1880, and California's selective enforcement of the

state laws against gambling: 'Would we be outraged if the
California State Police came barrelling through the door and
arrested us for violation of California's prohibition on gambling?
Of course we would. Because who is not supposed to gamble?
. . . them poor people, that's who. My God, they will spend the
milk money. They don't know how to control it. They can't
handle it. But us? We know what we are doing.' He might also
have mentioned the disproportionate effort the American justice
system puts into targeting crack cocaine, which is used by poor
people, compared to powder cocaine, the favourite drug of
Hollywood and Wall Street.

The same argument has been made in a British context – in
particular by Marek Cohn in his book *Dope Girls – the Birth of
the British Drug Underground*, which puts Britain's first drug laws
in the context of a racial panic over London's small Chinese
community. When I first came across Cohn's argument I'm
afraid I read it as: drugs + anti-racism = self-indulgence +
enjoyable hand-wringing. It took the *Daily Mail* to make me
ashamed of my cynicism. In a 'special report' of 12 January
1999 headed 'Suburbia's Little Somalia', Jo-Ann Goodwin
produced a classic of its genre, dealing with the arrival of
12,000 khat-chewing Somali refugees in the leafy streets of
suburban Ealing. This amphetamine-like drug dominated –
you might say rescued – what at times seemed a rather thin
exposé. 'Moslem and Arabic pronouncements cover the walls,'
noted Ms Goodwin, 'alternating with offers for bulk-buy
spaghetti and flyers for Italian grocers.' Blimey! 'Groups of
men drink milky African tea and order plates of lamb and rice.
Around 4 p.m. things pick up. The daily consignment of Khat
is due at any moment.' This provided some material for a
reporter faced with making bricks without straw in the absence
of anyone to talk to: 'Hostile, aggressive and suspicious, they
appeared antagonistic to any outsider.' Until, that is, she went

up to a young guy chosen at random and asked if he would sell her some khat. 'He walked me down a side street, dipped into his rucksack and produced two bundles. He hoped my husband would enjoy it. Women don't chew khat.' The feature cites a UN report linking khat with psychosis, liver damage and cancer and quotes the National Criminal Intelligence Service as suggesting that Britain is becoming a 'clearing house' for world-wide khat distribution.

For the Somalis in London in 1999 read the Mexicans who came looking for work in the south-west of the United States from 1915 onwards. In his speech to the Californian judges, Professor Whitebread quoted a couple of statements for the debates over laws against marijuana in the individual states. A speaker in the Texas Senate told his fellow legislators: 'All Mexicans are crazy and this stuff is what makes them crazy.' The Montana State Assembly heard a similar claim: 'Give one of these Mexican beet field workers a couple of puffs on a marijuana cigarette and he thinks he is in the bullring at Barcelona.'

Although Britain had laws against cannabis, there were few prosecutions until the start of post-war immigration from the West Indies. Then British newspapers began running pieces which display quite as much discomfort about black people as they do about reefer smoking. The *Sunday Graphic* ran inadvertently hilarious exposés two Sundays in a row, on 16 and 23 September 1951. The reporter John Ralph told readers: 'After several weeks I have just completed exhaustive inquiries into the most insidious vice Scotland Yard has ever been called up to tackle – dope peddling.'

Detectives on the assignment are agreed that they have never had experience of a crime so vicious, so ruthless and unpitying and so well organized. Hemp, marijuanha (*sic*) and hashish represent a thoroughly unsavoury trade.

'One of the detectives told me: "We are dealing with the most evil men who have ever taken to the vice business."

'The victims are teen-age British girls and, to a lesser extent, teen-age youths . . .

'The racketeers (or peddlers) are 90 per cent coloured men from the West Indies and west coast of Africa.

'How serious the situation is, how great the danger to our social structure, may be gathered from the fact that despite increasing police attention, despite several raids, there are more than a dozen clubs in London's West End at which drugs are peddled.

'As a result of my inquiries, I share the fears of detectives on the job that there is the gravest danger of the reefer craze becoming the greatest social menace this country has known.

'The other day I sat in a tawdry West End Club.

'I was introduced by a member, a useful contact both to me and the police.

'Drinks sold were nothing stronger than lukewarm black coffee, 'near' beer or orangeade.

'I watched the dancing. My contact and I were two of six white men. I counted twenty-eight coloured men and some thirty white girls. None of the girls looked more than twenty-five.

'In a corner five coloured musicians, brows perspiring, played bebop music with extraordinary fervour.

'Girls and coloured partners danced with an abandon – a savagery almost – which was both fascinating and embarrassing.

'From a doorway came a coloured man, flinging away the end of a strange cigarette.

'He danced peculiar convulsions on his own, then bounced to a table and held out shimmering arms to a girl.

'My contact indicated photographs on the walls. They were of girls in the flimsiest draping.

' "They are, or were, members," I was told.
'We went outside. I had seen enough of my first bebop club,
its coloured peddlers, its half-crazed uncaring young girls.'

Doesn't it sound your kind of place? The following year saw the
publication of the glorious *Indian Hemp – A Social Menace* by the
Tory MP Donald McIntosh Johnson. Taking his cue from
American Cold War fears that the Reds were using drugs to
subvert the American young, Johnson drew attention to an
obscure statistic: Board of Trade returns for flour imports from
the Soviet Union, measured by the hundredweight: 13,440,277
in 1948, down to 4,067,842 the following year, but rising steeply
to 13,504,079 in 1950. His suggestion was that the Soviets might
use cannabis-treated flour to brainwash Britain's population.
How? He referred to the possibility of altered brain-wave
patterns created by reefer-smoking in hot jazz clubs: 'For the
rhythm of the bass drum substitute the rhythm of totalitarian
propaganda and the point which I wish to make will be
appreciated.' (In the event it was Mr Johnson's American allies
who took up the idea of psychedelic drugs as a chemical warfare
agent, with the CIA's sometimes lethal use of unsuspecting
agents and servicemen as LSD guinea-pigs.)

One of the prescient pieces of reporting in that decade was
carried by the *Evening Standard* on 5 September 1951. The paper
noted: 'This year dope peddlers are reported to have searched
Oxford and Cambridge to see if there is a market for hashish
among undergraduates taking examinations.' Perhaps students
actually facing their finals papers weren't the most obvious
consumer group; but the dealers had clearly improved their
marketing by the time Howard Marks went up to Balliol less
than a generation later.

These days people who encountered pot-smoking at university hold public office, but legalization seems if anything more

distant than when the previous generation was in power. When it was running its legalization campaign under Rosie Boycott's editorship, the *Independent on Sunday* wrote to Labour cabinet ministers asking if they'd ever smoked pot. A large majority refused to comment. In 1998 Phil Woolas, a former student politician, now a Labour MP, was invited on television to discuss his claim that gangs of cannabis addicts were on a crime spree. The producer, Clare Handford was so outraged by his remarks in the green room that she passed them on to the diary writer of the *Independent*. Woolas had told her, she said, 'People like us could smoke a joint and it wouldn't do us any harm but if you're a working-class kid from Manchester it's a different matter.' Four years earlier Woolas had fought a bitterly contested by-election at Littleborough and Saddleworth in Lancashire and lost it to a Liberal Democrat called Chris Davies. Davies is that comparative rarity: a forty-five-year-old who is adamant that he's never smoked a joint. None the less he had spoken at the Lib Dems Party Conference in 1993 in favour of the policy that there should be a Royal Commission to study the question of legalizing drugs. He asked: 'If even soft drugs are bad, why is it at conference time that there's a queue a mile long whenever the Scotch Whisky Association holds a reception? As politicians we're a bunch of hypocrites – out of touch, trailing behind our law enforcers, and too frightened to stick our heads above the parapet. And with good reason, because we risk being shot at. Rival politicians are all too ready to score cheap political points against any opponent who dares to address this issue seriously.'

Davies soon found out the truth of his prophecy when he faced a Labour election machine personally directed by Peter Mandelson. 'During the Littleborough and Saddleworth campaign it came up every single day. It was on almost every single piece of Labour literature. I did one public meeting and the question came up directly. The Tory and Phil Woolas gave their

weasel words – then I gave my position and why I regarded the
current policy as going nowhere. I got a massive round of
applause.' After being elected, Chris Davies found himself one of
only two MPs who openly called for decriminalization. The
other is Paul Flynn, the Welsh Labour MP whose geniality is
unimpaired by abstinence, not only from pot, but from alcohol
and, despite chronic arthritis, from pharmaceutical drugs as well.

Davies says he keeps as battle honours the mound of Labour
literature from the by-election campaign – a petition form saying
'No, I do not want rave parties in Littleborough and Saddleworth', stories headed 'Families must be protected, says Labour
MP', 'Storm as Lib Dem calls for legal drugs', 'Lib Dems go to
pot', 'Top cop says Davies is wrong', etc., etc. One phrase came
to symbolize the campaign: 'Chris Davies – high on tax and soft
on drugs.' Later I discovered that a friend of mine had coined it
with Peter Mandelson during a hilarious session in a pub. He
explained that the problem had been to re-brand Phil Woolas as
something other than a student politico. 'The basic idea was to
sell him as a local hill farmer,' I was told. Hence campaign
literature picturing a grinning Woolas with two prize pigs, the
assertion that 'Phil Woolas's Pennine roots go deep', a photo of
him with the same grin beside 'Booth Wood dam built by his
grandfather, Thomas White'. I should say that in the many years
I've known my friend I can't ever remember seeing him spliffing
up. But he did spend his year before university travelling to
Afghanistan in a VW van christened 'Pigpen' in honour of one
of the original members of The Grateful Dead.

12

Luck of the Draw

I'm experiencing feelings of confusion, disorientation and panic – a kind of flashback to my misspent student years. It's the recurring nightmare where you're sitting an exam for which you're underprepared. What was the Morgan Report? Can I distinguish between Drug Action Teams and Drug Reference Groups – or between Tackling Drugs to Build a Better Britain and Building a Better Britain: A Ten-year Strategy for Tackling Drug Misuse? There are four of us in a small room on the ninth floor of New Scotland Yard – Nicky Redwood, a young woman trainee, who notes down the conversation, Lisa-Jo-Deyt-Aysage from the Metropolitan Police's public relations branch, and London's own drug czar, Commander Andy Hayman, the recently appointed head of the Met's Drug Directorate, a department which, at the time of our interview, is just a fortnight old.

Andy Hayman is young and spiky-looking, with a sparse moustache. He looks hard at me and pounces when I ask him to explain the phrase 'arrest referral'. It would have helped, I'm fairly gently informed, if I'd done my homework before turning up.

But I'm not prepared to accept all the responsibility for the interview going somewhat adrift. Commander Hayman has just launched a poster campaign costing £250,000 with the theme 'A crackdown on drugs is a crackdown on crime'. A skinny, sinisterly lit guy is pictured above the words 'I am a heroin addict. I only mug people when I'm desperate. I get desperate every thirty-six hours.' The point is to get the public to ring an anonymous number with 'any information they have about the misuse of drugs'. I want to hear that this has a more precise goal than to build up a London-wide database of drug users. And if this is his somewhat chilling aim, I'd mean-spiritedly prefer him to maintain files on heavily addicted smackheads, as being in more urgent need of funds, and hence more criminally disposed, than on the sort of people I know. He appears to be infringing Professor Charles Whitebread's Iron Rule of Prohibitions that they are something We do to Them. But Andy Hayman can't offer this reassurance. 'You're making massive assumptions,' he replies, when I suggest that television producers don't need to go in for crime to pay for cocaine, any more than they need to pay for Chablis or single malt whisky. He's out to challenge such accepted wisdoms; one successful foray, he tells me, has been against the idea that drug-related crimes are linked to 'youth culture' as represented by nineteen to twenty-four-year-olds; he thinks the main correlation takes place among the older, twenty-eight to thirty-five age group.

Actually I would associate 'youth culture' with the less dangerous drugs, perhaps because I've been conditioned to believe in people 'graduating' to more dangerous drugs. But this distinction between addictive and non-addictive drugs and their behavioural consequences is one that Commander Hayman is resisting. (A colleague of his later tells me, with a grave air of revelation, that cannabis is regularly found in the urine samples of street robbers.) 'There's no such thing as a safe drug,' he says. 'I must remind you of a view expressed by Keith Hellawell (national Drug Czar, or Drug Policy Co-ordinator): "Why are we saying soft and hard drugs?" '

I'm grateful to get this interview. The Customs Investigation Unit shillied and shallied, saying that Government policy did not make cannabis a main priority, asking for a list of questions and then returning written replies so uninformative you wonder why they bother to staff a press office (perhaps it's used to train civil servants in obfuscation). Keith Hellawell wouldn't do it either (his interview in the *Guardian* a week or so earlier had carried almost no discussion on drugs policy). But this new-style cop, freshly arrived at the Met from Essex police, and proudly putting MA after his name on his business card, has mistaken me for someone worth making his mark with (perhaps because Lisa-Jo Deyt-Aysage bought my wine book for her husband the Christmas before last – nice one, Lisa-Jo).

My analysis is that Commander Hayman's newness in office makes him willing to be interviewed but not to talk revealingly. (The most heartfelt talk I ever had on this subject was with a Home Office official nearing retirement in the early 1980s, when he confided his regret that Britain stopped supplying heroin addicts on prescription.) Andy Hayman is annoyed at my lack of interest in targets, strategy documents and multi-disciplinary teams; I'm disappointed that he'll barely discuss cannabis (though I hardly expect him to scuttle his career by mentioning, as old sweats in drugs squads sometimes do, that he thinks it ought to be legalized).

What I'd like is a justification of the role of the police in regulating drugs. The poster campaign would be a good start. This breaks new ground in telling people that they're at risk of assault from heroin users, rather than taking the usual course of denouncing pushers, or the unusual one of regarding addiction primarily as a personal disaster. When I later call Mike Goodman, director of Release, he describes the heroin poster as 'Absolutely fucking awful. It implies that the majority of people involved with heroin are not only likely to commit crime but are likely to go out and mug people, which just isn't true.' So I call Andy Hayman back at his office to ask for the evidence to support the 'muggers' poster. I expect him to be furious, but actually he thanks me for the opportunity to defend his brain-child from a critical mauling and says he'll ring back when he's found the statistics behind the heroin poster. He later calls me back and disarmingly tells me that there aren't any.

Earlier I'd asked him whether he believed that police action reduced the overall level of drug use, instead of displacing it from targeted areas. He told me this was 'a philosophical argument. It doesn't add much to doing the job out there. It's a very complex area of policy.' So all sorts of 'philosophical' questions are ruled out. We both know that in cases of assault, the drug that is overwhelmingly implicated is alcohol. It's also undeniable that the police make heroin more expensive by their attempts to 'stifle its availability', in Keith Hellawell's phrase, so making it more profitable to dealers and giving addicts more reason to have to steal to pay for it. The official line that there are no soft and hard drugs makes Commander Hayman cast a net that will catch nearly half the population, if his target is drug-related crime and smoking cannabis is, as he tells me, a drug-related crime. I think he realizes the lack of underlying logic. However, the drug bureaucracies need cannabis partly for institutional reasons, as the scale of use turns drug use into a 'massive problem' requiring a commensurate response. (One charity currently solicits funds with posters saying 40 per cent of children will use drugs – which is true only if you count weed – and a huge image of a syringe.) This is what he says when I suggest that when it comes to enforcement, many police have stopped seeing cannabis as a real crime.

'I'd describe it in a different way. We've got to recognize that there are competing priorities. In the UK the priority is putting greater emphasis on those who supply those drugs that cause the most harm: heroin or crack cocaine. It shouldn't be taken that cannabis has fallen off the agenda. What it is is recognizing the feedback: does society want us to be targeting cannabis when compared with heroin or crack cocaine? It's illegal and it's not good sense to be legitimizing its use, but nevertheless we haven't got infinite resources.'

What does this mean in practice? There may not be 'infinite resources', but cannabis offences still make up a large majority of all drugs prosecutions in Britain. The Met spent a fortune on its operation against the gangsters with their highly lucrative business selling £10 draws of weed and 'black' to members of the Back Beat club. Yet despite a total of forty-seven arrests and the seizure of £250,000 worth of cannabis and £150,000 in cash, two months later only two people have been charged. This seems a scant return for an operation involving six months of photographic and videotape surveillance culminating in a raid by more than 500 police, many of them armed, and led by a Deputy Assistant Commissioner.

But David didn't manage to slip through the net after he was caught red-handed with six kilos of home-grown weed, and I had the opportunity to witness his treatment at the hands of the criminal justice system. He came to trial in a modern Outer London Crown Court only a few weeks after we first met on a pavement in Brixton. I couldn't remember his surname and spent some time puzzling over the lists pinned up in the corridor, but it turned out to be easy to find him: his friends were the nice young people in the corridor who looked out of place. When the case was called I sat with them at the back of the court, then moved up to the press bench so I could see David. He'd cut his ponytail and put on an antique suit, but looked bedraggled and red-eyed. Nothing much happened at the hearing. It turned out that its point was to hear David's plea (Guilty), to order probation service reports and to set a date for the court appearance at which he would be actually sentenced.

★   ★   ★

The judge at the first hearing didn't 'reserve' the case to himself, so when David came back to court six weeks later he had no way of knowing if he'd be facing a liberal or a hard nut. The same gaggle met in the corridor, then went for a coffee in the courtroom canteen, trying to arrange themselves sociably on benches bolted into place on the floor. David's brother Jim was there, looking so clean-cut it seemed a pity he couldn't change places in the dock with his rumpled and hungover brother. In the cafeteria I started to try to pump Jim for the details of his two trials in India, how he'd come to be arrested in the bus, the mechanics of the witness-bribing. David glowered uncomfortably. 'Not here, mate.' Stupid of me.

This judge looked worse than the first one: thin-lipped and old-maidish. Counsel for the Crown got on his feet. David was not just up for sentence; he also faced the provisions of the Drug Trafficking Act which provides for forfeiture of dealer's proceeds. He said: 'It's right to say that the basis of the plea was notified to me and to the court on the basis that there were no financial transactions taking place and he had made no financial gain.'

As I know that most of the large sums David made from his growing operation went to spring Jim from jail in India, I have no difficulty in maintaining a grave expression while this farrago is paraded before the judge, who now looks puzzled but not unsympathetic. The Crown have inadvertently knocked ten years off the youthful-looking David's age, making him nineteen rather than twenty-nine. The judge tries to imagine himself into contemporary campus life. 'So it's that he had possession with intent to supply in order to, er, share the smoke that he was growing with his student friends?' Well, yes, m'lud.

The prosecution counsel is being tremendously nice. He keeps using a phrase much loved by barristers – 'It's right to say' – which can mean nothing, but in this case signifies that he's accepting the defence case. He says: 'It's only from the basis of the plea that the Crown can say that he was responsible for the growing' – in other words, give David credit for his frankness: generous credit seeing that he was found with (unwired-up) lights, various whole plants, hashish powder and hashish-making equipment.

He was also found with £4,840 in the flat. In the last six weeks David has somehow managed to account for most of this money – which was, as the police rightly suspected, part of the proceeds of selling his weed. He has a copy of a vehicle registration document to show his car passed out of his hands at that time and he is claiming that nearly all the cash in the flat is the money he got for it.

Now the Crown barrister says something which ought to ensure David at most a brief stay as guest of Her Majesty and the return of the money. 'It is the view of the police after investigation that the defendant has not benefited financially. For these reasons and because of the state of the evidence the Crown submits that it would be wholly inappropriate and a waste of court time to go through the procedure of a Drug Trafficking Act hearing.' In other words, the prosecution do not believe they can contest David's claim that he was working on a no-profit basis and so it won't pursue a request that had already been put in for forfeiture of the money.

It's going swimmingly. But then the judge interjects: 'Is *nobody* going to tell me what 5.95 kilos of herbal cannabis in the condition in which it was found is worth – or not? I know the case is that he's going to supply it for nothing, but do I get *any* indication as to value? I mean, is it worth £2.50 . . . or £250 . . . or £2,500?'

The truth is that it's going to be hard to massage the figure down to anything like as little as £2,500. And when confronted with a much higher figure, can the judge still believe, or even pretend to believe, that students today, however idealistic, make such generous presents to their friends? It's essential to get him off this tack. The defence guy tries to assure him of the plants' low quality, then warns of an interminable delay and a defence demand for Legal Aid to challenge any value the Crown arrives at. But the judge, increasingly riled at the realization that defence and prosecution have sewn things up before stepping into his court, is having none of it. He adjourns the case for three weeks pending a lab report on the value of David's seized plants. 'Three weeks?' snorts one or other of the barristers as they sweep out of court. 'With the speed the lab's working at they won't have a result in three months.' The open air has a horrible effect on David, who is still weak from last night's session in the pub, and he's sick in the shrubs around the Crown Court car park.

Because all his friends have so recently taken time off, I'm the only person who can accompany David for the unplanned sequel three weeks later. He gives me his girlfriend's work number and asks me to let her know if he's sent down there and then. This seems to be on the cards, following a change of prosecuting counsel. The new man would like to rip up the deal done by his predecessor. He tells the judge, who is also new: 'I have to say that having come fresh to this case today I find that an unusual matter, to have accepted quite so readily nearly six kilos as not involving personal gain.' I can't look at David. 'If my predecessor does absolutely feel that the basis of the plea is accepted, both should have signed a note.' In other words, no note, no deal.

But David's barrister swats away the challenge. The previous prosecutor had spoken in open court and his concession is recorded. If his successor doesn't believe it he'll ask the court officials to play through the tapes till they find it. So as fast as it arose, the danger passes; the prosecutor is reduced to stating his 'strong reservations'. To no one's surprise the Crown has not come up with a detailed costing, just the Drugs Intelligence Unit's note of current drug prices per kilo, and it is no surprise either that the defence won't accept this. So, another adjournment.

Each of these hearings has provided a kind of snap poll on whether the key people think it ought to be a crime to grow cannabis. My guess is that David's defence barrister, an Ulsterman, hates the stuff. (Protestantism and pot don't mix, as shown by the campaigning role of the US Bible belt. And the Northern Ireland poet Tom Paulin is one of the few people I met while researching this book who expressed a real horror of cannabis.) David had been lucky to get a sympathetic prosecutor at his second hearing, but his chances of leniency had been cancelled out by the judge: he'd only got two of the necessary three lemons on the fruit machine.

It was between David's first and second Crown Court appearances that Exodus decided to launch their legalization campaign under the name of CANABIS (Campaign Against Narcotic Abuse Because of Ignorance in Society), and they held their inaugural conference at Haz Manor soon after this third hearing. I went to Luton and afterwards horrified David by passing on the campaign's idea of attending all cannabis trials. 'Bunch of hippies banging tambourines – no thanks, man. It wouldn't do me any favours.' But this wasn't at all the flavour of the event. It's true that a very large amount of ganga was chuffed, as Exodus would put it. After all, you would expect heavy smokers to form the vanguard of the legalization movement. Also, with parties on Exodus's farm both evenings, nothing got going before 2 p.m. on either day. But there was also an underlying realism verging at times on ruthlessness.

The main hall of Haz Manor – the communal area of the former old people's home – was full of people and smoke when I arrived on the Saturday. The stand-up comedian Tony Allen was the chair – actually the only person constantly on his feet – a big tall man in tight black clothes with cropped grey hair, a pork-pie hat and a voice like Bob Hoskins. First people introduced themselves: veterans like Tim Malyon of earlier legalization movements; a Norwich contingent (Norwich is home to both the CL-CIA, a split-off from the Legalize Cannabis Campaign, and UK-CIA, which runs the main legalization web-site); lots of members of Exodus; lots of people from *Squall*, an occasional journal 'for the intelligent itinerant' which has documented Exodus's various battles over the years; the 'Sexual Freedom Coalition' (I strained to check I hadn't misheard), comprising Tuppy Owen, the sex therapist and former porn star (who thinks pot is good for sex but not much else) and a stately Dickensian bloke with a ponytail called Tim. Tuppy's younger boyfriend was a leading light of Class War, the anarchist group that became a household name after the Trafalgar Square Poll Tax riots of 1990. Plus individuals: a local journalist, a publisher of adult comics (for adults, not 'adult'), a recently jailed grow-manual writer and, an hour or two after everyone else, Free-Rob Cannabis. This was my first glimpse of the thirty-year-old former Rob Christopher who turned out, with his short hair dyed rich yellow, his red-cheeked face and his primary coloured sweater, to look somewhat like a cuddly toy.

The various groups piled a table with their different publica-tions. These weren't all popular with the residents. One Exodus member glanced at the cover of *Consenting Adults*, published by the Sexual Freedom Coalition, with its (unsexy) image of a small-breasted naked violinist and muttered: 'Bit much with kiddies around.' The journal *Class War* caused bigger problems. Its page three featured a news photo of an injured policeman and a gloating caption. Glenn resolved that in no circumstances would *Class War* be allowed to steward a CANABIS demon-stration (and Glenn's interventions were never opposed by other

Exodus members, who formed the biggest single bloc). Someone – possibly the Movement Against A Monarchy – had
produced this gem of a sticker:

> Society is Mentally Ill
> Cure your Diseased Festering Mind
> Destroy Society
> Disrobe outside Buckingham Palace
> Protest Naked for the Right to be Naked in Public

When I arrived I thought, 'What a strange collection of people,'
assuming it was a homogenous gathering whose members all
knew each other. Actually almost everyone reacted in the same
way (I expect to me as to the other participants), and the constantly
circulating joints didn't paper over people's differences. The local
journalist – a redoubtably uppity woman called Candida – tried to
stage a coup against Tony Allen 'on behalf of the sisters', claiming
to detect 'a lot of testosterone in the air', physically upstaging him
by blocking his view and asking the meeting to brainstorm ideas to
write on an upright scribbling pad. 'Is there something I'm
missing?' Tony Allen growled, darkening with anger, and wrested
back control – though Candida stayed on her feet in the wings,
watching for a fresh chance to rush him.

The majority, grouped around Exodus, were resisting pressure
on two opposed flanks. On one side were the purists, almost as
keen to attack alcohol as to promote cannabis, and who twigged
only slowly that they were out on a limb. A second conference
took place in January 1999 to plan the May Day legalization
festival on Clapham Common. 'I don't understand the reason
we're planning to have bars,' a supporter asked sadly. 'I suppose if
it's to raise money that's all right.' He can't have enjoyed the
excesses at the party later that evening, which culminated in
heroic bouts of vomiting (the women at Haz Manor seemed

especially susceptible – I heard two conversations in the morning about what had 'set them off again': orange juice and toothpaste respectively). On the other extreme, *Class War* hated all the stuff about cannabis spirituality, but had to accept it in the draft statement of principles, drafted 'in the light of the discussion' mainly by Tim Malyon and Glenn at some time during the small hours of Sunday morning. This went:

The New Deal for Cannabis

The ganga culture is here to stay. We demand:

1. The Road to Safety
   The immediate end to international cannabis prohibition and a binding Royal Commission to investigate prohibition in general and regulated legislation.
2. Free the Weed
   Personal possession, cultivation and non-profit distribution to be unlicensed.
3. New Dealers
   Commercial trading to be regulated according to ethical/ecological trading standards.
4. Free the Seed
   No patenting or genetic engineering of cannabis seeds.
5. Free the Holy Herb
   The right to burn the herb as a sacrament enshrined under Article 18 (Universal Declaration of Human Rights).
6. Set the Captives Free
   Free pardon for all cannabis offenders and destruction of all cannabis-related records. A full apology from the Government for the grievous crimes committed against its citizens in the name of the War on Drugs.

7. Chant down Babylon's War on Drug users
   An inquiry into the effects on society of prohibition and into the reasons why the War on Drug users have been pursued for so long.
8. Testing for Safety not Social Control
   An end to irrelevant testing by use of body samples. Relevant testing methods should be developed which can determine aptitude whilst under the influence.
9. Youth use
   Sixteen-year-old age limit only on commercial supply. Sanctions against supplier only.
10. Cut the Bullshit
    Fair and factual drug information – just say KNOW.
11. Healer of the Nations
    Ethical medical and industrial use of the cannabis plant.

Some of these items were a shoo-in. Yes to the holy herb (unless you're *Class War*), Yes to hemp, No to random drug-testing. But points 2, 3, 4 and 11 were the product of quite a long discussion. Two impulses were in conflict: the idea that cannabis should be free from state control and the desire to keep it from the hands of commerce. There was an early bid for import controls to give a monopoly to EU suppliers, which gave the meeting the air of a group of small-scale growers sniffing legalization and trying to stake a privileged place in the sun. Fortress Europe was quickly vacated in favour of trade links with co-operatives in Jamaica and elsewhere. Hip capitalism found few friends: 'We know that big business don't do us any favours; are we going to let them have a licence by not putting any restrictions on it?' As Glen said on another occasion, 'We don't want everything to be commercialized like Amsterdam. Amsterdam is the opposite of what we want.' But one of the young women from *Squall* felt 'It shouldn't be illegal to create a lifestyle out of something that's positive.' And everyone wanted to give the hemp industry a helping hand.

The solution was to sketch out two markets. There would be a tightly regulated commercial market, possibly taxed, which would be forced to compete with a profit-free, low-cost alternative market. In effect, the cheap ganga grown on a small scale would drive out expensive ganga from Benson and Hedges. Glenn said: 'It's crucial that the point of change isn't whether you grow three or ten plants: it's whether you make a profit from it.'

Describing a world of legal cannabis is still rather like trying to answer the proverbially ludicrous medieval theologians' question as to how many angels can fit on a pinhead. It's inspiring to think that legal cannabis would bring with it an alternative to both modern capitalism and current gangsterism. And yet there's something a little strange about the solution put forward by CANABIS. Big business would be regulated, while the good guys would be left to get on with it. But how would the body which some wit at the conference called 'Ofpot' be able to satisfy itself that Exodus, to take just one example, really was non-profit-making?

Till very recently the police in Luton have been satisfied of no such thing. I find the Exodus people straightforward and convincing, but I'm worried when I realize I positively want to take them on trust because I find their philosophy congenial. (To my lasting shame I once wrote in a student newspaper article that Virgin Records 'took decisions collectively', because someone in the Virgin press office had assured me so.) As it happened I had just been talking to the cynic Zelda when the phone rang again and Luton's deputy divisional commander, Superintendent Ivor Twydell, was on the line.

It's obvious that Ivor Twydell finds Exodus attractive in the way I do. The previous week he had gone to the Marsh Farm

Estate to look at the building they want to turn into the
community centre to be known as The Ark. He said: 'I thought
it could be quite positive for the town. I'm quite impressed with
the community aspect and their plans for The Ark: all that seems
to me something exciting, something you can't argue with.
Some of my colleagues say, "It's just a cover, it's just a front."
Some think I'm being taken in. I think the drugs issue is
unfortunate in that it almost gets in the way.'

Gets in the way? I've been told repeatedly that the local cops
know all about Exodus and spliff – that they saw the outdoor
plants when they visited Haz Manor (though not the ones under
lights) and had the ten plants per person rule explained. Guy, the
ex-blacksmith with 'love' and 'hate' tattoed on his knuckles,
made a point of insisting they've made no secret that if The Ark
comes off they'll be smoking openly. Has Ivor not been told or
has he not been listening? The conference on Sunday had
moved from a discussion of principles and demands to ideas
for direct action. Glenn had said: 'Me and Biggs are going to
spliff up at the police station on Saturday night. I'm going to ask
for 70,000 and Biggs is going to ask for 80,000 other offences to
be taken into consideration.' This obviously hasn't happened
yet: Ivor Twydell is maintaining his policy that with cannabis a
less urgent priority than addictive drugs, it wouldn't be a sensible
use of resources to bust Exodus. He might search and find
cannabis, but then he might in any Luton pub. He tells me what
he thinks are the groundrules: 'I said to Glenn Jenkins who seems
to be their main spokesperson that the cannabis issue is poten-
tially a source of great conflict. They have to be completely
discreet about any individual use of cannabis. That sounds like a
fudge. I don't want it to be a fudge. It's a very fine line. Does that
make sense?'

I wish it did. Superintendent Twydell is the last person you'd
want to see caught in the crossfire between Exodus and the law

on cannabis. If you characterized Commander Andy Hayman as a New Labour sort of cop, with his fondness for managerial theory and poster campaigns, Ivor Twydell is more New Age. Before joining the force he used to play in a band for a living, and he's not scared to speak 'as an individual and not as a police officer' about the need to change the Misuse of Drugs Act, and about his disappointment with the new Labour government and with Keith Hellawell, the Drug Czar. 'I think we are still a reactionary society. One of the difficulties I have is that people smoke cigarettes, and we know the damage that causes to people; people drink alcohol; if alcohol and cigarettes were now discovered they'd be banned immediately, so I find it difficult to say that one drug which appears to be far less harmful isn't OK. I know as a police officer that tonight alcohol will be the cause of a fair bit of crime and a fair bit of violence and suffering. I don't think cannabis does that.

'Individually, personally, I think it's a real shame that this whole issue does create a very big gulf between the criminal justice system and the person in the street. The vast majority aren't people who are criminals: they're not people who want to commit a wilful act; they're people who want to live their lives like anyone else.'

If all local police commanders were like Ivor Twydell, there would be no need to do anything about changing the law on cannabis; it could just be left to wither away from operational neglect – or, one of the better suggestions I've seen (from Harry Shapiro of the Institute for the Study of Drug Dependence), the UK police could keep us in line with international treaty obligations by giving offenders a laminated card outlining the dangers of drugs. If they re-offended, they could be given another card in bigger print.[1]

But most people don't live in Luton; what if you're a pot-smoking single mum in Orkney where, according to Linda Hendry of the Scottish Legalize Cannabis Campaign, the police are prepared to threaten loss of contact with your child to get you to inform on your dealer? This is part of the discretion of local chief constables, and applies, according to the Home Office, to all laws, not just cannabis. I told a friend of mine who's a lawyer and married to the pot-smoking professional who inspired this book about the amazing leniency of the prosecuting counsel at David's second court hearing. She said: 'They can be quite helpful to well-educated middle-class guys like the people growing skunk in that film *Lock Stock and Two Smoking Barrels*. But it's different if you're black and covered in gold jewellery.' David had a hard-boiled south London solicitor with a lot of experience of drugs cases. I put this theory to him, and he forcefully claimed that British justice was colour-blind; in fact he came across more like a cop than either Commander Hayman or Superintendent Twydell.

David's fourth court appearance. Every other time I've hung around for hours waiting for his case to be called; this time the court is already sitting. Once again there is a complete change of cast. This time there isn't even the usual defence lawyer, and I'm a bit disoriented, but write 'defence' and start trying to get the gist of what the guy's saying. It sounds as if the prosecution have stopped trying to overturn the fiction that David made no money from dealing: 'It's right to say that on the 10th, the Crown – I must put this most correctly – whilst they could not agree the basis of the plea, certainly weren't in a position to gainsay it.' Phew. The next issue is the value of the weed. Of course there have been no lab reports. The barrister, who sounds every bit as efficient as his predecessor, is trying to get the judge to accept that only two-thirds of the stuff was actually saleable: two kilos at an estimated value of £1,500 per kilo. The judge has bought it! Surely David will now be spending Christmas at home with his dad (still ignorant of either of his sons' brushes with the law) rather than in jail. The judge is 'minded' to go for a community service order, but needs to check that the law allows him to. Even the prosecution barrister seems caught up in the Christmas spirit, with a speech which refers to David's career as a student and his ambition to become a teacher (which apparently he invented on the spur of the moment when talking to his probation officer). There's a brief, tense adjournment. Then the judge returns. First he addresses David, concluding: 'The law is there to be obeyed. If you think it should be otherwise you should use your intelligence and energies to persuade others – not break the law.' Finally the sentence: 120 hours of community service, and a £1,000 fine. The police will even hand David back the money that actually came from selling his weed. David's solicitor has thawed and he smiles to me: 'It looks as though your theory was borne out.'

And it's only as we're walking away from the courtroom that I realize I got the lawyers mixed up and that the 'defence counsel' who saved David from prison had actually been the barrister from the Crown Prosecution Service.

Postscript

I was going to end the book with David walking free from the Crown Court. But all the time I've been researching and writing it I've been putting off making one particular phone call. It's to someone who's five years older than me called Jean-Paul, whose parents were friends of my parents. We went on one holiday together to Alsace, which is where his father came from, and the families used to visit each other for Sunday lunches. There were three children, and the one who was closest to me in age was Philippe. When we got into our mid-teens we both started trying to be counter-cultural, and I remember once inviting him up to my room for a surreptitious pre-lunch joint. Philippe was funny, warm and very intelligent; I say 'was' because during the 1980s he started taking heroin, got addicted, and later shot himself.

It sounds tasteless and melodramatic to say this, but I find that there's a slight physical resemblance between David and Philippe; enough to make it hard for me to picture them simultaneously. The phone call to J-P is to ask if he thinks his brother would still be alive if he'd never smoked pot.

J-P was immediately inclined not to blame Philippe's cannabis-smoking. 'What fucks you up is what's in your mind,' he said. He had himself smoked three joints a day during the eight years he'd spent in Nigeria as a foreign language teacher – among other things, genuflecting at the shrine of Fela Kuti's genius – and hadn't suffered at all by giving up when he moved to

London. J-P had actually hoped that Philippe would use cannabis to help him get off heroin (not an impossible hope in many
people's experience), and during the last days of his life, when
they had been together, he had said, 'Take as much dope as you
want, as much alcohol as you want – but no heroin.'

When I first smoked a joint, hardly anyone in Britain took
drugs. There are now more than 500 heroin-related deaths a
year and more than 40,000 heroin addicts,[1] some of whom are
committing thefts worth scores or possibly hundreds of millions
of pounds a year to pay for their habit. I accept that the taking of
cannabis in the 1960s made it more likely that people would take
more dangerous drugs. While I can understand the libertarian
position on hard drugs I don't accept that they should be freely
traded, any more than I agree with the American Rifle Association when it says that 'It isn't guns that kill, it's people.' Nor do I
believe that prohibition is impossible. By attacking cannabis the
Swedes have also delayed the age at which people experiment
with hard drugs. In America the War on Drugs produced
measurable results, with marijuana used by 12th grade high-
school students (seventeen- to eighteen-year-olds) falling to
almost half the levels in 1992 of those reported at the peak in
1979, before rising again later in the 1990s. With political will
and the new technology of drug-testing it would be possible to
roll back the tide.

But I don't want to, and more to the point, nor do most
people. With their tradition of regulation by social codes rather
than legal sanctions, the Dutch have shown that it's possible to
give people the freedom to use drugs that only hurt themselves,
if they hurt anyone, and that such a policy actually reduces the
general consumption of socially damaging drugs (in which
category I'd have to include alcohol, much as I love it). The
thing is: I don't want to live in Sweden or Saudi Arabia. Drugs
can destroy societies: the classic example is alcohol when used by

certain non-European cultures. But what really shattered the lives of the indigenous peoples of North America was not whisky but the fact that the European settlers who introduced it constituted a hostile presence. Knowledge of the right use of any drug has to be acquired, transmitted from culture to culture, learned from person to person. As the National Institute of Mental Health researchers found in the late 1960s, where a drug has a strong associated culture, which is true of ganga in both Nigeria and in Jamaica, people can consume lots of it without harming themselves. It's when drugs are traded impersonally for profit that they are likely to become lethal.

Prohibition is itself a drug culture: it doesn't stop drug use, but it communicates a blunt message – a fear of chaos and disapproval of unregulated self-indulgence. Many honest and thoughtful politicians want to continue putting out this message, just as they want laws against racist behaviour to communicate a view of a healthy society. But the message conveyed by the laws against cannabis today lacks realism, sophistication or respect for our citizens. The alternative approach is the one Western countries take with alcohol, which is controlled partly by legal regulation but mostly by engrained social codes. We need to evolve our cannabis culture, not repress it.

J-P says that Philippe might well have linked pot to his troubles. Apparently he used to say: 'I'd have been all right if it hadn't been for 1968' (Philippe being French, May '68 = the Anglo-Saxons' Summer of Love). Nineteen sixty-eight was a time when an old order went into the melting-pot before a new one had been born, and many people were more adrift than they let on. Perhaps he had a point – if so the answer is to develop our cannabis culture, not repress it.

Appendix

Further Reading

Books

The two current books on cannabis that I've seen distributed most widely are Jack Herer's *The Emperor Wears No Clothes* (11th edn, AH HA publishing, tel: 001 512 5337), or read selections online at www.jackherer.com), and *Marijuana Myths, Marijuana Facts: A Review of Scientific Evidence* by Lynn Zimmer and John P. Morgan (The Lindesmith Center, New York, 1997). Both are a good read; they represent respectively the tie-dye and suit-wearing wings of the American legalization movement. Thanks to Chris Conrad's work as editor it's easier than in the past to source the *Emperor*'s eye-popping claims (though I've had to admit defeat over the 'Turkish smoking parlours' for hashish, supposedly an everyday feature of American city life in the late nineteenth century). Jack also, has a web site (jackherer.com). The only thing wrong with *Marijuana Myths* is the authors' shyness about telling readers where they're coming from as pillars of NORML.

Hemp: as an author in his own right, Chris Conrad has published *Hemp, Lifeline to the Future* (Creative Xpressions Publishing), which is sounder than the *Emperor*, if less fun. *Hemp Today*, edited by Ed Rosenthal (Quick American Archives) contains a wealth of gripping information; there's also the diverting spectacle of Rosenthal parading revisionist views while paying tribute to hempist orthodoxy, rather as when Deng Xiaoping tried to present capitalism as an extention of Maoism.

Medicine and science: The key text is Lester Grinspoon's *Marihuana, The Forbidden Medicine* (L. Grinspoon and J. Bakalar, Yale University Press, revised ed., 1993), which offers a comprehensive guide to the many claims made by patients. The story of the American medical marijuana movement is told by the founders of the Alliance for Cannabis Therapeutics, Robert C. Randall and Alice O'Leary, in *Marijuana Rex*, (Thunder's Mouth Press). (The American

ACT web site is marijuana-as-medicine.org) Late in 1999 the American wing of the Oxford University Press is due to publish *The Science of Marijuana* by Professor Leslie Iversen, who was the scientific adviser to the House of Lords committee on cannabis. The committee's report, *Cannabis – The Medical and Scientific Evidence* (HL Paper 151, the Stationery Office, London) is a well-written and useful summary, though a bit dear at £7 for only fifty-one pages. Much the same ground was covered by the United States Institute of Medicine, which reported in March 1999 to the White Houses's Office of Drug Control Policy. Their full report is *Marijuana and Medicine: Assessing the Science Base* by John A. Benson Jr and Stanley J. Watson Jr (National Academic Press). Or you can read it online (book.nap.edu). The really hard science is to be found in *Cannabinoid Receptors* by Roger Pertwee (The Academic Press, 1995).

Cultivation and connoisseurship: *Hashish!* by Robert Connell Clark (Red Eye Press, 1998) is a bit like the classic work on ampelography (the science of vine classification) by Pierre Galet, in that while indispensable, it's not truly user-friendly and cries out for some slick publisher with a large budget to redesign it and winkle out the inappropriate pictures (English sahibs smoked tobacco, not ganga, even if the word they used for their hookahs was a 'chillum' (see Thakeray's *Vanity Fair*). Get in there, Dorling Kindersley/Mitchell Beazley/Ebury Press.

The grow manuals form the biggest-selling category. The Mel Frank/Ed Rosenthal partnership has split up and each author now produces both a general book and a guide to indoor cultivation. The advantage of *Gold Harvest* by George Mayfield (Green Magic Productions, 1997) is that it's written with UK conditions in mind and has the appropriate electrical measurements, etc. I liked the look of *Guide to Growing Marijuana in a Cool Climate* by D. Irving (Knockabout Comics, tel 0181 969 2945), but critics point out that it was first published more than twenty years ago and could use updating. At the other extreme, *Sea of Green* by 'Hans' (*High Tmies*) is a slickly presented guide to high-tech indoor cultivation.

Select Bibliography

Abel, Ernest, *Marijuana – The First Twelve Thousand Years* (Plenum Press, New York, 1980)

Barr, Andrew, *Drink, A Social History* (Pimlico, 1998)

Bonnie, Richard J. and Whitebread, Charles H., *The Forbidden Fruit and the Tree of Knowledge – the Legal History of Marijuana in the United States* (The Lindesmith Center, 1999)

Cherniak, Lawrence, *The Great Books of Hashish*, vol. 1 (And/Or Press, Berkeley, CA, 1979)

Clarke, Robert C., *Marijuana Botany* (And/Or Press, Berkeley, CA, 1981)
De Monfried, Henri, *Hashish – A Smuggler's Tale* (Random House, London, 1935)
Gray, Mike, *Drug Crazy – How We Got into This Mess and How We Can Get Out* (Random House, New York, 1998)
Grice, Trevor and Scott, Tom, *The Great Brain Robbery* (Aurum Press, 1998)
Grinspoon, Lester, *Marijuana Reconsidered* (Harvard University Press, 1971)
Heaney, Sara and Rogers, Dominique, *A Plant of Contention* (University of Essex, 1998)
Johnson, Donald McIntosh, *Indian Hemp, A Social Menace* (Johnson, 1952)
Kamstra, Jerry, *Weed*: Adventures of a Dope Smuggler (Bantam, 1975)
La Valle, Suomi, *Hashish* (Quartet, 1984)
Marks, Howard, *Mr Nice* (Martin Secker and Warburg, 1996)
Mechoulam, Raphael, *Marijuana* (Academic Press, New York 1973)
Nahas, Gabriel G., with an introduction by Sir William Paton, *Keep Off the Grass* (Futura, 1983)
Norris, Mikki, Conrad, Chris, and Resner, Virginia, *Shattered Lives – Portraits from America's Drug War* (Creative Xpressions, El Cerrito, California, 1998)
Rozenthal, Franz, *The Herb – Hashish versus medieval Muslim Society* (E. J. Brill, Leiden, 1971)
Rubin, Vera (ed.), *Cannabis and Culture* (Mouton, The Hague, 1975)
Schofield, Michael, *The Strange Case of Pot* (Harmondsworth, Penguin, 1971)
Tart, Charles T., *On Being Stoned: a psychological study of marijuana intoxication*, (Science and Behaviour Books, Palo Alto, California, 1971)
Tendler, Stewart and May, David *the Brotherhood of Eternal Love* (Panther, 1984)

Magazines

Canada

Cannabis Culture (formerly *Cannabis in Canada*). Old back issues published online on cannabisculture.com, which also has a book store. Subscription inquiries tel: (1) 604 669 9069.

UK

cc:news published by Bodaiju, PO Box 2700, Lewes, E. Sussex. Website: www.schmoo.co.uk/ccnews.html. Non-glossy monthly news-sheet. Useful updates for activitsts. There is other cannabis information on the schmoo website.

Weed World. Tel: 01974 821518. Website: www.users.dircon.co.uk/~weed1/Semi-glossy with news, features and ads from seed companies.

USA
Hemp Times. Website: www.hemptimes.com.

High Times. Trans High Corporation, 235 Park Avenue South, 5th Floor, New York NY 10003. Website: www.hightimes.com

UK organizations

Pro-legalization
CANABIS, the Campaign Against Narcotic Abuse Because of Ingorance in Society (see Chapter 12) can be contacted c/o Haz Manor, 1–2 Bramingham Lane, Streatley, nr. Luton, Bedfordshire, LU3 3NL. E-mail: exoduscollective@csi.com.

Cannabis in Avalon PO Box 2223, Glastonbury, BA6 9YU E-mail: cannabisinfo@gn.apc.org. Free-Rob Cannabis's new group.

CLCIA, the Campaign to Legalize Cannabis International Association is the Norwich survivor of the old London Legalize Cannabis Campaign, but has contacts throughout Britain. 63 Peacock Street, Norwich NR3 1TB. E-mail: webbooks@paston.co.uk.

The Legalize Cannabis Campaign, Scotland c/o 2A West Preston Street, Edinburgh EH8 9PX. Tel: 0131 667 6488.

Transform. The UK's chief campaigning organization against the War on Drugs, offering a well-argued case for legalization of all drugs. Box 59, 82 Colston Street, Bristol BS1 5BB. Tel: 0117 972 7428. Website: legalize.org/global/britain/transform.

Medical
The Association of Cannabis Therapeutics, PO Box CR14, Leeds, LS7 4XF. Fax. 0113 237 1000.

The London Medical Marajuana (sic) Support Group is at 88–90 Farringdon Road, EC1R 3EA. Tel: 0171 863 7223. E-mail: medicalmarajuana@hotmail.com.

The Medicinal Marijuana Collective, the group founded by Colin Davies (see Chapter 3) can be contacted at PO Box 209, Stockport, SK5 8FB.

Legal
The independent Drug Monitoring Unit provides research and expert

evidence in the criminal justice system. Freepost NWWIIIII Wigan, WN2 3ZZ. E-mail. idmu@netgates.co.uk. Website: www.idmu.co.uk.

The Fair Trials Abroad Trust. Much of this organization's work is with overseas drug arrests. Bench House, Ham Street, Richmond, Surrey TW10 7HR. Tel: 0181 332 2800.

British Government National Drugs Helpline 0800 776600.

Release advice line 0171 729 9904 10–6 Monday to Friday.
Emergency hotline 0171 603 8654 all other times.

Institute for the Study of Drug Dependence and the Standing Conference on Drug Abuse, 32–36 Loman Street SE1 0EE. Tel: 0171 928 1211. There's a good library.

Some other information sources

UK
The UKCIA run a website with a library and a well-maintained news-cuttings service, turning up nuggets such as a University of Toronto study showing that moderately stoned drivers are only barely more dangerous than sober drivers. Website: www.ukcia.org.

United States
Dr Dave's Hemp Archives. A lot of cannabis information gets passed across numerous websites. Dave West's passion for his subject means that his site at www.pressenter.com/~davewest/hemp.html is full of stuff you won't see anywhere else.

There is an extraordinary amount of historical material available online at the site run by the Drug Reform Co-ordination Network (the DRCNet) at www.druglibrary.org including the text of many of the numerous govern-ment commissions on the subject, from the Indian Hemp Commission onwards.

The Drug Peace Campaign is a new San Francisco group campaigning against the War on Drugs. Website: www.drugpeace.org.

The August National Organization for the Reform of Marijuana Laws (NORML) is at www.norml.org.

With the Soros millions, the Lindesmith Center runs an informative website at www.lindesmith.org. The Drug Policy Foundation, whose separate function I've never quite got straight, is at www.dpf.org.

One important source of statistics on the scale of US cannabis use is the school leavers' surveys run by the University of Michigan. The information is posted on the 'MTF Home Page' reached via www.isr.umich.edu.

France
Observatoire Geopolitique des Drogues. This Paris-based research group publishes annual reports on trends in the global drugs trade. The website has an English language version. Tel: (33) 140 366 381. Website: www.ogd.org.

The Netherlands
The International Hemp Association. PO Box 75007, 1070 Amsterdam publishes a scholarly journal on industrial hemp which can be viewed online at www.commonlink.com/~olsen/hemp/IHA. The same URL with 'IHA' has many hemp links.

www.drugtext.org is the site run by Mario Lap and includes a history of Dutch decriminalization.

Anti-drug campaigns

The Partnership for a Drug Free America (see Chapter 10) are at www.projectknow.com.

The White House Drug Policy Site is at www.whitehousedrugpolicy.gov.

The Drug Enforcement Administration home page is www.usdoj.gov/deal/.

Drug Watch International regularly brings together leading anti-cannabis campaigners, including Dr Gabriel Nahas. The website is www.drugwatch.-org, and includes links to other groups such as European Cities against Drugs. The postal address is PO Box 45218, Omaha, Nebraska 68145–0218.

Notes and References

Chapter 1: Wine of Haydar

1. Of course it is also relevant that the volume of illegal drug-taking does not approach the scale of legal drug use.
2. See ' 'Magico-religious use of Tobacco among South American Indians', by Joannes Wilbert in Vera Rubin *Cannabis and Culture*, Mouton, The Hague, 1971. Wilbert quotes what is possibly the first ever western description of tobacco smoking, by Girolano Benzoni in his *Historia del Mundo Nuovo* (Venice, 1565) which makes it clear that tobacco was originally an intoxicant: 'So much do they fill themselves with this cruel smoke that they lose their reason. And there are some who take so much of it, that they fall down as if they were dead, and remain the greater part of the day or night stupified.'
3. Attributed variously to the 13th century poets Ibn Khamis and to Ibn al-A'ma. These lines are quoted in Franz Rosenthal, *The Herb: Hashish versus Medieval Muslim Society,* 1871.
4. Quoted in Roger Joseph 'The Economic Significance of Cannabis Sativa in the Moroccan Rif', in Vera Rubin, ibid.
5. 'The Political, Economic and Social Stakes in the Production of and Traffic in Drugs in Morocco', for the Drug Unit of the General Secretary of the European Communities, March 1994.
6. The EU report threatens the growers of Ketama with an even more sinister prospect, quoting allegations, widespread in the Rif in the early 1990s, that the authorities were mounting a 'war on drugs' in the Rif in order to shift production to new industrial-scale production in the south of Morocco.
7. The EU report lists five grades of this 'hamda' powder, from double-zero to zero through to No 4, the lowest quality.
8. During the 1912–56, the years of Spanish rule, Spain 'cut more trees in a decade than the local tribesmen had cut in a century': (Roger Joseph op. cit.)

9. Ernest L. Abel *Marijuana, the First 12,000 Years*, Plenum Press, New York.
10. David Jones, 'The Herb and the Mystic – Cannabis in East Religions, in *A Plant of Contention*, ed. Dominique Rogers, University of Essex 1998.

Chapter 2: Mugglesborough

1. One observer in the 1960s found hippies so dreary that he tried to demonstrate that medieval 'hashish' had to be a different drug to the one that they consumed. After a distinguished career as a scholar on the team studying the Dead Sea Scrolls, John Allegro published *The Sacred Mushroom and the Cross* (Abacus, 1973), with its studiedly offensive thesis that the origins of Christianity lay in a fertility cult centred round the use of hallucinogenic mushrooms. In it he wrote, 'It is difficult to believe that the "pot"-smokers of today, the weary dotards who wander listlessly around our cities and universities, are the spiritual successors of those drug-crazed enthusiasts who, regardless of their safety, stormed castles and stole as assassins into the strongholds of their enemies.'
2. Lambros Comitas, 'The Social Nexus of Ganga in Jamaica' in *Cannabis Culture*, op. cit.
3. Mezz Mezzrow, *Really the Blues*, Carol publishing group, 1981.
4. *Cannabis Culture*, op. cit.
5. Anna Bradley and Oswin Baker, *Drugs in the United Kingdom – a Jigsaw with Missing Pieces*, Institute for the Study of Drug Dependence, 1998.
6. George Orwell, *Inside the Whale and other essays*, Penguin books, 1990.
7. Don Aitken, 'The Cannabis Market and Dealers' in *Cannabis, Options for Control*, ed. Frank Logan, Quartermaine House, 1979.
8. This claim is made in *Big Deal, the Politics of the Illegal Drug Business* by Anthony Henman, Roger Lewis and Tim Malyon with Betsy Ellore and Lee O'Bryan, Pluto Press, 1985.
9. Three gang members were found shot dead in a metallic blue Range Rover in Essex in December 1995. See Matthew Colin, *Altered State the Story of Ecstacy Culture and Acid House*.
10. Anna Bradley and Oswin Baker, *Drugs in the United Kingdom – a Jigsaw with Missing Pieces*, op. cit.
11. *The Exodus Story*. Loftus Productions for Radio One.
12. Luton, whose name derives from the local river Ley is historically a centre of the hat-making industry.
13. 'Chuffing' is Exodus-speak for smoking pot. I thought of using it in the title of this book. However my editor consumer-tested it on his younger colleagues, asking them if they'd been chuffing. They thought he was accusing them of farting.

14. Bob Marley's records have sold 2.5 million copies since 1991 in Britain.
15. Quoted in E. P. Thompson *Witness Against the Beast, William Blake and the Moral Law*, The New Press, 1995.
16. At this time the Ottoman governors of Egypt had decreed the death penalty for tobacco smoking. An Egyptian historian, Ibn al-Wakil al-Milawi, quoted in Franz Rosenthal op. cit., tells the story of two old men surprised by the governors retinue in a park where they'd gone to eat hashish and smoke tobacco. The hashish goes unremarked – the point of the story is their comic and painful attempts to hide the hot tobacco pipe under clothing.

Chapter 3: 'Medi-Pot'

1. J. G. C. van Amsterdam, J. W. van der Laan and J. L. Slangen 'Residual Cognitive and Psychotic Effects of Prolonged Heavy Cannabis Use'. National Institute of Public Health and the Environment, Bilthoven, The Netherlands. Paper presented to the House of Lords, translated from a literature survey published in Ned. Tijdschr. Geneeskunde 142 (10), pp.504–508, 1998.
2. A study at Hammersmith Hospital in 1997 on an individual patient found that his demand for morphine was much lower when he was treated with cannabis oil than with a placebo. Holdcroft A. et al. Pain relief with oral cannabinoids in familial Mediterranean fever. *Anaesthesia*, 1997, pp.52, 483 (quoted in the House of Lords report).
3. The Lancet, 1998; 352; pp.785–6. The figures showed 35 per cent of men and 19 per cent of the women surveyed currently using cannabis.
4. The text of Proposition 215, drafted by Dennis Peron, is:
a) This section shall be known and may be cited as the Compassionate Use Act of 1996.
b) The people of the State of California hereby find and declare that the purposes of the Compassionate Use Act of 1996 are as follows:
A) To ensure that seriously ill Californians have the right to obtain and use marijuana for medical purposes where that medical use is deemed appropriate and has been recommeded by a physician who has determined that the person's health would benefit from the use of marijuana in the treatment of cancer, anorexia, AIDS, chronic pain, spasticity, glaucoma, arthritis, migraine, or any other illness for which marijuana provides relief.
B) To ensure that patients and their primary caregivers who obtain and use marijuana for medical purposes upon the recommendation of a physician are not subject to criminal prosecution or sanction.

C) To encourage the federal and state governments to implement a plan to provide for the safe and affordable distribution of marijuana to all patients in medical need of marijuana.

2. Nothing in this act shall be construed to supersede legislation prohibiting persons from engaing in conduct that endangers others, nor to condone the diversion of marijuana for nonmedical purposes.

c) Notwithstanding any other provision of law, no physician in this state shall be punished, or denied any right or privilege, for having recommended marijuana to a patient for medical purposes.

d) Section 11357, relating to the possession of marijuana, and Section 11358, relating to the cultivation of marijuana, shall not apply to a patient, or to a patient's primary caregiver, who possesses or cultivates marijuana for the personal medical purposes of the patient upon the written or oral recommendation or approval of a physician.

e) For the purposes of this section, 'primary caregiver' means the individual designated by the person exempted under this act who has consistently assumed responsibility for the housing, health or safety of that person.

5. George Soros wrote in the *Washington Post* (2 February 1997) that he had contributed $1 million to the drug policy ballot initiatives in California and Arizona. He denied a personal stake in the issue – 'I tried marijuana and enjoyed it but it did not become a habit and I have not tasted it for many years.' Instead he put the issue in the context of his support for the concept of 'the open society'. Soros claims that the 'war on drugs' is a classic example of the 'closed society' mentality he deplores, producing adverse, unintended consequences (mass incarceration, gangsterism and the spread of disease), that cannot be addressed because of its defenders' unquestioning self-belief.

Chapter 4: The Hard Science

1. John Rae, *Letters From School*, Collins, 1987.
2. Gabriel G. Nahas, *Keep Off the Grass*, Futura, 1993.
3. *The Drug and Alcohol Review*, 1994, 13, pp.209–16.
4. Author's conversation with Aidan Hampson, researcher with the US National Institute of Mental Health (*see* Chapter 8).
5. Quoted in Virginia Berridge and Griffith Edwards, *Opium and the People, Opiate Use in 19th Century England*, Yale University Press, 1987, p.214.
6. The most important of these is Gas Chromatography, developed in the 1950s.
7. D. J. Harvey (ed.) asssited by William Paton and Gabriel Nahas *Marijuana 84 Proceedings of the Oxford Seminars on Cannabis*, IRL Press, Oxford, 1985.

8. G. G. Nahas and D. J. Harvey, Psychoactive Cannabinoids and Membrane Signalling. A Putative Mechanism'. *British Journal of Pharmacology*, 1999, pp.126, 299.
9. Tom Scott and Trevor Grice, *The Great Brain Robbery*, Aurum Press, 1998 p.39.
10. Lee Butcher, *Accidental Millionaire, The Rise and Fall of Steven Jobs at Apple Computers*, Paragon House, New York, 1987.

Chapter 5: Arouser of Thought

1. Thomas Wentworth Russel KBE, *Egyptian Service, 1902–1946*, John Murray, 1949.
2. From the written evidence presented by David Copestake, a methodist minister, to the House of Lords select committee on Cannabis, 1998.
3. G. G. Nahas, *Marihuana, Deceptive Weed*, Raven Press, New York, 1973.
4. G. G. Nahas, *Keep Off The Grass*, op. cit.
5. Mentioned in Robert C. Clarke, *Hashish!*, Red Eye Press, 1998.
6. William H. Ukers *The Romance of Coffee: An Outline History of Coffee Drinking Though a Thousand Years*, Tea and Coffee Trade Journal Co., New York, 1948.
7. William Ukers, ibid.
8. David Jackson 'Cannabis Cures all?' in *Drug Link* September–October 1998, Institute for the Study of Drug Dependence.
9. Attributed variously to the 13th-century poets Ibn Khamis or Ibn al A'ma.
10. Nasir ul Din Ibn al Munayyir – quoted in Rosenthal ibid.
11. See the article on Mezz Mezzrow by Albert Goldman, reprinted in *High Times*, 1998 Cannabis Cup supplement.
12. My experience would have come as no surprise to one of the earliest western students of hashish, Dr Jacques-Joseph Moreau (1804–84), who experimented on its use as a treatment for psychiatric patients. He wrote, 'I saw it as a means of effectively combatting the fixed ideas of depressives, of disrupting their chain of ideas, of unfocussing their attention on such and such a subject' and, 'The hashish intoxication, after turning the thoughts of the patients in an unusual direction and causing a slight excitement, may be followed by calm and several hours of lucidity during which he accurately appraises his situation.' *Hashish and Mental Illness* pp.211 and 215, tr. Gordon J. Barnett, Raven Press, New York, 1973.
13. *Keep Off the Grass*, op cit.
14. I have heard though that very recently Algeria has developed, not exactly a *kif* but a ganga culture, with Bob Marley a cult figure and Brixton a place of pilgrimage.

Chapter 6: Objects Tilt to the Left

1. According to Jacques-Joseph Moreau (ibid.), being stoned may involve (1) general feelings of pleasure (2) increased excitement combined with heightening of all senses (3) distortions of the dimensions of time and space, generally a magnification of both (4) a keener sense of hearing combined with a greater susceptibility to music and the phenomenon that ordinary sound can be enjoyed as though it sounded sweet (5) persistent ideas verging on persecution mania (6) disturbance of emotion, most often in the form of an increase of pre-existing feelings (7) irresistable impulses (8) illusions and hallucinations of which only the former are evidently related to the real world.
2. Charles T. Tart, *On Being Stoned, A Psychological Study of Marijuana Intoxication*, Science and Behaviour Books, Palo Alto, California, 1971.
3. Paul B. Wilkinson, 'Cannabis Indica, an Historical and Pharmacological Study of the Drug' *The British Journal of Inebriety*, Vol XXIII 2 October 1929, quoted in Donald McI Johnson *Indian Hemp A Social Menace*, 1952.
4. Hashish and intricate geometric designs both became current in the Islamic world at about the same time. Could any self-respecting pot-head regard this as a coincidence?
5. *The Robert Crumb Coffee Table Art Book*, Bloomsbury Publishing, 1997.
6. Thomas Thompson, *The Bible in History*, Jonathan Cape 1998.
7. Jacques-Joseph Moreau: 'Once the orderly chain of association of ideas is broken, the most bizarre and extravagant thoughts, the strangest combinations of ideas are formed and take control of the mind. They can be induced by the most insignificant cause, as in the dream state. The city of Die is dominated by a cliff called 'U'; a young man desires to add the letter 'u' to the word Die and all the inhabitants of Die are gods (Fr: dieu) in his mind'. ibid. p.35.
8. Roberto Williams-Garcia, 'The Ritual Use of Cannabis in Mexico' in Vera Rubin, *Cannabis and Culture*, p.143.

Chapter 7: The Religion of Hemp

1. J. W. Roulac, *Hemp Horizons*, 1997, quoted by Sara Heaney in 'The Modern Uses of Hemp' in *Cannabis Plant of Contention*, University of East Anglia, 1998.
2. Dave West, 'Fiber Wars: The Extinction of Kentucky Hemp' in *Hemp Today*, ed. Ed Rosenthal, Quick American Archives, 1994.
3. 'Hemp Realities' in *Hemp Today*, op. cit.

Notes and References 235

4. Burning general waste to generate power is opposed in Britain by such groups as Greenpeace because of the risk of generating carcinogenic dioxins.
5. Expounded by Jakob Böhme (1575–1624) in his 'Signatio Rerum'. For example, the white patches on Lungwort are supposed to evoke a diseased lung, and the trilobed leaf shape of *Hepatica* to indicate that it should be used in liver conditions.

Chapter 8: Strains and Stresses

1. Although male cannabis plants contain THC they are universally discarded in favour of the later-maturing and higher-cropping females.
2. Richard Evans Schultes, William M. Klein, Timothy Plowman and Tom E. Lockwood 'Cannabis as an example of taxonomic neglect' in *Cannabis and Culture*, ed. Vera Rubin, op. cit.
3. In Professor Ashton's written evidence to the House of Lords committee in 1998.
4. The standard strength grown by the University of Mississippi is 1.8 per cent THC; strong, 4 per cent THC.
5. A. J. Hampson, M. Grimaldi, J. Axelrod and D. Wink, 'Cannabidiol and delta-9-tetrahydrocannabinol are neroprotective antioxidants' Proceedings of the National Academy of Sciences, Vol 95, Issue 14, pp.8268–8273, 7 July, 1998.
6. J. M. McPartland and P. P. Pruit, An herbal 'synergistic shotgun' compared to a synthetic 'suilver bullet': medical marijuana versus tertrahydrocannabinol. Proceedings 1998 symposium on the Cannabinoids. International Cannabinoid Research Society. Burlington VT p. 112, 1998.
7. It's an especially bad idea to eat raw hand-rubbed hashish as comes, for example, from the Kulu district, as even slight faecal contamination from the farmer's hands can cause hepatitis.
8. Zuardi A. W. Shirakawa I., Finkelfarb E., Karniol I. G., 'Action of cannabidiol on the anxiety and other effects produced by delta 9-THC in normal subjects' in *Psychopathology*, Berlin 1982.

Chapter 9: Cup Fever

1. The Californian-based Thomas Chong and Richard 'Cheech' Marin made several successful comedy albums in the early 1970s and three movies including *Up in Smoke* between 1978 and 1981.

Chapter 10: Pot of Gold

1. Advertisement in the *Illustrated London News* quoted in the booklet accompanying Channel Four's 'Pot Night', broadcast on 4 March 1995. One factoid that the House of Lords report helpfully squashed was Queen Victoria's alleged use of cannabis to relieve period pains; this idea presumably arose because Sir John Russell Reynolds who was for many years the queen's personal physician, wrote on cannabis in his five volume *System of Medicine* (second edition 1866–79) and especially recommended this application – but the report can find 'no actual proof at all' that tincture of cannabis was eligible for the Royal Warrant.
2. Baudelaire moved across to opium and finally gave up both drugs, at which point he denounced hashish in biting terms: 'Like all solitary habits it makes the individual valueless to society and society superfluous to the individual. Hashish never reveals to the individual more than he is himself.' (The second point is spot on; the first is necessarily true in a culture in which only a few individuals are dabbling in the drug.)
3. Cynthia Cotts 'Hard Sell in the Drug War', *The Nation*, 9 March 1992.
4. Associated Press, 23 February, 1999, dateline St Paul Minnesota.
5. This anxiety recalls the plot of *Lock Stock and Two Smoking Barrels* – but to Oscar Wilde's axiom that life imitates art, David hadn't seen the movie.

Chapter 11: Conspiracies

1. 'Selling Pot: The Pitfalls of Marijuana Reform Reason, 25.2 (1993) pp.20–9.
2. National Institute of Drug Abuse National Household Survey and the NIDA's High School Senior Survey.
3. This following section draws heavily on the relevant chapter of Virginia Berridge and Griffith Edward's *Opium and the People: Opiate Use in 19th Century England*, Yale University Press, 1987.
4. A. D. Harvey 'Towards a Potted History of Pot' *London Quarterly*, December 1995 – March 1996.
5. *Indian Hemp A Social Menace*, op. cit.
6. Lane Edwards, *An Account of the Manners and Customs of the Modern Egyptians Written in Egypt During the Years 1833–1835*, Darf, 1985.
7. Quoted by Matthew Atha in his article of prohibition history on the UKCIA website (www.ukcia.org).
8. 'Like his Hindu brother, the Musumlman Fakir reveres bhang as the lengthener of life, the freer from the bonds of self. Bhang brings union

with the Divine Spirit. 'We drank bhnag and the mystery I am He grew plain. So grand a result, so tiny a sin.'

9. T. S. Clouston 'The Cairo Asylum: Dr Warnock on hashish insanity,' Journal of Mental Science, 42 (1896) quoted in Berridge and Edward, op. cit. p.213.

10. Speech to the California Judges' Association, 1995 Annual Conference, available on the Schaffer Online Library of Drug Policy (www.druglibrary.org).

Chapter 12: Luck of the Draw

1. In 'What's in a sausage? The Roots of Cannabis Prohibition', *Drug Link* September–October 1998, Institute for the Study of Drug Dependence, 1998.

Postscript

1. Anna Bradley and Oswin Baker, *Drugs in the United Kingdom – A Jigsaw with Missing Pieces*, Institute for the Study of Drug Dependence, 1998.

Index

A Note on the Author

Patrick Matthews is a freelance writer and journalist. He has contributed to numerous publications, including the *Independent*, the *Mail on Sunday*, the *Guardian* and *Time Out*. He won the 'Wines from France 1995 Premier Cru' award for wine writing and was shortlisted for the Glenfiddich and André Simon awards for his book *The Wild Bunch: Great Wines from Small Producers* in 1998.

He is also a television producer and director, with credits on *The Late Show*, *Dispatches*, *Arena Food Night* and *Food and Drink*.

A Note on the Type

This book is set using Bembo. The first of the Old Faces is a copy of a roman cut by Francesco Griffo for the Venetian Printer Aldus Manutius. It was first used in Cardinal Bembo's *De Aetna*, 1495, hence the name of the contemporary version. Although a type cut in the fifteenth century for a Venetian printer, it is usually grouped with the Old Faces. Stanley Morison has shown that it was the model followed by Garamond and thus the forerunner of the standard European type of the next two centuries.